VISION Paperbacks

First published in Great Britain in 1998 by VISION Paperbacks,
a division of Satin Publications Limited.

VISION Paperbacks,
a division of
Satin Publications Limited
20 Queen Anne Street
London W1M 0AY
E-mail: 100525.3062@compuserve.com

Cover design and layout: Justine Hounam.
Typesetting and design: Pixel Press.
Printed and bound in Great Britain: The Bath Press, Bath.
Photography Rex Features

©1998 Colin Challen/VISION Paperbacks
ISBN: 1-901250-18-0

PRICE of POWER

The Secret Funding of the Tory Party

Colin Challen

THE AUTHOR

Colin Challen was born in Scarborough. He served in the RAF and he later graduated from Hull University.
In the 1970s, he became a political activist, and has been a member of the Labour Party for the last fifteen years.
Colin Challen now works full-time as a Labour Party Organiser in Leeds. *The Price of Power* has been written independently of his Labour Party work. It represents part of a longer-term project "to explore the covert organisation of Labour's main rival".

Other works by Colin Challen:
The Quarrelsome Quill: Hull's Radical Press from 1830
(with Mike Hughes)
In Defence of the Party: The Secret State, the Conservative Party and Dirty Tricks

ACKNOWLEDGEMENTS

I am very grateful to the following for their help in the preparation of this book: Colin Burgon MP; Peter Hounam; Mike Hughes; Neal Moister; Robin Ramsay; John Spellar MP; the staff of Leeds City Library and of the Brynmor Jones Library, Hull University, as well as to many other people who have sent me cuttings and other materials.

CONTENTS

FOREWORD

Most of this book has been researched from published sources, which is clearly a strength and weakness. The strength is that over time, one can usually have the benefit of seeing a contemporaneous response from the Conservative Party. The weakness is that because so much has not been revealed, any account based on such sources will be incomplete to some degree.

It would take a deep throat of mammoth proportions to provide the real history of Conservative Party funding. Such an investigation is unlikely to appear - not merely because the Treasurers of the Conservative Party have been chosen for their unswerving loyalty, but also because the Party's strict adherence to a policy of secrecy has kept most party servants in the dark. Even the one example in this book of a Party Treasurer who has left the Tories for another party, Alastair McAlpine, has been remarkably reticent about the funding of the party – barring a serious brainstorm, he will take the real secrets with him to the grave.

But we have entered a new era. There are two organisations which have kept their pledge of secrecy paramount despite the growing fear that such behaviour is an affront to democracy. One organisation is the Conservative Party. The other is the Freemasons. Now, facing the danger of being found in contempt of Parliament, the Masons have been forced to provide the names of members who may have been involved with various police investigations involving alleged miscarriages of justice.

If it takes such a threat to get such information out of these organisations, the question most people would ask is why? What have they got to hide? In these circumstances, normal methods of research do set some limitations. Nevertheless, relying just on published sources over the best part of this century does provide sufficient material to raise more than serious doubts about the claims the Conservative Party has repeatedly made about the legitimacy of much of its financing. Their serial denunciations of their accusers just won't wash any more.

INTRODUCTION

In the 1997 general election, the Conservative Party's crushing defeat brought a century of Tory supremacy to an inglorious end, which barring occasional lapses, had made the organisation appear a potent weapon to be loathed and admired. But the truth about the organisation of the Conservative Party is that it has always been a carefully nurtured deception, whether the deception related to its democratic legitimacy, to the use of covert methods and the unaccountability of its funding, or its inter-dependence on the state and more particularly, the secret state.

The scale of the 1997 disaster has laid bare the true level of support enjoyed by the Conservative Party, not so much electorally (it was nowhere near being pushed into third place as the Labour Party nearly was in 1983) but in terms of its active support. There was an indicator here of how the Tory Party had come full circle this century – the fewer people it attracted to work for it seemed to be in inverse ratio to how much money it could attract. Rich people would dip into their pockets on an unprecedented scale, but "ordinary" people couldn't find the time to come to the aid of the party. In 1909 Winston Churchill described the Conservatives as "The party of the rich against the poor."[1]

A similar charge today would not ring hollow, given that most people now might class themselves as poor in comparison to the despised 'fat cats' of recent provenance. Similarly, the defeat of the Conservatives in 1906 was against a backdrop of what we would now call 'sleaze' – the sale of honours and favours for party funds leading to much comment in the press.

Lord Woolton, Party Chairman in 1945, was caught fortuitously (if that is the right word to use in the context of the Tories' second major defeat of the century, in an era when real organisational change seemed possible) when it seemed there was a mood in the party which would genuinely welcome aboard 'ordinary people'.

Price of Power

But despite the top-down affirmation of reform then given, it can be seen that no sea-change took place. Power within the party was not redistributed and accountability was not introduced, even though party membership grew enormously. Lower-case conservatism, combined with unquestioning respect for the powerful still prevailed. Most of the powerful, of course, had served their apprenticeships under a rather different aegis and no doubt anticipated that they would plough the same furrow as soon as the public's post-war enthusiasm for collectivism waned.

Until now, the wisdom of the Conservative approach has only been internally challenged by tiny fringe groups such as the Charter Movement, who wish to "set the party free". They were held in a patronising regard by the leadership, which clearly felt the function of the members was to blindly obey rather than ask awkward and often pointed questions. Point number four of the Charter Movement's 10-point charter reads: "Full control over all the Party's money must be exercised by the elected officers, who must be accountable to the members."[2]

Demands such as these have struck a double blow at the very heart of the Conservative Party, which invests so much power in its Leader. The Leader appoints the senior officers, including the Party Treasurer, and has routinely denied that there is any need to tell anyone where the money comes from. Accountability, it was thought, would lead down the slippery slope of interfering with the individual's basic civil liberty to give their money away as they see fit with the promise of complete anonymity. After all, as has been pointed out on numerous occasions by party leaders, it is not illegal to make donations to political parties and the Conservative party is a paradigm of honour.

But staying within the letter of the law and appearing honourable were not qualities which could stave off public disgust; the rising stench of feculent patronage had practically swamped the once apparently democratic public domain by the 1990s. It would become clear that if the Tories had ever once, experimented with the idea of an open form of internal democracy prior to their crushing defeat of 1997, then the experiment would have been doomed to failure – because it would have denied the party's financial backers the private influence they expected.

William Hague's pledges to reform the party, including a limited

form of one-member-one-vote for the leader, and the ending of
foreign donations, are clear signs of crisis management. Such ideas
were anathema to the leadership prior to the 1st May 1997, partly
because of the "if it ain't broke don't fix it" view; more importantly
because the constitution of the Conservative Party has provided
great freedom for its leader to do precisely just what he or she
wanted without interference.

On the other side of the leadership/grassroots coin, the autonomy enjoyed by local Conservative Associations has been jealously
guarded. So, on matters of dispute between the two, a stalemate
could often prevail, allowing both sides to continue as before until
the heat of the argument had evaporated.

In every internal respect the party had reached an all-time low
by 1997, in terms of both morale as well as organisationally, urgent
steps were needed to revive its fortunes. William Hague would have
little else to do in any case in the coming years but re-organise his
party. For without some show of re-invention, few people would be
attracted into joining it. With a local base which saw in 1996 the
party's tally of councillors pushed into third place behind the
Liberal Democrats, and parts of the country without Conservative
representation of any description, there could be little or no incentive for those who wished to further their career in politics to join.
Even the door to quango membership had slammed shut.

In these circumstances, only the hard core will be around to
rebuild the party in the new millennium – a hard core who know
that it will take years of unrewarding work to make any recovery.
For the patient, long-term careerists, there is no better time to get
involved of course, for they will accrue an influence which can only
grow as the party grows again – assuming that it does.

***

This study attempts to pull together much of the published
material on the funding of the Conservative Party and some related
issues, and as such depends heavily on what must in many cases be
speculative accounts. The deeper internal workings of the
Conservative Party are shrouded in greater secrecy than many
aspects of the state. Party servants such as Sir Joseph Ball ensured
that there would be no party equivalent of the "30 year rule" after
which state documents would be made public, by employing the

3

simple expedient of destroying all records of his activity. In more
recent times the shredders at Conservative Central Office have no
doubt given sterling service. The culture of secrecy was described
in former deputy party chairman Emma Nicholson's aptly titled
Secret Society, where she noted that "the Treasurer's Department
did everything in secret: even the secretaries were sworn to confi-
dentiality... Everyone else – including the directors of other
departments and the most senior agent of the whole party organisation – was kept in the dark."[3]

A political party run on this 'need to know' basis will find it difficult to change, but the experience of the five years 1992 to 1997
should assist: public interest in what became known as "sleaze"
grew unabatedly, and forced the House of Commons to take
unprecedented measures to curtail the peddling of influence, a
trade which had become synonymous with the workings of the
Conservative Party under John Major.

***

Could a similar history be written about the funding of the
Labour Party – in the interests of balance? Probably most
Conservatives would say 'yes'. Indeed, there is a funding history of
the Labour Party, but it would be rather a different animal to that of
the Conservatives. The major themes of this book would be largely
excluded – the sale of honours, the secrecy, the foreign donations,
the auction of parliamentary seats, the lack of donors' democratic
accountability – the sheer scale of the Conservatives' murky financial past far surpasses anything any political rival managed since
the days of Lloyd George. This is not to say that the Conservative
Party's opponents were innocent of malpractice – one only has to
recall the name of John Poulson to see how all parties encountered
similar difficulties regarding their probity from time to time. There
is of course one very clear reason why a sharp contrast exists
between the two main parties – the finances of one were in effect
regulated by law, whereas the other's were not. Labour's historic
source of finance, the trade union political levy, has been the
subject of legislation almost from the time of Labour's birth. As a
consequence of this, Conservative politicians have been able to
point to 'Labour's paymasters' whilst claiming that their side got
most of its money from a wide variety of sources, mainly W.V.S.

types running bring and buy stalls if you believe their propaganda. At least the 'union barons' had names, and you could see how much their members contributed. Indeed, in 1928 the Tories gave these trade union omnipotents' members the right to contract in, as opposed to contract out of paying the political levy. The effect of this was to reduce the Labour Party's trade union 'membership' by a third, but during the Second World War more than half of that lost ground was regained. The 10-yearly political levy ballots introduced in the 1980s by Margaret Thatcher have, without exception, given affirmative support to the principle of maintaining the political levy. But it would be wrong to suppose that it was merely because they had to obey the law that Labour's funding was more transparent: as noted in British Political Facts, "The Labour Party has always published Accounts in its Annual Conference Reports." Thus the party voluntarily disclosed that its income in 1912 was £12,000. The first accounts the Tories issued appeared in 1968, and even that was a halting commitment, later withdrawn after a change of Treasurer to one less committed to openness.

Thus, a history of the financing of the Labour Party would not offer quite the same picture of devious subterfuge as that of the Conservatives. This is not to deny that Labour's chief funders did not use their support to seek to influence the Party – far from it. It was their support which helped establish the Labour Party in the first place. The history of that relationship – and this is the point – is well documented, it is on the record. The Conservatives' record has only been explored in the most fragmented of ways, each fact having to be drawn out like a rotten tooth.

Colin Challen

Price of Power

Chapter One

MONEY FOR HONOURS

If success as a Conservative Party Treasurer could be measured by longevity in office, then Earl Farquhar is in the top rank. In the twentieth century, only two others served longer. Farquhar, an undisclosed bankrupt, ended his tenure unhappily, a fate which also befell one or two of his successors. Farquhar's rise in the party hierarchy owed much to his contribution to metropolitan Conservatism, and in particular his role in the establishment of the London Municipal Society, which organised Conservatives to fight London local government elections. But whilst he was always deeply involved in Conservative organisation, Farquhar never had the good fortune to fully convince others of his worth. This was brought home when he sought honours for his work. Whilst he was well adorned with honours – Baronet, Baron, Viscount, Earl – his colleagues tended to be less than fulsome in his praise. When he was seeking ennoblement, for example, he dutifully listed his contribution to the cause:

"I gave and collected £7,000 for the Elections in July [1895]... more than half of the whole £30,000 has come out of my own pocket and if you were to count what I had guaranteed much more . . . out of the £30,000 odd I had given and collected since 1891 – £21,000 had been given and collected by me since the middle of 1894 – £14,000 for the LM Society resulting in great measure in the victories at the LCC elections last March... "[1]

And so on. Farquhar got what he wanted, but it was noted that he "recapitulates at wearisome length all his services (chiefly imaginary)". The author of *Local Politics and the Rise of Party*, who studied the Bonar Law papers, cryptically concluded that "in his ultimate relationship with Unionist party funds, Farquhar to some degree redressed the balance of these early generous contributions."[2] Since Farquhar had also been linked in the press with 'homosexual scandals', he was always going to be an awkward member of the Conservative hierarchy.

Farquhar had the honour of serving the Tories between 1911 and 1923, a period which matched the ascendancy of Lloyd George. During that period, the Conservatives were only to taste power in a wartime coalition with the Liberals, which continued for another four years after the 1918 general election. By the time of his death, Farquhar was portrayed as being very much allied to Lloyd George, so distancing both him and Lloyd George's methods from the Conservatives, at a time when those methods epitomised the corruption of the coalition. Farquhar's mental faculties were diminished as a result of senility by the time the coalition was drawing to a close. However, it would be wrong to suggest that this was the only reason why he risked compromising the honour of the Conservative Party in a dubious relationship with Lloyd George's political fund or Lloyd George's sale of honours. The Conservative leadership knew about and participated in most of what was being done to fill their coffers.

The Conservatives, long before Lloyd George cynically catered for the bauble addiction of the plutocratic *nouveau riches,* were themselves waist-deep in the trade of honours. It was the done thing, even though occasional examples are available to delineate the scope of the trade. For example:

"[Salisbury, Tory Leader until 1902] rejected a suggestion from Richard Middleton, head of Conservative Central Office, that a peerage should be sold to an Indian rajah in return for a donation, but he did encourage Middleton and Lord Abergavenny (then one of the trustees of Conservative Party funds) to accept large sums of money from men whose only objective in donating it was to receive honours. As a result the party became considerably indebted to men like William Waldorf Astor for a gift of £20,000 in 1900... for the election fund."[3]

After Salisbury, Balfour showed a similar willingness to engage in the trade[4] and his successor, Bonar Law saw party funds swelled by those queuing up to take honours in the Conservative Party's allocation. It was in the first three years of Farquhar's reign as Treasurer that the Party Chairman, Sir Arthur Steel-Maitland (a friend of

Maundy Gregory, the honours broker) added £160,000 each year to party funds through honours sales.[5] As far as Farquhar was concerned, life as party Treasurer could hardly have got off to a more promising start.

By the standards of the day, this trade was largely accepted as normal practice – only occasionally would voices be raised against it, when honours seekers came forward who were so self-evidently unsuited. Even then, they were sometimes rewarded. In 1919, Bonar Law established the doctrine that Conservative Party leaders were to follow right up to John Major who made a virtue of it in the 1990s. Law told the House of Commons: "I do not believe that any government would be prepared to admit the principle that subscription to Party funds should debar subscribers, who would otherwise be suitable, from recognition at the hands of the Sovereign".[6] Clearly, it would be advantageous for Party donors to camouflage their generosity with gifts to charitable bodies. Indeed, in order to draw attention to oneself, charitable donations may be deemed a prerequisite, since charity balls and committees provided all the right opportunities to mix with the right people – as Maundy Gregory would demonstrate so well.

Bonar Law was speaking to the Commons in a debate on a motion to compel parties to publish the sources of their funds. The motion was defeated, as were all the similar motions that came before the House in the decades that followed. But during the debate, Bonar Law demonstrated either his utter contempt for the House, or a level of ignorance it is barely possible to countenance in a Party leader. He told the House:

"The Prime Minister (Lloyd George) has made, and will make no recommendations to His Majesty as a reward for contributions to Party funds. I wish to say, not only do I not know of any such bargain, direct or indirect, but I have asked the Whips, and they have told me that there has been and will be no such bargain."[7]

This disingenuous reply is carefully crafted to evade the issue of whether *his* party had received funds. As early as 1910 Law knew the trade was going on as his new Party Chairman, Sir Arthur Steel-Maitland had sent him a memorandum regarding the achievements of the then outgoing Chief Whip Sir A. Acland Hood: "He started (in 1902) without any invested funds and left a nest egg of over £300,000. A year's peerages are hypothecated, but still this is a very fine performance." Steel-Maitland then outlined his plans to raise an income of £100,000 at least:

"Towards this, Lord Farquhar and I have at present got about £30,000 a year more, mostly in a few big subscriptions. I am at present organising with him systematic collections from (1) Peers (2) the City. We ought to reach say £80,000 a year by July, as the autumn has been an unfavourable time. After that I hope to tackle provincial centres, and perhaps from local funds in Lancashire, Yorkshire and Scotland, thus relieving the centre. It is preposterous that these rich places should, as now, come yelping to London for help. I may be too sanguine, but I hope by the end, say of 1913, to have an income, irrespective of the Liberal Unionists, of £120,000 to £140,000 a year. This should be to a large extent, but not wholly, irrespective of future honours." [8]

During much of Bonar Law's leadership period, Lord "Ned" Talbot, later Viscount Fitzalan of Derwent, was Chief Whip. There cannot be any doubt that he too was well practised in the trade. In a letter sent by Sir George Younger, Chairman of the Party, in January 1921 to Bonar Law, he complains bitterly of the activities of the coalition Liberals "poaching" Conservative honours seekers:

"I should never have grumbled if we had half the list, but considering how Talbot had to work to secure to his modest lot, considering the men we had to take down to let in fellows like... there is little wonder that I am protesting. Not only should we have half but it wouldn't be unreasonable if we expected rather more than that, & I hope you'll insist on at least half for the future & also suggest a much smaller list.

There must be a stop to Freddie poaching our men. I haven't a doubt that if I had got Mills a seat, & got him into the House he would have proved a generous annual subscriber, & it was for us & not for Freddie to give him something more later on. Freddie has written in reply to my letter about the £2500 & stating its purpose." [9]

The "Freddie" referred to here is F.E. "Freddie" Guest, Lloyd George's Chief Whip. But Younger was fighting a battle on two fronts, since his own Treasurer, Lord Farquhar had proved, certainly in his last years, to be a rather recalcitrant party treasurer. Younger and Bonar Law were keen to clarify whether Farquhar had given money intended for the Conservatives to the Lloyd George fund, as there appeared to be some doubt as to whether Farquhar had decided that they shared the money in a way that was not intended, particularly for election purposes. Eventually, Law wrote to Fitzalan in 1923 (by then Talbot had been elevated to Viscount Fitzalan):

"You have noticed the trouble there was with poor old Farquhar. I have seen him twice and there is now no question of his hesitating to sign cheques for the actual party funds but I still have a strong suspicion that he has handed sums, and perhaps large sums, to L.G. for his party while he was acting as our Treasurer. He is so "gaga" that one does not know what to make of him..."[10]

Specifically in contention was a sum of between £80,000 and £200,000 given by Lord Astor (who shortly before he died in 1919 had been made a Viscount). Fitzalan replied that he had not been handed £80,000, as Law queried, saying "I was not consulted as to what should be done with the money. The thing was a fait accompli when I heard of it. He [Farquhar] simply happened to tell me what had been given and what had been done with it."[11] "He certainly cannot be relied on" concluded Fitzalan. Law wrote about Farquhar as Treasurer in the past tense, but the "poor old man" was stubborn to the end. The Times reported that Farquhar was unhappy with Younger's control over the party's funds[12] – presumably Younger was keen to get his hands on any accounts that Farquhar was hanging on to, with another election looming. Two weeks later it was reported that "The little incident raised by Lord Farquhar over the administration of the Unionist Party is closed. It was almost a personal matter between Lord Farquhar, the trustee of the fund and Sir George Younger as representing the spending department – the National Unionist Association. Lord Farquhar's interview with Mr Bonar Law removed the misunderstanding."[13] But two months later, Farquhar's reign as Treasurer, during a period in which the Tories clearly endeavoured to profit as much as they could from the trade in honours, came to an inglorious end. In March 1923 Law announced that Farquhar had resigned and that he had been replaced with Younger. The next day, The Times printed a statement from Farquhar, issued through the Press Association: "It is not true that Earl Farquhar has resigned the position of Treasurer of the Unionist Party funds. Lord Farquhar has no intention of resigning. His position has always been one of difficulty and delicacy inasmuch as he personally collected large sums, much of which was subscribed, and was expressed to be subscribed, for Coalition purposes. Lord Farquhar absolutely refuses to resign his office until his position, which is obviously fiduciary, is sufficiently protected." Two days later it was made clear that the position of Treasurer was solely up to the Prime Minister. On the issue of the transfer of ex-coalition funds, Law said "compared with the party chest as a whole, this is a much smaller matter."[14]

Following Lord Talbot's departure in 1921, Leslie Wilson was appointed Chief Whip by Bonar Law's successor, Austen Chamberlain. In 1927 Chamberlain had entered into a spat with Lloyd George over who should take the blame for the sales of honours; the matter was still causing public concern. In response to a letter from Chamberlain, Lloyd George had drafted a response saying "I recollect two cases presented by Leslie Wilson in your day about which I had grave misgivings.... Subsequently I was informed... that substantial cheques had been passed in respect of both cases to the managers of your party fund." [15] There can be little doubt therefore that Bonar Law was entirely au fait with where the money had come from during his period in office. But he established the doctrine which Conservative leaders were to follow, which ensured that nosy MPs would be fobbed off with obfuscating half-truths, and which was to ensure that even after the passing of the 1925 Honours (Prevention of Abuses) Act a culture of money for honours would still permeate the Conservative Party.

During the final days of the coalition, the scandal of honours sales led to several debates in Parliament, possibly the most noteworthy being the debate held in the Lords on 29th June, 1922. In this debate some of the methodology of the honours touts were revealed: the furtive letters to potential aspirants, the hints of "delicate matters of a complimentary nature," references to recently honoured individuals, and last but not least, the scale of charges, from £10,000 for a knighthood up to £40,000 for a baronetcy. The debate was primarily about an offer of a peerage for Sir Joseph Robinson, a South African mine owner, well into his eighties, who had a less than honourable past. Because of the publicity surrounding his case, Robinson declined the 'offer', and the government obfuscated the issue by referring at length to all the recent honours that had been given which were perfectly justifiable.

Following the debate, the issue of honours for another expatriate was raised. A peerage had just been conferred on Sir William Vestey, the butcher to shipping magnate, who had chosen to avoid paying income tax by upping sticks and settling in Argentina. Lord Strachie drew the attention of the government to the contents of a Report of The Royal Commission on Income Tax, itself reported in the press. The Royal Commission's report related that Vesty ran a business whose capital was in excess of £20,000,000, and that in 1915 (in Vesty's words) "taxation was imposed which made it impossible to continue working from England." Asked where he was now domiciled, Vesty replied "I am abroad. I pay nothing."[16] As a consequence of his business's move abroad, Vesty estimated that between 3,000 and 5,000 men were unemployed. In the words of Lord Strachie: "I think the feeling of most people would be that this was not the sort of man who ought to be rewarded for evading taxation and thereby throwing a heavier burden of taxation upon those who have to pay taxes."[17] Vesty, who was in the Chamber, sought to defend his position by referring to competition from the Americans, who didn't have to pay such punitive taxes, and to the contribution of his business to the war effort. But the latter defence has been found wanting, and his first line only highlights where his loyalties lay during the years of the war – when others sacrificed their lives. The Vesty family tradition was thus established, and in the early 1980s the Vesty business once again achieved notoriety for continuing to avoid British taxation. As will be seen later, this form of behaviour was, if anything, encouraged by the Conservatives, who became increasingly dependent on donations from businesses which were run by people whose use of British domicility rules enabled them to pay less, or no tax at all.

The honours scandals occurred against a background of two inter-related forces tugging at the political establishment during the inter-war period. On the one hand were the new, organised forces of labour, who were not only threatening to take control of the state through democratic means but also appeared ready to rise in revolutionary fervour. On the other hand were members of the ancien regime, who not only feared the new, assertive working class, but also despised the nouveau riches, particularly when it came to "devaluing the coinage" of their power, particularly in the House of Lords. The latter threat to the old order had seen its greatest exponent in Lloyd George, who clearly couldn't give a bugger about the noble Lords' self-esteem. But the plutocrats and the old aristocrats

13

were joined in a unifying cause – facing the threat to capitalism itself. Thus, whilst the promise of honours always remained a useful tool in encouraging donations to party funds, after the 1925 Act it would be harder to develop the large reserves necessary for modern political warfare from this source alone.

The Conservative Party tried to adapt to the changing, more volatile times by meeting the threat head-on. In 1923, Sir Herbert Nield, Chairman of the Association of Conservative Clubs, announced the launch of a fund to promote "Conservative working men candidates at the next election." 500,000 members of 1,500 clubs were asked to donate a penny a member a year. The fund would not be used to fight 'forlorn' hopes but where seats offered a "reasonable and probable chance of victory."[18] The fear was that unless the Party could find good working class candidates, the Party's image would help drag down its electoral chances, particularly in the cities. After a major publicity drive, sufficient funds were raised through this appeal to support two candidates in 1922 and one candidate in both the 1923 and 1924 general elections. But it has been noted that "it proved impossible for any of the candidates to be found a 'safe' Conservative constituency. Two – West Rhondda and Silverton (both 1922) – were hopeless, while the two others – Walsall (1923), and Preston (1924) – were marginal."[19] After this paltry effort, the scheme appears to have been wound up, and it remained generally true that 'working class' parliamentary candidates were anathema to Conservative Associations. This was also true in local elections. The problems encountered by wage-earning aspiring Conservative candidates were not merely confined to election expenses, since party meetings would often be held when they were at work, and no allowance was made for loss of earnings. But these difficulties must have palled beside the major political obstacles which faced Conservative Party working class organisations. John Greenwood's study of these organisations depicts a history of failure upon failure, best summed up by the thought of such an organisation, whose sympathies were inextricably tied to the interests of, for example, the mine owners – then trying to recruit and retain miners as members. Some did join, but in insignificant numbers. The main role of Conservative trade union organisations eventually fell to propagandising, campaigning against the political levy and acting as "a not very convincing piece of window-dressing for a party that thought of itself as "classless." The irony of course, is that a lot of working class people voted Conservative. But the "classless" claim is belied by the attitude of those who ran the Associations, who clearly felt nothing but discomfort when confronted by Conservative working class voting fodder seeking parity."

Thus it was clear that the availability of independent means, if not a fortune, was a crucial characteristic of successful aspirants to Party candidature. The Times summed up the mood of many in the bourgeois ranks of the party in 1924:

"Has the Conservative machine fully recognised the arrival of democracy? In how many constituencies is the party association really representative of the whole party, including the rank and file? In whose hands is the selection of the candidate? Is it in the hands of half-a-dozen rich men, who will be expected to provide the election funds themselves unless they can find a candidate rich enough to do everything himself? Is there a bad old tradition, born of rich candidates, that everybody who does work for the party may reasonably expect to be paid for doing it? Are the funds of the party, if not provided by the candidate, obtained by appealing to a few dozens or scores of wealthy men instead of appealing to all members of the party in the constituencies?"[20]

This was a theme that was to be aired over much hand-wringing on many occasions well into the 1950s. But for much of that time words, not deeds, were the order of the day. Perhaps the rank, if not the file, felt too affronted by the possibility of a sudden influx of working class men and women into positions of authority in the party. As ever, the threat was that working class men and women would move into positions of authority in the state, not the party, side-stepping the unattractive Conservatives altogether.

Before the challenge of the new enfranchised working class had been taken up publicly, the ground had been prepared by the party hierarchy for a secret offensive shortly before the First World War ended. In concert with Lloyd George and their coalition partners, the Conservatives played their part in an organisation "'concerned with Anti-Bolshevism and Increased Production Propaganda' intended to incite public hostility against the trade unions and political left wing."[21] The organisation was headed by Sir William 'Bronco Bill' Sutherland MP, Lloyd George's press agent "noted for his foul mouth, uncouth manners and outsize cigars,"[22] and membership consisted of Sir Robert Horne, Coalition Conservative Secretary of State for Labour, Lord "Ned" Talbot, F.E. Guest and Lord Riddell. According to the historian Keith Middlemas,

"Sydney Walton, a former undercover agent and government fugleman was appointed to run it, with a fund of £100,000 subscribed, not from government funds but industrial sources, chiefly members of the Engineering Employers' Federation, headed by Sir Vincent Caillard. Walton took the main propaganda role from a variety of front organisations, set up during the war, such as the British Empire League, the British Workers' League, the National Democratic and Labour Party, and the national Union Movement, all of whom had been in receipt of industrial subscriptions, and his 'information service' fed, without any restriction from the Official Secrets Act, on the government's most private sources of information, Special Branch and Secret Intelligence Services. [23]

The novel feature of this organisation was that it was privately funded. In days gone by, the activities of the government of the day's whips' office would be directly funded by the "secret vote." [24]

The use of front organisations was an important aspect of the Conservative counter-attack throughout the best part of the century, and the secrecy which has attended their funding is inextricably linked to the secrecy surrounding Conservative Party funding. Given Farquhar's handling of money at this time, it is probable that money was switched at a whim between the party and its sister, front organisations. That having been said, a theme taken up by a number of industrialists throughout the course of this history was expressed by Sir Vincent Caillard, when he moaned about the danger of the Whips' presence giving the organisation a "political colour". Industrialists, by some paternalistic logic, often saw themselves as somehow "non-political" but simply working for the "larger interest". This is, of course, one important self-defining aspect of true 'Conservatism.'

The Conservatives' appeal to the wider interest did not seem to be making much ground. By 1923, Bonar Law, the "Unknown Prime Minister" retired from the leadership of the party for the second time, and Baldwin took over the reins. In the short, first period of his premiership – ended by the election of the minority MacDonald Labour government in 1923 – Baldwin did little to change the culture that made his party seem so unattractive to working class electors (to say nothing of their attitude towards Conservative Party policies of course, but that's another matter). Although he had commenced the process of putting the anti-sale of honours bill through Parliament, it failed to reach the statute book before he went to the country in December.

Baldwin's reputation of 'safety first' in so many matters, left an impression that here at last was a leader who was more in tune with the electorate's desire to clean up politics. He was undoubtedly something of a breath of fresh air after the worst excesses of the Coalition years, but even if his honest reputation has managed to survive relatively intact through the years it would not be right to conclude that he had brought the Conservative Party into a new state of honesty and accountability. Indeed, Baldwin's pedestrian, plodding nature was as much a foundation of his reputation as it was the cause of his inability to decisively deal with the problems he faced modernising the party.

He certainly recognised the problems insofar as they were summed up by The Times editorial already quoted. In 1927, he told the Tories' National Union:

"Local organisations and associations I know are mostly self supporting and many of them can do no more than support themselves. We cannot look to them to provide additional funds for headquarters organisation... There is a popular feeling that our old friend Lord Younger has half a dozen millionaires around the corner ready to open their purses at any moment. The trouble with a millionaire is that has made his money and knows how to keep it."[25]

Our 'old friend' Younger indeed had at one time some fairly well-heeled funders around the corner, for during the Coalition period he was able, mainly through honours sales, to double party funds; from £600,000 to £1,250,000 by his own admission. But by the mid twenties, these generous supporters were "old and dying off." Younger wrote to Baldwin in 1927, telling him:

"...the actual responsibilities of the Treasurer consisted in safeguarding and maintaining a Party fund by collecting special subscriptions for each general election, and that the Chairman of the Party Organisation superintended the collection of annual subscriptions and the contributions occasionally made by the medium of the honours List. I never, so to speak, sold an honour, nor did I ever make any bargains; but from time to time I did raise a substantial contribution and I agree with old Lord Salisbury that no great Party can be run unless the Fund from time to time can be so strengthened.

"The charge against [Lloyd George] is not that he raised such subscriptions but that he used his position as PM to fill his own political coffers, which ones were placed in trust and solely used for the necessities of the Party to which the donor belonged. The Fund since I ceased to be Chairman has been very seriously depleted and requires to be strengthened."[26]

It would be harder to find – at least until the 1990s – a more confused and contradictory statement on the subject of Conservative Party funding. In his desperation to distance himself from Lloyd George's coat-tails to which it is clear Younger's party were closely attached, he not only confesses that he has used precisely the same fund-raising methods but then points the finger at the office of the Party Chairman, and even throws in a character-building reference from the demonstrably compromised Lord Salisbury.

Younger's letter was written to Baldwin in order to allow Baldwin to consider a replacement for the position of Treasurer. In the words of Robert Rhodes James, "Baldwin at once hastened to write to Younger to express the hope that he would not resign as Treasurer."[27] Whilst it is unlikely that Baldwin was uninitiated in the ways of the honours scams before this time, we nevertheless can thus show beyond doubt that he knew what the score was by 1927. Younger not only kept his job but held on until only the Grim Reaper relieved him of it two years later.

Younger's letter nevertheless gave J.C.C. Davidson, the new 'puritan' Party Chairman (1926–1930), a soft 'get-out'; if it was the case that the Party Chairman raised money for the organisation and the Party Treasurer raised money for general elections, then it may have been possible for 'tainted money' to be kept out of the Party's general funding. Since the central headquarters costs each year would be less than the peak spending nationally and locally for general elections, it could be conveniently and almost truthfully argued that 'the Conservative Party is not funded by tainted money'. In 1927, the Tories were working assiduously to keep the public attention focused on Lloyd George's activities and away from their own connivance in them. There was no "joint coalition fund", "the coalition had led to no changes in the financial arrangements of the Conservative Party". Despite the 'poaching' of Conservatives, Younger could always tell the press that he had "no financial interest" in his erstwhile colleagues' money.[28]

Further confusion is created by the existence of a list of 56 donors to a special election fund of £156,000 given in 1929. The list, found in Davidson's papers by Michael Pinto-Duschinsky, an authority on party funding, gave rise in Pinto-Duschinsky's mind to two questions: "(1) were the donors motivated by a desire for titles or by fear of socialism? and (2) did contributions come from businessmen in their individual capacities or from their companies and corporations?"[29] In addition, one is also bound to ask whether Davidson's determination to get rid of Maundy Gregory was motivated by the memory of Gregory's friend and Liberal Coalition Chief Whip F.E. Guest "poaching our men." It could have been a cause for concern, since many of those on Davidson's list had received honours in the latter unwholesome years of the Coalition.

As is the case for all parties, when the general election looms, it becomes easier to raise money, not least on the back of promises that cannot always be kept. At the same time, with the growth of front organisations, which could also play ancillary roles in fighting general elections, there would be little difficulty masking the accountancy trail. But it is interesting to note another reason for obfuscating the accountancy trail – to conceal how the money is used. No history of Conservative Party funding would be complete without the inclusion of Lord Randolph Churchill's comment made in 1884: "I should like all the finances of the Tory Party to be open to inspection for anyone who may wish to look at them, be he friend or foe. Where you allow secret expenditure you will certainly have corrupt expenditure; and where you have corrupt expenditure you will have vitiated elections, disfranchised boroughs, party disgrace and public scandal."[30]

Younger's role as a paymaster in the Zinoviev Letter Affair provides a good proof of Randolph Churchill's thesis, and perhaps also explains in part Baldwin's reluctance to let him go. The Zinoviev Letter, a forged, seditious missive allegedly signed by Grigory Zinoviev, president of the Third International and addressed to British Communists, came into the hands of the Conservative Party through the efforts of Major Guy Kindersley MP. Whilst it had also been passed to MI5, via the Foreign Office, the Conservatives had it in time to make good use of it to smear the Labour Party in the last few days of the 1924 general election. It was Younger to whom Kindersley took his accomplice, Donald im Thurm, and it was Younger who as Party Treasurer was asked to find £7,500 for the procurement of the letter. [31]

Publication of the letter was indeed embarrassing to Ramsay MacDonald, and may have played some part in his defeat, although this is not satisfactorily demonstrated psephologically. But what is of interest is that the Conservatives should engage in the transmission of a forgery (they of course deny at the time that they knew it was a forgery, but neither did they try to find out), for which they had paid a considerable sum, and that they then geared up their election organisation before its publication to deliver leaflets around the country denouncing the foreign, Bolshevik 'demon' Zinoviev. Later, Kindersley was to seek a knighthood for im Thurm for his part in the affair.

The intrigue that lies behind the tale of the Zinoviev Letter demonstrated not only how much the Conservatives had the support of the secret state – MI5 and the like – but also how much money they might have available for covert activities of this kind. Would it be fair to assume that this was the only time a Conservative Party Treasurer was asked to meet some shady dealer in politically sensitive papers?

Another example of Baldwin's acceptance of 'tainted money' occurred in 1928 when Beaverbrook approached him on behalf of a friend for a knighthood. Beaverbrook made out a cheque for £10,000 to J.C.C. Davidson after Baldwin promised to give the matter his 'personal attention'. Davidson "cautioned that there might be some delay in putting the honour through" and indeed nothing happened during the six months the Tories remained in office. Davidson returned the cheque after their election defeat saying "I have had no occasion to make use of the money."[32] Clearly, Beaverbrook or anybody in a similar position would go away thinking "maybe next time, then." Davidson, with only a few months left as Chairman, could hardly have been more equivocal.

Perhaps this was more of a policy of not wishing to burn the boats, whilst at the same time recognising in public the need for reform. In his speech to the National Union, already referred to,

Baldwin said he would prefer to have a shilling apiece from 100,000 supporters rather than it coming in a few gifts of £5,000. Davidson was of a like mind: "I would rather raise £1,000 by half crown subscriptions in the constituencies than by one cheque from a rich industrialist."[33] But this revolution in Tory fund-raising hadn't quite arrived yet, as Davidson made clear in a letter to Neville Chamberlain (who was keen to get rid of him, and shortly did thereafter):

"… The City has raised already something like £150,000 and are continuing to raise further funds for the Party for the simple reason that they are thoroughly frightened at the prospect of a Socialist Government.

The way the City was worked was that I went down to a private meeting, and told them that only big money was any good to me. The result was that at a lunch given in November £130,000 had already been raised in £5,000 subscriptions. Stanley made a short speech on the dangers of Socialism to finance and credit, one of those inimitable little speeches so free from party bias that the danger seemed all the greater as no allowance had to be made for partisanship."[34]

Once again, we see the presentation of the Conservative interest as being non-political – thus making it more attractive to industrialists, financiers and the like who prefer to be identified with the 'larger interest'. But coming three years after Baldwin's appeal for half-crowns from the 'hundreds of thousands' as opposed to £5,000 gifts from the few, it must have been clear how the party was still failing to garner the wider financial backing and therefore greater credibility it yearned for in public. Perhaps Baldwin's earlier efforts could only be stymied by the well-meaning help of supporters like Lady Elveden, who in response to Baldwin's stirring appeals, called upon women to "stretch out a helping hand", remarking that "many women do not realise how socialism is making in-roads into the poorer constituencies."[35]

As those in-roads became ever wider, Baldwin appealed to the City for more help. An appeal committee was established by the Metropolitan Division of the National Union of Conservative and Unionist Associations in 1926, and a target of £25,000 a year was set. Membership of the appeal committee was dominated by banking and insurance interests, with oil, brewing, shipping and tobacco also in evidence.

The Conservatives' appeal to the wider audience could hardly be assisted by Davidson's rather crass top-down approach. His handling of a motion calling for more democracy in the party, moved at the 1928 annual conference is indication enough. The motion was timid: "that the executives of all Conservative and Unionist Associations should be informed of, and have the opportunity of considering, any contemplated departure of a substantial character from the recognised policy of the party, and that they should be able to forward their conclusions for the consideration of the Central Council."[36] From the podium, Davidson delivered a suitable dressing down: "... it did not appear to be recognised that the Conservative Party was the most democratically organised association in the country, and that its leaders were always available for consultation by the rank and file. They had elected their leader, and they must trust him. If the resolution were carried, the position would be very much the same as that which existed in Russia." Davidson concluded by telling the proto-Bolsheviks of the National Union: "the general in the field could not afford to have his strategy interfered with by his staff." The motion was duly defeated. But at the same conference other anxieties were present – anxieties that grew stronger each year, but which were never taken too seriously until the Tories went down so badly in 1945.

This was the issue of financing the local associations, most of which, if they had an MP, would expect that MP to fund not only their own general election expenses, but to pay the annual expenses of the association too. In many cases, there was no likelihood of being selected as a candidate unless prior commitments to these arrangements were given. According to the MP Duff Cooper: "It is as difficult for a poor man, if he be a Conservative, to get into the House of Commons as it is for a camel to get through the eye of a needle."[37] At the 1928 conference one of the first efforts to address this problem was made, in a motion which 'viewed with anxiety the scarcity of wage earning MPs and candidates.'[38] Cirencester & Tewksbury claimed that they managed to avoid their MP paying anything by virtue of their scheme in which 7,000 'working class people' had contributed 6d or 1s a year since 1918. Conference had to reject the charge that the Conservative Party was a rich man's party. The motion could hardly fail to be carried, since few could defend the status quo – but the status quo in many cases had paid for their status, and there was no enthusiasm to do anything as a result of a vote on this motion. With a general election looming, Ramsay MacDonald could make hay at the Tories' expense: "There is nothing more encouraging to me in this life than to read a Tory circular appealing for money to help them fight the next general election. The Tories will go into the next general election with literally millions of pounds behind them. They will spend it – I would not like to say wisely – but they will spend it well, and in spending it they will not be too scrupulous about the limitations the Corrupt Practices Act imposes on them."[39] With statistical justification, Macdonald could claim that Labour's £1 would go further in votes than the Tories £10 or £20.

The common touch of Baldwin was noteworthy – but his attempts to portray the party as classless were on the whole futile. A report of a pre-general election preparation meeting of the Conservative's Central Council in 1929 at the Drury Lane Theatre noted that 'members invited included a weekly wage earner and the wife of a weekly wage earner.'[40] A post-election appeal to women to contribute to the costs of the next general election was supported by Lady Iveagh in the following terms:

"The object of the appeal is to raise the necessary funds to carry out a greatly increased and intensified campaign of education among the women electors of the metropolitan area [who had, the appeal stated "after the extension of the suffrage come into an unexpected inheritance and did not know quite what to do with it."] Funds are specially required to enable this work to be undertaken in the poorer constituencies... recent events have shown only too clearly the dangers which beset our uninformed electorate." [41]

The "dangers" referred to, of course, were simply Labour candidates attracting more support – not, as one might assume some subversive element at work.The Conservatives rallied to the cause of the poorer constituencies with bridge tournaments in Belgravia, advertised in the Court Circular column of The Times.

The plea to support the poorer constituencies, oft repeated in the 1930s, ran parallel to the growing unease about the appetite for rich candidates elsewhere. Both conditions could be seen as examples of the Party losing touch with the electorate, and indeed especially that part of the electorate who were women. If having to fund your own campaign was a bar on wage-earning men standing as Conservative candidates, how much worse must it have been for wage earning

Price of Power

women – or wives of wage earning men? At the annual conference of the Women's Unionist organisation in 1930, a Miss Headlam-Morley moved that "this conference feels that as long as Conservatives expect their Parliamentary candidates to bear much of the cost of local associations, and the whole of the their election expenses, it will never be possible for many of the ablest and most suitable men and women to stand for the House of Commons in the Conservative interest." Lady Astor concurred: "Did they realise how short they were of women in the House of Commons?"[42] Since Central Office had to approve candidates, the hierarchy must have been satisfied with the standard. But who (apart from the opposition) was going to get specific and name the names of suspect candidates? There wasn't yet enough pressure on the organisation to mend its ways, and in any case any move to reduce or remove the autonomy of the local associations would have been met with howls of protest, and probably outright revolt. Once again, The Times, being slightly detached from the Party, was able to recognise the dangers of not changing:

"A small local caucus operates a languid association and deems it its duty to offer the "privilege" of a safe seat only to a candidate able to contribute heavily to its funds. The seats which should cost a candidate least – since there is no lack of Conservatives with the power to pay – turn out in practice to cost him the most. By the same arrangement they stand to attract and to be saddled with the least competent candidates."[43]

Thus it seems it was not merely a case of proving your financial worth – but either entering an auction, or facing the danger at least of being 'gazumped'. G.R. Hall Caine MP, a multiple company director indicated the costs involved: "Being the member for East Dorset has cost me £37,000 in the last seventeen years, and deducting the amount received in salary, I have paid the nett figure of £31,000... Many MPs spend far more than I do in their constituencies... It is lamentable that Conservative seats should be put up for auction and sold to the richest candidate."[44] Sir Reginald Blaker concurred when he lamented: "In my opinion . . a married man with an income of £2,000 a year, apart from his salary as an MP, cannot afford the expenses which a Member of Parliament has to meet."[45] Blaker was consequently not seeking re-election, although when his association raised a fund to meet his election expenses he changed his mind and was re-elected in 1935. It was not good enough, but how could

Baldwin, who favoured change, achieve it?

Blaker was not alone in his difficulty making ends meet. Sir Samual Hoare, (later Visc. Templewood) who had served in the Cabinet – and would do so again – was given £2,000 a year by Lord Beaverbrook following a begging letter from Lady Hoare, who "had cleverly raised the point that due to the time-consuming activities and low pay of a politician, her husband might have to leave politics for more lucrative positions . . Hoare's biographer has identified three payments of £2,000 and observed with considerable understatement that had they [the payments] been publicly known at the time the accusation of corruption would undoubtedly have been made."[46] There is always the danger that low paid politicians may be susceptible to corruption, particularly if they feel a high financial reward is their due. However, given Parkinson's second law, which states that expenditure will always rise to meet income, which then became de rigeur in the 1980s and 1990s, no upper limit on income could ever be adhered to by Conservative MPs nursing their lucrative connections and consultancies.

In his first public political speech since the formation of the National Government, given at the Ilford Skating Rink, Baldwin praised the organisers of the meeting for taking the "very proper democratic step" of charging for admission, with seats at 1 shilling and two shillings each. Standing room at the back was free. He told his audience:

"To my mind, our party, representative more than any other party of all classes in the country ought to depend financially on all classes and all people who believe in what we support. Just as our Labour opponents make use of their meetings – and very properly – to raise funds to support their work, so tonight you are doing the same thing. It is far better and far more independent to do that than depend upon the pockets of a few rich men, which is all wrong... That spirit of independence which you are showing will sound the death knell of what has been a curse to our party – and that has been the setting up of seats in certain places to auction – that they became merely the pocket boroughs of rich men. I have always maintained that all should have an equal chance to be chosen as candidates to represent the great democratic constituencies of our country."[47]

This was Baldwin's strongest statement yet of his desire to rid the party of the excessive influence of "rich men" – but it was just a statement of desire, rather than action. He may have hoped that the party organisation – of which he was personally in control, might have picked up the drift of his thinking, but if they did, they were reluctant to act. Indeed, he recognised that his pleas were falling on deaf ears, telling the Conference of Women of the National Union in 1932: "I have preached on this theme so far without very great results, but I shall go on preaching in the hope that after my time at least some future leader may find himself in the position of leading a party absolutely independent and financially stable and secure."[48] Clearly, Baldwin was held back by the fact that a root and branch assault on the funding methods then in use would have destabilised the organisation and further undermined his own leadership at a time when in the wider policy domain he was already under attack from his own ranks.

Although the Conservative Party in the 1930s general elections saw its electoral support rise to over 50%, its parliamentary party was still dominated by the "cousinhood" – that well-connected group of MPs who were aristocrats, heirs to titles or were themselves landed gentry. Thus, whilst Baldwin's claims about the classless party may have had some psephological credence (particularly given its alliance with MacDonald) it nevertheless continued to draw a line in the sand when it came to encouraging "classless" candidates. In fact at a time when Labour's strength was increasing, the Conservatives were choosing more public school educated MPs than ever before – and they were being chosen for the safest seats, i.e. those which were more likely to have "auctions" to choose the candidate. (In the 1945 'wipe out', the public school educated Tory MPs largely held on to their seats, pushing their percentage membership of the Parliamentary Party to its highest level before or since.[49] Only 4% of Conservative MPs in the inter-war years were "rank and file workers", as opposed to 72% for the Labour Party. Apart from the image projected by the party by remaining so much a creature of the upper classes, it could also be seen that such a reputation could engender apathy amongst its natural allies from whom it would normally expect to receive money (similar thoughts come to mind when looking at the party's decline in the late 1980s and 1990s). Austin Hudson, Chairman of the Metropolitan Area wrote:

"Realising the wide area in which I would appeal, and the large number of comparatively wealthy people who live or work in

London, I did not anticipate any great difficulty in raising the sum which was required... I reckoned without the apathy of the average 'Conservative'. It is amazing to me to find the number of wealthy men and women who would be prepared to lose quite large sums of money at cards in a single evening, yet who will not subscribe £1 a year to assist those who are fighting a battle in which they are so vitally interested."[50]

The apathy was widespread. Mr Walter Stutters, Vice Chairman of the 1912 Club (formed to help the cause in the poorer constituencies) wrote that the Conservative Party "in many districts was being rapidly brought to a standstill for want of funds and because of niggardly financial support for Conservative Associations... to starve the only political party which stood between existing society and a policy of spoilation and confiscation was little short of madness."[51] Perhaps the complacent attitude of some of the party's wealthy backers had been induced by the diminishing threat of a socialist take-over with the arrival on the continent of fascism, or perhaps they preferred to fund directly those front organisations associated with the party which could nevertheless be passed off as 'non-political'.

But whilst the party was in power, there was little incentive to do much about the progressive wish-list of some members. A report of a "full examination" of the issue of parliamentary candidate selection was given to the annual meeting of the Central Council in 1935, and "the conclusion come to was that the whole matter was closely bound up with the question of finance."[52] It was felt that associations should become independent of candidates for financial support, to which end it was agreed that a standing advisory committee would be set up to ensure that "only the best possible candidates" would be selected. Later that year, at the national conference, the national party was called on to assist where the local party couldn't afford not to select on financial grounds.[53] The Conservative Party, by now in power once more in its own right, prevaricated on the issue yet again, and so by 1937 a resolution urging the Executive Committee of the National Union to set up a committee of inquiry into the "existing practice of constituencies making extensive financial demands on Parliamentary Candidates" was to be moved. It was evident that some seats were still being bought. The matter was dragged up again at that year's national conference, where the mover of the relevant resolution called for a variety of reforms to improve constituency organisation, adding for good measure that so far as the quality of candidates was concerned, "Money does not bring brains."[54] Seconding the motion, a former MP, W. Nunn from Whitehaven, said he had no objection to a candidate "paying a large sum of money" but he did object to the local organisation thereby doing nothing. In theory it was wrong for a man to buy a constituency, said Mr Nunn, leaving open the question whether in practice it was something that could be tolerated for quite a while longer. As a result of the 1937 conference resolution, which was passed with only three votes against, yet another committee was set up, but in the absence of a national conference in 1938, it was not until January, 1939 that it reported to the Party Leader, Neville Chamberlain. With war imminent, another general election would not be held, and the issue rumbled on until a Central Council meeting 1941 finally established a policy that "it is contrary to the interests of the party that the choice of candidate should be determined by any promise he may make either in regard to contributions to the funds of the association or provision of election expenses." The sanction available to the national party to uphold this policy was the option of withholding endorsement as a Conservative candidate, but this of course was only a possibility if it could be proven in the first place that an association had used finance as a criteria in making its choice. It is more than probable, in reality, that many associations, which had remained "languid" for so long would continue to protect their prized organisational autonomy by simply keeping quiet about it. But one or two were caught out. The Worcester Association issued a questionnaire to potential candidates asking "whether [they] would be prepared to subscribe to the local association an amount equal to the salary of the agent; and whether he would be prepared to pay all his election expenses if nominated."[55]

In fact, the policy of the party had only shifted to the extent that upper limits would be set on how much a candidate should pay for the election expenses and running costs of the constituency. These were still tidy sums and further reforms appeared necessary, and so the 1948 conference, which kicked off with the hymn, "Lead kindly knight amid the encircling gloom", heard Henry Brooke say "there are still too many [associations] which denied even an interview to a potential candidate who had not promised in advance to pay half his election expenses – perhaps £400 – and to pay a subscription of £100 to the association."[56] A resolution to finally end the system of candidates' and MPs' contributions, (if over £25 and £50 a year respectively) with a deadline of January 1st, 1949, was agreed. Lord Woolton, the Party Chairman at the time, took the credit for the change, having noticed himself that "sometimes harassed treasurers had been influenced by the amount the candidate could afford to subscribe to his election expenses... I decided to put this problem to the Executive Committee of the Party, and ask them to appoint a committee to advise on it."[57] The committee, under David Maxwell-Fyfe, apparently put the final nail in the coffin of the local associations' selection auctions, but even then, after the first flush of enthusiasm for change waned, could it have been possible that some slipped back into their old ways? Maxwell-Fyfe was perplexed by the drop in candidate's calibre in the mid-Fifties: "I think we had reason to hope that the general standard would not have declined as abruptly as it did. What made the situation particularly annoying was that many excellent candidates, who would have made first-class Members and probably Ministers, were left to fight utterly hopeless seats not once, but two and even in some cases three times, while the safe seats went to men of far lower calibre. This was to cost the party dear."[58] Maxwell-Fyfe thought it must be due to the "tyranni-cal" grip local associations had on their selection processes, which led them to pick "obscure local citizens with obscure local interests" or worse, like in the Labour Party, "tedious local worthies or party hacks".

The length of time it had taken the Conservative Party to tackle the problem of selection auctions after it was first raised was something like 20 years – and the party was only finally moved to act when it had been thrown out of office, this time with Labour in power in its own right. Being in opposition concentrates the mind wonderfully on organisation, but it is clear that the Tories were so unused to the condition that despite repeated resolutions and complaints – even from the party leader – it could only be something so drastic as a landslide defeat which could make reform a reality.

Chapter Two

THE TRIANGULAR RELATIONSHIP

Maundy Gregory has been remembered largely as an honours broker. The departure in 1922 of Lloyd George, his mainstay in that trade, is seen as the start of a slide in Gregory's fortunes, both in actual influence and income. This is despite the fact that in the following ten years there is considerable evidence that Gregory enjoyed a luxurious lifestyle and ran his business affairs as if nothing had changed. Blackmail probably helped in some way, since Gregory would have had ample information at his disposal for that purpose. But another feature of his career in these years also bears closer inspection, and that is his relationship with various right-wing networks. Pinto-Duschinsky summarises Gregory's position thus:

"The web of personal contacts that has been outlined is a good illustration of what can for convenience be called the 'triangular relationship'. In the inter-war years, it linked parts of (1) the secret service, (2) Conservative Central Office, and (3) some right-wing business lobbies. They were united in their fear of left-wing or Communist influence. It was evidently felt that Gregory was in a position to reveal scandalous information that not only would harm the Conservative Party and some of its business supporters but also might damage the national interest."[1]

It will not be the argument here that Gregory was a key player in these networks, in the sense that he was, for example, a policy-maker or a politician. But a good case can be made that he was never far behind the key players, and was capable of making connections which served the far right-wing cause of many fellow Conservatives, be they British or foreign. Given also that Gregory earned his living from taking a commission from the various activities in which he engaged, it is not unreasonable to assume that he continued to act as a conduit for funds from one place to another.

His membership of the Thule Society, a seemingly esoteric German society, may have given him ideas.[2] The Thule Society was founded in 1918 by Rudolf Blauer, a wealthy anti-Semite. The creed of the Thule Society was based on a myth of a lost island civilisation, the secrets of which could be gained by initiates through occult rituals. It propagated the idea of Aryan supremacy, and sought the extermination of "inferior" races. Through the Thule Society a number of wealthy Germans were able to channel their support into the new nazi movement, particularly Hitler's National Socialist German Worker Party (NASDAP).[3] The Thule Society provided an excellent cover for those who wished to support Hitler, but whose position demanded discretion. That Gregory joined the Society demonstrates a certain perspicacity, given the fact that it was both well endowed and well connected with the rising powers in Germany. Whilst the rise of Hitler caused some concern in British Conservative circles, the majority of the Party's leadership welcomed this new force in Germany which it believed would stave off Soviet expansion. Until his fall from grace in 1932, Gregory had certainly tied his colours to the most fashionable new movement in right-wing circles.

Perhaps through his membership of the Thule Society, but certainly through his trips to Germany, Gregory developed other relationships which it is not unreasonable to suppose may have borne fruit. He made friends with Count Werner von Alvensleben, who "had not only schemed to get von Papen appointed Chancellor of the Reich but had put Hitler in touch with the senile President Hindenburg."[4] Alvensleben was well placed in 1932 to warn Hitler of a possible coup by General Schleicher, whom Hitler had been negotiating with to gain the Chancellorship.[5] In comparison to these events, Gregory might appear out of his depth - a rather ridiculous figure. But he nevertheless was committed to the cause, and this would have done him nothing but good within those circles where support for fascism was increasingly seen as a respectable thing. Gregory's magazine the Whitehall Gazette & St. James Review in 1932 summed up the feelings of a great many Conservatives at the time when it said:

Price of Power

"Apart from the considerations of foreign policy an essential advantage which must be recognised universally as proceeding from the Hitler movement is that of having constrained all the forces of the Left to unite against the government . . and of having taken upon themselves in every way possible the defence of the national interests against purely brutal and subversive aims."[6]

Gregory attended the formation in Germany of the League for the Protection of Western European Culture which "must help all efforts tending to the maintenance and creation of private property."[7] In November, 1930, Gregory rapturously reported on a further rally of the League, at which Brig. General Sir William Horwood, the former Commissioner of the Metropolitan Police, spoke. Donald McCormick, whose book Murder by Perfection opened up the possibility of Gregory committing two murders, makes the valid conjecture that "All these activities may have helped Gregory maintain his influence in certain circles, but they did not bring him in any money, nor the hoped-for well-paid post of roving agent for the British Secret Service."[8] Whilst it is not clear whether the conjecture is true, so far as money or MI5 is concerned, Gregory's positioning of himself at the centre of the far right must have had some tangible benefits. Is it conceivable that his special issue of the Whitehall Gazette of September/October 1932, celebrating "Mussolini's great achievement: the tenth anniversary of the fascist regime", featuring signed articles by Italian Ministers and an autographed portrait of Il Duce, went unrewarded? At this stage, even the likes of Winston Churchill were still in awe of Mussolini. As late as 1933, Churchill could be found praising "the Roman genius", "the greatest lawgiver among living men", even if fascism wasn't a model appropriate for Britain, which could depend on its democracy to protect its freedom without recourse to extreme measures.[9]

These views were expressed by many Conservatives, most of whom also extended their admiration to Hitler. Some went further than merely an expression of view; Oliver Locker-Lampson MP, for example, formed his own fascist-like organisation called the "Blueshirts".[10] Others met Alfred Rosenberg, the Nazi ideologue on his many visits made to Britain to enlist support, including a visit to the Carlton Club. Indirectly, Rosenberg helped to finance Gregory, with money channelled through the Ukrainian Nationalist movement, headed by Paul Skoropadsky, the "Hetman of the Ukraine."[11]

The Triangular Relationship

Gregory's relationship with Skoropadsky went sour in 1932, allegedly because of a stupid remark Gregory had made whilst visiting the right-wing Herrenklub in Berlin. This led to the rapid demise of his reputation amongst some of his German friends, who realised he was not all he made himself out to be. Nevertheless, up until that point, Gregory was pursuing a policy which was for all intents and purposes what became government policy shortly thereafter. In the words of McCormick, "Making use of his right-wing friends in England he put forward the plan of arranging a secret understanding with extreme right-wing movements in Germany, the idea being that if Britain came to terms with these organisations, she could form a bloc against the spread of Bolshevism in Germany or France."[12] Given that Hitler had not yet achieved power in Germany, it is clear that Gregory was in the forefront of thinking about this "secret understanding" which was to be the hallmark of Neville Chamberlain's collusion with Hitler several years later.

Thus, Gregory placed himself so far as he could at the centre of British support for east European nationalism. His connections on one much earlier occasion had almost literally made him a kingmaker, when it fell to him to try and find a suitable person to fill the vacant Albanian throne, on behalf of his mentor, Sir Basil Zaharoff (the arms dealer), and Lloyd George. After Zaharoff consulted Sir William Sutherland, Lloyd George's uncouth press agent, Gregory was given the task. But no suitable 'English country gentleman with an income of £10,000 a year' could be found, and the deal fell through when the Italian-backed Zog took the throne.[13]

It was to Sir Basil Zaharoff, a sinister influence in European affairs up until his death in the 1936, that Gregory owed his rise in society. Zaharoff funded Gregory's original interest in the private detective agency business, and no doubt his help made it easier for Gregory to serve Sir Vernon Kell, head of MI5 during the First World War. More importantly perhaps, in the current context, was Zaharoff's role as head of the 'Vickerage'. The Vickers armaments company had flourished under Zaharoff's tutelage, and the growth of the company cannot be isolated from the unconventional or downright immoral methods used by Zaharoff to gain business. The company (which later became Vickers-Armstrong, after Armstrong's were taken over) exercised considerable influence with the government - to the extent that the Foreign Office would operate as agents for Vickers.[14] Key

33

employees of the company got key jobs with the government. For example, a friend of Gregory's, Lord Southborough was a technical advisor to Vickers before the First World War, then became Civil Lord of the Admiralty. We have already seen how another member of the 'Vickerage', Sir Vincent Caillard, with Sir William Sutherland and other friends of Gregory amongst the Coalition Whips set up an anti-communist group, funded to the tune of £100,000. Later we find an indirect link between Vickers and the financing of Hitler:

"The Hitler movement was financed not only by Hugenberg [a former director of Krupps and following WWI, a leading German newspaper publisher], who dealt out the subsidies of the heavy industry, but also by Pintsch, a Berlin firm controlled by Vickers, who from the very first had an agent at Hitler's headquarters."[15]

Whilst a statement of the political objectives of this Vickers subsidiary is not available, it might be reasonable to assume that it would have been motivated in much the same way as was another foreign company associated with Vickers, the Spanish armaments and shipbuilding company La Sociedad Espanola de Construccion Naval. Sir Charles Craven, Chairman of Vickers-Armstrong explained the situation to the Nye Commission on Armaments in 1934:

"Of course things look very stormy in Spain at present, and I sincerely hope nothing will be done to check the swing to the Right which has recently taken place, because the present Government look as if they were going to be most sympathetic to the Sociedad and give us a modest Naval programme, which, I can assure you, is very sorely needed to keep the place going."[16]

As illustrated in Tory MP, by Simon Haxey, published in 1939, a number of leading Conservatives were shareholders in Vickers, and Sir John Anderson MP was a director before being appointed to the Cabinet in 1938. Following the forced disclosure of company donations in the 1960s, Vickers emerged as one of the Conservative Party's more generous benefactors, as it had connections with and supported the Right during the inter-war years. It would be reasonable to assume that it provided support to the Tories in that period. Arguably, given Sir Vincent Caillard's involvement, Vickers support would have found its way to one of the 'front' organisations which worked alongside, and in harmony with the Conservative Party.

Another sinister figure known to Gregory was Sir Joseph Ball, the so-called eminence grise of Neville Chamberlain, and a key

Conservative Central Office officer - serving as its Director from 1930 to 1939. Although Ball was appointed by Davidson in 1924, having been persuaded to leave the direct employ of MI5, he long outstayed his former boss's tenure at CCO. Indeed, given Ball's close attachment to Chamberlain, it is probable that Ball did all he could to force Davidson out of office. Ball tapped funds for the indirect use of the Party, since he was able in 1936 to take over a publication called Truth, a long standing political weekly. Ball wanted a vehicle for his pro-Chamberlain and right wing views. The shares in the Truth Publishing Company were bought by Lord Luke of Pavenham, Chairman of the Business Committee of the National Publicity Bureau.[17] The National Publicity Bureau was set up in 1934 to promote the policies of the National Government during the 1935 general election, and as such, was nominally non-partisan. As Ball remarked, "The funds collected by the Bureau come to a very large extent from Joint Stock Companies, the executives of which regard themselves as precluded from subscribing to any party organisation."[18] Once again, therefore, the fears of the likes of Sir Vincent Caillard had been addressed, and in the case of the National Publicity Bureau a simple mechanism was established by which donations could be received for use on behalf of the Conservative Party, even if some of the hierarchy of Central Office whom Ball didn't like were firmly shut out of the arrangements.

The ownership of Truth was generally a well-kept secret; indeed even after the start of the Second World War, and despite his extreme right wing views, Ball was able for a while to be appointed to the Committee (18b) which oversaw the internment of suspected nazi sympathisers. Whilst he was serving on that committee, Truth was to describe Hitler as "the most unassuming and probably the most efficient dictator"[19] but earlier it had done what it could to allay fear of Hitler's intentions:

"The bogey of German 'aggression' does not seem so dark and dangerous if one remembers that it has been used, so far, to regain German sovereign rights within her own frontiers and that there is little evidence of any intent to cross other people's frontiers by force of arms."[20]

That was in 1937, but Ball was obviously fearful that his message, and inter alia the message of Chamberlain was not sinking in. In a memorandum in 1938 he wrote that:

Price of Power

"steps should be taken immediately to secure finance, possibly from National Publicity Bureau funds, for the formation of a national organisation, ostensibly non-political in character, with the avowed object of providing accurate and impartial information about foreign affairs, but with the secret objective of combating the dangerous propaganda of, and eventually smashing, the League of Nations Union and the pernicious Youth Organisation controlled by it."[21]

Securing the funding for such an organisation should not have been difficult since Ball was himself well-connected in the business world, being the director of a number of companies, particularly in mining. Indeed, after the war he became a director of Consolidated Goldfields, which, when the time came for disclosure of company donations, was found to be one of the biggest contributors to Tory Party funds. So far as Ball's proposal for a new organisation went, he estimated its costs to be about £15,000 annually, becoming self-financing after two years. Since nothing more has been heard of it, one can only suppose that the advent of war brought down the League of Nations faster than Ball could.

Another little charted aspect of the Triangular Relationship must be the role played by the City in the inter-war years. The network operating between the City and the Conservative Party, and their combined support for fascism still remains shrouded in mystery. One of the oldest merchant banks, Brown, Shipley, nevertheless provides a clue into the networking possibilities available. Brown, Shipley had been an employer of many prominent Conservatives - perhaps the most prominent being Edward Heath. Many of the bank's partners were or became Conservative MPs. Sir W. R. Stuttaford was Chairman of the Conservative Political Centre. Another Conservative MP, who became Speaker of the Commons, was Sir H. Hylton-Foster, who married into the Clifton-Brown family of Brown, Shipley. For good measure, the 12th Baron Farnham, a director since 1991, is the Pro Grand Master of the United Grand Lodge of Freemasons. Also for fifteen years a partner at Brown, Shipley was Montagu Norman, the future Governor of the Bank of England, who served in that post for an unprecedented 24 years.

In 1926, Brown, Shipley were represented on the Tories' City Appeal Committee by Edward Clifton-Brown, who was also a director of the Westminster Bank Ltd., the Standard Bank of South Africa and Royal Exchange Assurance. In 1926, the merchant banks and assurance companies dominated the City Appeal committee, and by the 1990s their sector was still the largest known group of corporate donors to the Conservative Party. A study in 1973 found that the 381 directors of 17 merchant banks held between them a total of 2,211 directorships altogether.[22] These networks were of course crucial to the funding of the Conservative Party, if the membership of the 1926 Appeal Committee is anything to go by, and in the case of Brown, Shipley's connections, this appears to have been the case with regards to support for Hitler as well. Through their intimate connection with Brown Brothers & Co of the United States, which merged in 1931 with W.A Harriman & Co Inc. and Harriman Bros & Company, becoming Brown Brothers, Harriman, there is a now well-charted network which not merely traded with or lent money to the Nazi regime, but proactively assisted in the promotion of Nazism outside of Germany.[23]

Just as Neville Chamberlain led the political wing of the Conservative establishment into its collusion with the Nazis, it could be said that Montagu Norman led the financial wing of the Conservative establishment into a similar mode. Whilst Norman, who never cast his vote, undoubtedly considered himself outside the party political frame - as did so many industrialists whose contributions to the party were designed to defend free enterprise, rather than the Tory Party - he nevertheless had such a background and held such a position that his influence in assisting the implementation of government policy would be immense. Although at times he felt he was no more than a 'financial technician', Norman's policies were highly political. After the First World War, for example, his high interest rate policies, then as now designed to slow down an overheating economy, led to greater unemployment. Nor could he conceal - try as he might - his distaste for a Labour government. Once again, this was not 'political'; a colleague overheard him say, after Labour came to power in 1924:

"This means the beginning of the end of all the work we have been doing. It was not a political utterance, for I never heard him express any political opinions. He was, in my judgement, referring to his work of preserving the City as a body whose independent judgement should be respected by reason of its manifest integrity."[24]

His pro-German sympathies appeared similarly to stem from a 'non-political' banker's desire to ensure economic stability in

Price of Power

Germany, but also from a hatred of all things French. His support for Germany, predating the rise of Hitler, continued up to the very outbreak of war. And, whilst his sympathetic biographer, Andrew Boyle, describes Norman as being one of the last of the 'sleepwalkers', (Boyle deprecates the use of the 'retrospectively wise smear' of 'appeaser' with regards his hero) it is clear that Norman's sympathy with various aspects of Nazi ideology left him open to the suggestion that he was not unduly concerned with what was happening in Nazi Germany: not that is, concerned enough to reverse the financial support which he had approved. And what Norman approved, other lesser City mortals were likely to follow. Norman's authority has been summed up thus:

"Being a completely closed system, the City spoke out rarely - and then ex cathedra - through its appointed high priest, the Governor of the Bank. Individuals who held contrary views or talked out of turn were cold-shouldered and utterly disregarded; those ill-advised enough to dissent publicly were few. The fear of losing business by offending the hierarchy and thus being labelled as wayward and unreliable was not so strong a motive as the herd instinct of attachment to a community with its own code of understanding and loyalty."[25]

Norman had a number of highly placed connections with the Hitler clique. One very close friend was Dr. Hjalmar Schacht, one-time President of the Reichsbank, whose grandson was named after Norman. Schacht had become a long term supporter of Hitler, although by the time the war started he was to suffer a similar fate as had many others who for one reason or another were to fall foul of the Führer. Prior to his estrangement however, Schacht had convinced foreign financiers that Hitler's Germany was a sound destination for credit, and his relationship with Norman, whose world-wide reputation was unimpeachable, must have helped instil the necessary backbone into the 'herd instinct' of his colleagues. But Schacht's domestic reputation was not all that it could have been, since he was blamed by some for building up an unsustainable raft of credit which would become the undoing of Nazi Germany - indeed, even without another war, Germany's finances were headed for the rocks.[26]

Norman also met Alfred Rosenberg, who on one of his visits to London was seeking to gain acceptance for Hitler's bid for power.

The Triangular Relationship

Part of that mission necessarily involved trying to convince London financiers and bankers that a Hitler government would be creditworthy. In this objective, Rosenberg's task would be made easier by the interlocking relationships between British and German bankers. Rosenberg followed up his talks with Norman to meet representatives of the British end of the Schroder Bank. Subsequently, an associate of the Schroder Bank, Baron Kurt von Schroder, hosted a meeting at his Cologne home in 1932, at which "The arrangement to cover the debt of the Nazi Party and finance their expenses until they were in power was made among Hitler, von Papen and von Schroder."[27] The importance of this meeting may be gauged from a comment by Fritz Thyssen, the leading pro-Nazi German industrialist, who recorded that "It is certain that huge expenditures had completely exhausted the National Socialists' party funds. This is also the reason why Herr Von Papen arranged the meeting between Adolf Hitler and the Cologne banker, von Schroder. The party finances, which just at that time were threatening to reduce the party to an unbearable position, had to be remedied. Its subsequent success in obtaining the necessary funds was complete."[28] Without this support at such a crucial juncture - just as Hitler was about to seize power - Hitler's task would have been far more difficult. Much of the money for Hitler's propaganda effort was found to have been provided indirectly and directly by Western sources and companies.[29]

A director of the Schroder Bank, as well as the Bank of England, was F.C. Tiarks. Tiarks was a member of the Conservative Party's 1926 City Appeal Committee, and later served as the British member of the Bank of International Settlements (BIS). Throughout the Second World War, the BIS, later implicated in the Swiss Nazi banking scandal, continued to lend money to Germany - somewhat revealingly in order to maintain the international financial order. An example of the banking world's amoral fiscal rectitude came to light in 1938, when after Hitler's invasion of Czechoslovakia, Czech gold deposits held in London were handed over to Germany. When pressed in the House of Commons, Chamberlain denied that this was the case. But it wasn't true: Norman had approved the transfer, which was carried out by the BIS.[30] Doubts about Tiarks' connections with the Nazis had to be confronted as late as 1942, when "President Roosevelt... cabled to the Prime Minister, intimating that these reports were so persistent that they must be traced to source."[31]

Price of Power

Norman interviewed Tiarks twice, and was 'absolutely' reassured that there was no truth in the rumours. Indeed, so far as any meeting with Dr Schacht was concerned, this would have been impossible by 1942: by then the former President of the Reichsbank was in a concentration camp. Interestingly however, Andrew Boyle comments that "So long as Norman did not try to obstruct or interfere with the serious business of winning the war, Churchill would choose to leave him well alone."[32] Indeed, Norman was able to contribute to the Allied war effort: using his other connections, he introduced Ian Fleming, a stockbroker, to the Director of Naval Intelligence - and thus contributed in no small way to the creation of James Bond.[33]

There can be little doubt that the Conservative establishment did more than simply appease Hitler - they actively aided his rise to power and helped him stay in power in the first shaky period of his Chancellorship. This process has now been more aptly titled 'collusion'[34], rather than appeasement or at the other extreme, conspiracy. The avoidance of moral scruples in the pursuit of profit on the part of members of the Conservative establishment has not abated since the war: as the Scott Inquiry into arms sales to Iraq showed, the habit remains.

Chapter Three

Maundy's friends

G ood food and wine have been the stock-in-trade of lobbyists and political intriguers from the start of recorded history. As inducements or rewards, lavish meals with copious amounts of vintage wine provide excellent opportunities for deals to be struck in an atmosphere of well-being and bonhomie. Eating together is generally, though certainly not universally accepted as a means to forming a bond of friendship.

Maundy Gregory's capturing of the 'Eve of Derby' dinner has been seen as one of his greatest coups. The dinners, held on the eve of the race, were started in 1912 by the sportsman and Tory MP, Walter Faber. Until 1926 they were held at the Carlton Hotel, and by then had become one of the premier social events of the year. Gregory became the dinner's host by the simple expedient of co-opting two of its organisers, Faber and Lord Southborough, onto the Committee of Gregory's Ambassador Club. The dinners were held at the Ambassador Club from 1927 to 1932, the year before Gregory's downfall, and from 1933 moved to the Savoy Hotel.

The guest list of the dinners, running into the 150-mark, largely comprised leading politicians and other notables of the day, who for the occasion were pledged not to talk about politics but only about the forthcoming race. In this simple sense, they could be described as non-political events. Gregory's agenda would of course be merely to be seen discreetly (sic) mixing with his guests as an equal, of sorts.

The fact that Gregory was able to continue with this display of generosity, years after the Chairman of the Conservative Party, J.C.C.

Price of Power

Davidson had vowed to finish off Gregory's trade in honours seems odd. The impression we are given by Davidson in his memoirs (and his explanation of the relationship of Gregory to the party seems to have been universally accepted) is that the Conservative Party had washed its hands of the tout, and could, barring one or two misdemeanours, say that the corruption of the honours system had ended if not with Lloyd George, then certainly with the passing of the 1925 Honours (Prevention of Abuses) Act.

In fact the evidence given, albeit scant, in Davidson's memoirs only illustrates Davidson's disapproval for Gregory's selling of honours, and not for the idea that honours may yet still raise money for the Tories. And, for all that Davidson could have done to stop or at least isolate Gregory years previously, here we are in 1931 looking at the guest list of the Eve of Derby dinner which reads like a combined Carlton Club/Conservative Party membership list. The interesting thing about this list is that it contains not just Conservatives, nor even prominent Conservatives, but that it would be incredible for many of them not to have been aware of their host's background. How would one describe Gregory's situation in these circumstances? Had he hypnotised this noble gathering into a state of disbelief? Had he a blackmailer's stranglehold on them? Or was it simply his food and wine they were after, regardless of the question of how it was to be paid for?

What is not in doubt is that for Gregory, fine trappings aside, the Eve of Derby dinners must have been work engagements. The guest list (see end of chapter) tells us not only that his presence as host was not seen in any way as a danger, but it also tells us that Gregory still had considerable influence.

It would be wrong to apply 1990s standards on "sleaze" to 1930s political behaviour, since clearly many things that were acceptable then are no longer so. Indeed, whilst in today's climate professional lobbyists probably wouldn't publicise the guest lists of their events too much, Gregory could only see benefit in the above list being published in The Times, which it duly was.

Much of the list also reflects Gregory's right-wing political stance and connections. Whilst it is by no means an homogenous group of people, even the smattering of right-wing Labour MPs ties in with the hue of the event.

Here too are people who were close colleagues of Gregory during the glory days of Lloyd George's honours racket – F.E. Guest being the most significant. The nature of the game may have changed since the 1925 Honours (Prevention of Abuses) Act, but to see this group of people rubbing shoulders with Gregory in 1931 throws much light onto the reluctance of anyone in authority to deal with him. The truth is, he was there with them and it was only the mismanagement of his own affairs that led to his downfall, not the precipitate actions of any (like Davidson) who claim credit for it.

Of course, those who hold to the view that this purely 'social' event tells us little about the interaction of the guests have a point. One could look to the differences that were to emerge later over many of the guests' enthusiasm for fascism, for example. One could point to the fact that even though some prominent members of the Economic League were present, John Baker White, the League's Director, had investigated Gregory's background and wanted to get rid of him. But he didn't, and that was for much the same reason that nobody who supped at Gregory's table did – because even if they knew about his activities, they were never sure who else did, and moreover, who else co-operated with him. In the end, they paid his pension, a reward which must have given Gregory much satisfaction.

Indeed, the final, fitting irony is that it was one of Gregory's least distinguished guests at this dinner who paid all or something for his retirement. Julien Cahn was knighted during Ramsay MacDonald's premiership – under protest by MacDonald – in order to get Gregory out of the Conservatives' harm's way after his appearance in court and conviction under the 1925 Honours (Prevention of Abuses) Act in March 1933. According to MacDonald's diary for the 13th December 1933, Stanley Baldwin insisted that Cahn should be honoured with a knighthood. Baldwin argued that:

"Maundy Gregory's papers and Maundy Gregory's presence here would stir up such a filthy sewer as would poison public life ... that all parties were involved (I corrected him at once and said 'Not ours'. He smiled and said that unfortunately friends of mine were. I replied that if they were I knew nothing about it. Then I remembered that Clynes and Henderson were mentioned at an earlier stage); that people like Winston Churchill, Austen Chamberlain, Birkenhead were involved; that Gregory had been used by Ll. G. and Bonar Law." [1]

Baldwin told MacDonald that £30,000 was needed to clear the "dungheap" – and six months later acquiesced "Mr B... involves me in scandal by forcing me to give an honour because a man has paid £30,000 to get Tory headquarters and some Tories living and dead out of a mess." [2]

MacDonald by this time was ill and in any case was very much a prisoner of the Tories as a figurehead of what was essentially a Tory government. But the diary entry confirms that in all probability many of Gregory's dinner guests knew what his game was. But the Cahn episode in Gregory's career also illustrates the point that the Conservatives appeared to have had more to fear from exposure than did Lloyd George's Liberals. Whilst it may be true that Lloyd George wouldn't have cared too much either way if his earlier massive sales of honours had been confirmed (and so didn't feel he could be blackmailed) he wouldn't for one moment have missed the kind of money needed to purchase Gregory's retirement. Much of his political fund was still intact in 1933.

The fact that it was the Tories who paid such a high price – not merely from the personal coffers of Cahn, but in so blatantly compromising their own honour (surely honour was one of the supposed essential characteristics of Baldwin?) shows that Davidson's spin on the Gregory years leaves far too much unanswered.

As the guest list at the 1931 'Faber' eve of Derby dinner illustrates (and does again to an almost equal extent in 1932, the last that Gregory was able to host), the event was one which could attract in open company with this "dunghill" the most extraordinary grouping of elite Conservatives imaginable. In their midst we see senior figures from the Metropolitan Police and intelligence circles. They knew who their host was – contrary to the impression given by some writers. At the 1932 dinner for example, as recorded faithfully in the Whitehall Gazette, Maj. General Seely rose to pay homage to Gregory in the kindest terms.[3]

Davidson no doubt did wish to break Gregory, and was a contributory factor in his downfall. But he had to tread so carefully, it would not have been obvious to the Party at large what was going on, although breaking Gregory financially might mean "making enemies amongst the people – and some very well known people indeed – who were his clients, and who expected honours in return for their payments to him."[4] This comment, made in 1927, demonstrates how little impact the 1925 Act had made on these "well-known people".

Davidson provides an example of one high ranking Tory:

"He had paid Maundy Gregory a large sum down in order to become a peer, and he was in addition a good Tory and worked for the Conservative Party in the City. Although he paid his money to Maundy Gregory, he had also been recommended independently by the Conservative Association for an honour for the work he had done for the Party. The first thing I asked him was whether he had been approached before. I went on to say that he had a very good recommendation for the work he had done in the City and for the Party. He then admitted rather naïvely that he had paid a large sum on account to Maundy Gregory. I told him that that was not a very clever thing to have done, because Baldwin couldn't possibly recommend to the Sovereign for an honour a man whose name was on Maundy Gregory's list. I said it was equivalent to buying an honour through a broker. He said he hadn't quite looked at it in that light, and that he had been told it was quite a usual thing."[5]

It is most likely that it was Gregory that told this "good Tory" that his method of obtaining honours was the "usual thing"; but it is significant that this well placed seeker of honour was "naïve" enough to believe him. How many, and for how long, did all the other "well known people" adopt a similarly naïve attitude? Right up to the point of Gregory's public exposure, undoubtedly. Gregory's links with the hierarchy of the Conservative Party clearly never diminished, even during and after Davidson's tenure in office. (Davidson was forced out in May 1930, at the instigation of Neville Chamberlain, who saw Davidson as "not only useless, but a liability to the entire leadership."[6]

Perhaps Davidson had to go not only because he was causing discontent in the Party generally with his inept support for Baldwin after the defeat of 1929, but also because he was interfering with the long cherished beliefs of many of his highly placed colleagues that there were 'ways and means' of speeding up the recognition they felt they deserved. For a short period at least, many Tories after that defeat may have seen Gregory as the only available route for seeking honours, if they vainly assumed he had any power to influence Labour politicians in the 1929 Labour government. Interestingly, Gerald MacMillan, who wrote the first biography of Gregory in the 1950s, and so didn't have access to Davidson's account which was published in 1969, wrote of Gregory in 1932 that he "apparently tried to demand a higher commission or 'rake-off' for the part he played, and as a consequence quarrelled with whoever it was in the Party organisation that had charge of Honours business at the time."[7]

Why should any of these good Tories believe that money could buy honours after it became illegal? Davidson can share much of the blame. In the case of the "Persistent Commoner" (so-called by Davidson's biographer Robert Rhodes James) we find that although Davidson is not prepared to take this man's money in exchange for an honour, he does give some encouragement to the belief that, e.g. "his generosity to the Party would not be forgotten in the future" or "I should not forget the service which he had rendered to the Party."[8] In this particular case, the Persistent Commoner was repaid by the Party the sum of £100,000, after legal action was threatened when the honour never materialised. But later the Persistent Commoner's money started rolling in again, more than making up for the Party's temporary loss. There is clear evidence in Davidson's own memoirs, therefore, that Davidson's behaviour was not entirely dissimilar to Gregory's. Gregory's patter would necessarily have to include reference to the delicate possibility of failure, and occasionally he too was forced to hand money back to disgruntled customers. But Davidson was in a much stronger position than Gregory to give off conflicting signals and so reap the reward without any intention of honouring his vague encouragements. He could accept money for the Party, and not give any commitments at all – so much the better. In such cases he could, in his mind innocently profit from the naïveté of honours seekers, many of whom he would not wish to offend. In other cases, he clearly did resist large sums on offer. One such case recorded in his memoirs was a straightforward entreaty to swing a large naval engineering contract in return for a contribution of £200,000 to party funds. Davidson was not open to such blatant corruption.

Apart from Davidson's published memoirs, there is evidence in his unpublished papers of honours trafficking. These show that a rich Indian merchant, A.J. David bought his baronetcy for £30,000 from Davidson.[9] David's sponsor was Oliver Locker-Lampson – an acquaintance of Gregory's.

Since Davidson's own account credits himself with the downfall of Gregory, it is worth noting Davidson's attitude to his victim once he was trapped:

"Nobody knew to what extent Maundy Gregory would betray his

past in his desperation and financial stringency. We accordingly organised someone to go and see him, who told him that he couldn't avoid a term of imprisonment, but that if he kept silent we could bring pressure to bear on the authorities to let him live in France after his sentence had been served.

"When this occurred he was met at the prison gates by a friend of mine [Capt. R C Kelly, also a friend of Gregory's] who drove him in a motor car to Dover, took him to France, ensconced him in previously arranged accommodation, gave him a sum of money and promised him a quarterly pension, on condition he never disclosed his identity or made any reference to the past ... we kept him until the end..."[10]

In other words, they got Gregory to change a plea of "Not guilty" to "Guilty" in return for a light sentence, ensuring that evidence, which Inspector Askew, of Scotland Yard, hinted at in the court hearing,[11] was kept under wraps. Any attempts to further investigate the matter were quashed. When a Labour MP asked the Home Secretary in the House of Commons whether Askew's further complaints would be investigated, Sir John Gilmour (Conservative) replied "The complaints extended over a period of about three years – they have already been investigated by the police but no sufficient evidence has been obtained to justify criminal proceedings."[12] In this respect, if by "police" Sir John meant those in the charge of Sir William Horwood, the Commissioner of Metropolitan Police, then little would come of any 'investigation', since Horwood was a friend of Gregory's. This effectively made any charge difficult, as John Baker White, a former director of the Economic League and MI5 man has recorded. He accompanied Col. O. Harker, Deputy Director of MI5 to see Horwood with a file on Gregory which contained enough "to satisfy the Director of Public Prosecutions". However the two MI5 men bumped into Gregory on their way up to see Horwood in his Scotland Yard office, and without any further reflection Harker said "That does it – there's no point going up" and destroyed the file there and then.[13] Given that the Director of MI5 reports directly to the Home Secretary, it seems odd that superficially at least, other channels were not used to nail Gregory.

The phrase 'perverting the course of justice for the good of the party' probably never entered Davidson's head. That in obtaining the money to pay for Gregory's retirement was itself a criminal act also may never have entered Davidson's head. In the light too, of

Price of Power

contemporary suspicions that Gregory was a murderer (a full investigation of that was of course prevented by Gregory's absence abroad) a highly probable conspiracy to protect the interests of the Conservative Party can be established. Seen in this light, Davidson's reputation as a "puritan" have to be treated with caution. He was an obedient servant of the Party, with an overwhelming lack of scruples. As G. R. Searle put it in Corruption in British Politics, 1895 – 1930, "... though the Conservative Ministries of the 1920s prudently avoided the 'excesses' which had brought such opprobrium on the post-war coalition, one should view with some scepticism the claim that Baldwin and his colleagues were living on a much higher plane than their predecessors."[14]

Eve of Derby Dinner. 1931 Guest List:

Name	Club	Comments
Sir Walter Allen	Conservative	C in C Metropolitan Special Constabulary
Lord Ashfield	Carlton	Director of Midland Bank; ICI; Tory MP, ex Cabinet
Joseph Ball		Chairman of Conservative Research Dept; ex MI5
Brig. Gen. Hon. Everard Baring		Dir., Nat. Provincial Bank; Chair, Southern Railway
Capt. Woolf Barnato		Daredevil motorist, diamond heir
Lord Bayford	Carlton	Conservative MP; former minister
Detmar Blow	Athenaeum	Architect
Ralph Blumenfield	Carlton	Chair, Daily Express; founder of Anti-Socialist Union
Stanley S Bond	Carlton	Chair, Butterworth's Publishers Vice Chair, Central Board of Finance, Church of England
Prof. Tancred Borenius	Travellers	Much honoured
A C H Borrer		
Alfred C Bossom	Carlton	Nat. Conservative MP, elected 1931; Grand Prior of Primrose League; founder Anglo-Baltic Society
D A Bourn		
Sir Harold Bowden	Whites	Vice-Pres, Federation of British Industry
Sir Archibald Boyd-Carpenter	Carlton	Conservative MP; minister
Brendan Bracken		Conservative MP, to become a minister; He had bought with friends only weeks earlier a gift of a Daimler for their friend Winston Churchill on his return from a trip to the United States.
Quintin Bridge		
Sir George T Broadbridge	Carlton	Lord Mayor of London,1936/37; featured in Dec. 1925 Whitehall Gazette; Conservative MP
Warwick Brookes	Carlton	Conservative MP
H A Browne		
Viscount Burnham		Managing proprietor of Daily Telegraph; Liberal then Conservative MP; workedwith Davidson on General Strike-breaking British Gazette; founder of precursor to the Economic League, the Industrial League.
Col. H W Burton	Carlton	Conservative MP
Ald. Sir William Miler Burton		
Lt. Col. A T Butler		
T W Byford		
W C Bywater		
Sir Julien Cahn	Carlton	President of City of Nottingham; Conservative Association; one of the "Officials I have met" featured in Whitehall Gazette, Feb. 1927. Cahn's chief position to merit this treatment seemed to be as

		Master of Foxhounds, Burton Hunt but "also a first class cricketer"
Sir James Calder		Director of Distillers
Lord Camrose	Carlton	Editor in Chief Daily Telegraph; Sunday Times; close friend of Davidson; offered to help Davidson fund a newspaper to support the Tory line.
R H Carruthers		
Sir Austen Chamberlain		Leader, Conservative Party until Carlton Club meeting in 1922 that ended Lloyd George Coalition
Brig. Gen. J Charteris		Conservative MP – described as an incompetent intelligence aide to Field Marshall Haig in WW1.
Lt. Cmd. Sir Warden Chilcott	Carlton	Conservative MP; Wrote for Whitehall Gazette
Winston Churchill		A noted lover of the Eve of Derby dinner
J H Clynes		Labour Cabinet Minister; spoke at 1932 dinner: "I could not rise at such a gathering as this, as say a leader of the Opposition, but at this gathering there is no opposition. We here are as a National Government"
W H Collins		Chairman and Man. Director of Cerebos Ltd; Dir. Fortnum and Mason; Carreras Ltd; lauded in the January, 1931 issue of Whitehall Gazette as "An Ambassador of Commerce"
Henry F Compton		Conservative MP
Viscount Craigavon	Carlton	Conservative MP, first Prime Minister of N. Ireland
Douglas Crawford		
Sir Herbert Creedy		Civil Servant – private secretary to various ministers, including Lloyd George; sought to update Army Intelligence offices in preparedness for the election of Labour government in 1924.
Bernard Cuddon		
Eric Cuddon		
Dr F W M Cunningham		
Lord Cushendon		Conservative MP – a "Diehard"
J C C Davidson		Chairman of the Conservative Party – who left the impression that he would rather have choked than eat any of Gregory's food, but he was there anyway
Col. Harry Day		Eccentric Labour MP
Capt. F H J Drummond		
Lt. Cdr. Godfrey E Duveen		
Major H Piers Dyer		
Harold E Eastwood		Head of Communications Dept., Foreign Office, 1925+
Viscount Elibank	Carlton	Conservative MP; minister
Lord Fairhaven	Carlton	
Dr R Fielding-Ould	Carlton	
William J Firth	Carlton	Steel manufacturer, knighted 1932
Walter G Fish		Dir., Assoc. Newspapers, Editor of Daily Mail
Sir Charles Frederick	Carlton	
Lord Glanely	Carlton	Shipper, brewer
Sir William Godde		Unofficial financial advisor to Hungarian government, 1923 -1941; former joint news editor Daily Mail
C T Gordon		
Cdr. M Graham-White		
Charles Graves	Athenaeum	Possibly the Asst. Editor Punch; Spectator
David Greig		
Capt. Hon. F E Guest		Former Liberal Chief Whip during the Coalition government, a friend of Gregory's from the days of Lloyd George honours scandals; became Tory MP
Charles Gulliver		
H A Gywnne	Carlton	Editor of Morning Post; circulated a "Diehard Manifesto"; was a critic of Lloyd George over one of the honours scandals during the height of honours sales; worked with Davidson on "British Gazette"
Sir Sven Hansen		
Ralph Harwood		Deputy Treasurer to the King

Price of Power

Name	Club	Description
Sir Arthur Hazlerigg	Carlton	Conservative parliamentary candidate; member of Home Office Advisory Committee 18b 1939-41 – advising on internment of 'Nazi' and like sympathisers
Maj. Sir George Hennessey		Vice Chair of Conservative Party from 1931; minister; wrote for first issue of Gregory's Whitehall Gazette; 1st Baron Windlesham Copley de Lisle Hewitt
Jesse W Hind	Carlton	Colliery owner knighted in 1934; associated with the Economic League
Sir Clement Hindley	Athenaeum	Chairman of Betting Central Board
Frank Hodges		Labour MP; first Chair of Electricity Board; former secretary of Miners' Federation seen to have taken weak stand on behalf of miners
Col. Sir Arthur Holbrook	Carlton	Conservative MP; Chairman Portsmouth Conservative Association; Freemason
Vyvyan Holland		Son of Oscar Wilde. Later in life (in 1955) whilst facing bankruptcy, it was reported that his wife was an advisor to the Queen on make-up and beauty preparations. His presence at the dinner, along with others, shows Gregory's control of the guest list.
Sir Robert Horne	Carlton	Conservative MP; Cabinet Minister; shipowner
Brig Gen Sir William Horwood		Commissioner, Metropolitan Police 1920-1928 a friend of Gregory's; won the support of Lloyd George to bring Special Branch into Metropolitan Police – which led to the departure of Sir Basil Thomson
Lt. Col. Sir George A Hussey		Brewer
Sir Edward Iliffe	Carlton	Conservative MP; associated with Economic League, British Empire Union
Sir Joseph Isherwood		Shipwright
Julius Jacobs		
Lord Jessel	Carlton	Conservative MP; Whip
Col. H Driver Jonas		
Capt. R C Kelly		Economic League Central Council member, and the person who was eventually employed by Davidson to help Gregory into exile
B Kemp-Welch		
Maj. Guy Kindersley	Carlton	Conservative MP; stockbroker; involved in securing Zinoviev letter for Tories; member of the 1926 Conservative Party financial appeal committee
Sir Edward Knapp-Fisher	Carlton	Receiver General Custodian and Chapter Clerk of Westminster Abbey
Lt. Col. P R Laurie		Chairman, North-West Wiltshire Conservative Association; Deputy Assistant Commissioner, Metropolitan Police
Sir William JH Leese	Brooks	Solicitor
David Levi		
Sir Albert Levy		Treasurer of Royal Free Hospital Albert Levy Benevolent Fund
George Levy		
Lewis Levy		
Sir Maurice Levy		Radical MP
Capt. Ivor Stewart Liberty		Director of Liberty & Co Ltd
Marquess of Linlithgow	Carlton	Dir. of Bank of Scotland; Dpty Chair of Conservative Party 1924-26; signed "Diehard Manifesto"
R L J Llewellyn	Athenaeum	Notable medical expert
R W Lloyd		As above
Cdr. O Locker-Lampson	Carlton	Conservative MP; met Nazi ideologist Alfred Rosenberg; leader (1933) of "fascist-like Blueshirts"
Lt. Col. Sir Charles Lowther		High Sheriff, Northamptonshire
Lord Lurgan	Carlton	Chairman of Carlton & Ritz Hotels
Sir Edwin Lutyens		Architect
Sir Harry McGowan	Carlton	Director, Midland Bank; ICI; member of Anglo-German Fellowship; Central Council of Economic League; later Lord McGowan
Edward Marjoribanks		Conservative MP; seen dining with Prince Bismarck of the German Embassy the following month in the

		company of Doris Duke, a U.S. tobacco heiress; committed suicide not long afterwards.
Duke of Marlborough		Conservative minister in Coalition government
E H Marsh		Knighted 1934; Private Sec. to Winston Churchill
Reginald Mason		
R H Meatyard		
Lt. Col. J Seymour Mellor		Chief Constable of War Office Constabulary, MI5
H W Merckel		
Sir George Middleton	Athenaeum	Labour MP
Ralph Milbourn		
Sir Archibald Mitchelson		Banker; colliery owner; Dir. of Great Universal Stores
Marquis del Moral		Spanish marquis with military background
Hon Evan Morgan	Carlton	Conservative parliamentary candidate
Capt. G H F Nichols		
Leslie K Osmond		
Maj. Guy Paget	Carlton	Ind. Conservative MP
Sir Harry Peat		Accountant
George H Pinckard	Carlton	Proprietor of Yachting Monthly
H Pirie-Gordon		Worked for Gregory during his ownership of Burke's Landed Gentry
Lord Plender		Created a Baron in 1931, he could have been dubbed the original "King of Quangos" judging by his Who's Who entry; founded first chartered accountants' Freemasons lodge in 1906
H.E. Paul Popovitch		
Arthur B Portman		
Harry Preston		
O Pulvermacher		Night editor of the Daily Mail and later established northern edition of Daily Telegraph
Lord Queensbrough	Carlton	President of the National Union of Conservative and Unionist Associations 1928/29; obsessed with the "international Bolshevist plot"; a trustee on a secret Conservative trust run by Davidson and Steel-Maitland to finance propaganda; Chair, Seimans Bros.
G St. Quiton-Jones		
Daniel Radcliffe		Shipowner – died with outstanding Gregory debts
Marquess of Reading		Various high offices – as Lord Chief Justice he heard the Roger Casement case and passed death sentence. Gregory allegedly was involved in procuring the diary evidence of Casement's homo-sexuality which helped spoil any chance of a reprieve. Wrongly it seems implicated in Marconi scandal
Ernest Rechnitzer		
H F Robertson		
Sir Ernest Roney		Nat. Liberal
Sir Henry Rothband		
Maj. Gen. Earl of Scarborough	Carlton	Former ADC to the King
Maj. Gen. J E B Seely		1st Baron Mottistone, created 1933; a Liberal, then Conservative; member of Anglo-German Fellowship, an 'intimate of Ribbontrop' (German Ambassador)
Sir John Simon		National Liberal MP; Foreign Secretary 1931-35; member, Chamberlain's circle of Hitler collusionists
A F Sims		
Col. J L Sleeman		
Col. J Aubrey Smith		
W H Smith		
Lord Southborough		Name was mentioned as luncheon guest of Gregory's when trying to sell knighthood to Cmdr. Leake
Earl Spencer		
George A Spencer		Labour MP (?)
Eugen Spier		Founder of "Focus" – Winston Churchill's private intelligence network
Sir Arthur Steel-Maitland		Chairman of Conservative Party; minister; trustee of Davidson's trust (see also Queensbrough above)
Sir Nairne Stewart-Sandeman	Carlton	Director, Dawnay, Day & Co; featured in one of

Price of Power

		Gregory's "Officials I have met" columns in the Whitehall Gazette in July, 1929
Lord Strathspey		Chairman of Rottingdean Branch Conservative Association; Royal Empire Society
Sir Campbell Stuart		Managing Director of The Times 1919 – 1924. A Director (or Deputy Director) of Propaganda in Enemy Countries during the war
Duke of Sutherland		Paymaster-General 1925-1928; Grand Prior of the Primrose League since 1922
A J A Symons		Friend of Gregory's, who shared an interest in work of author Frederick Rolfe "Baron Corvo"
J H Thomas		Labour MP, then National Labour MP 1931 -1936 – credited with causing the collapse of the "Triple Alliance" in 1921, deprived of his union membership in 1931. Spoke to Davidson in 1931 of "smashing the socialist party completely"
Albert Van den Bergh	Jun. Carlton	Director of Unilever
Lt. Col. Sir Kenyon Morgan	Carlton	Conservative MP; director of MorganVaughan Crucible; Commissioner of Income Tax
Sir Herbert Walker		General Manager, Southern Railway 1923 -1937
W Dudley Ward		Coalition Liberal MP; minister
Sir Duncan Watson		Chairman Henry Heath Ltd
Vice Adm. P Wemyss		
Frank P Whitbread		Brewer; Chairman and Treasurer of the National Trade Defence Association – created amongst other things to "secure the election of MPs favourably disposed towards the brewing trade."
Jack Wilson		Private Secretary to Austen Chamberlain, 1914-34
Earl Winterton	Carlton	Conservative MP; minister
Corbett W Woodall		
Reginald Wright		

* Not all positions indicated here as being held by the individuals concerned were necessarily held by them in 1931 – but are listed here in order to indicate something of the background of the guests. Thus some may have ceased to be ministers for several years, others had yet to occupy a higher status or honour.

Chapter Four

A New Dawn

The Conservative Party had expected to win the 1945 general election on the sole merits of Winston Churchill as war leader. Having placed all its eggs in one basket, it took a short while for the party to wake up to the reality of the public's perception of The Conservative Party. As we have seen, its much reduced Commons presence had been reduced to a rump of people who could pejoratively be classed as 'upper class twits' – those MPs who had either bought their seats, were members of the 'cousinhood' or who at least had a public school background. The party had lost touch with the ordinary voter, and that fact reflected itself in the post-mortems which took place.

The concerns over the selection of candidates on grounds of finance led to calls to rebuild the party's funds to enable poorer associations to pick candidates who were to be judged on ability alone. These poorer seats were just as likely to be in the better-off areas as in the East End of London. Treasurers "must be carefully selected and backed by a live finance committee" reported The Times,[1] indicating that many were backed by dead or non-existing finance committees. Lord Woolton, the new Party Chairman certainly sought to give associations reasons enough to refresh themselves, when in 1947 he launched a Fighting Fund of £1million. He told that year's annual conference that the Party was spending five times more than its income, (whilst in the same breath and with unintended irony, he blamed the government for bringing about 'national bankruptcy').[2]

The £1million target was achieved within five months according to The Times in March 1948. By April, according to The Times, the target had been achieved in four months, and by October that year the £1million had miraculously been raised in only three months. It was clearly a matter of some flexibility, leading opponents to question from whence the money came – "I feel pretty sure there will be some fat cheques", said Herbert Morrison, who asked a question which was to dominate much of the debate on the subject until the late 1960s, "Who are the Tory benefactors who subscribe their large funds?"[3] The Tory response would usually be something along the lines of: 'lots of little people', 'cheese and wine parties' and so on, but few were convinced. After all, if some associations were almost at the stage where they would for the first time start having to convene "live" finance committees with the object of covering their own expenses, Central Office would not be at the top of their list of beneficiaries. But Central Office was still struggling to cover its own annual expenditure (as opposed to special election or 'fighting' funds) – the shortfall was £200,000 a year. David Maxwell-Fyfe (later Lord Kilmuir) proposed a quota system of funding the centre from the constituency associations, which would fund Central Office to the tune of 3d a Tory vote at the preceding general election.[4] In later years, as we shall see, the 'quota system' became a useful measure of how healthy the party was in the country, given the increasing number of associations who failed to send anything at all.

No doubt the fund raising techniques used to achieve Woolton's target were much the same as the tried and tested techniques of Davidson and Younger – tapping the City and commerce, although it would seem less likely at this time that the promise of honours would have featured highly, given the size of Labour's majority. Morgan Phillips, Secretary of the Labour Party nevertheless claimed that individual sums of £10,000 had been received in response to Woolton's appeal.[5]

Woolton fails to mention it in his memoirs, but he can also take the credit for establishing in 1948 a method of paying money to the party which ensured that tax could be avoided – with the added bonus of creating a further veil of secrecy around the source of funds. It was only in 1988, through the efforts of Rosie Waterhouse, an investigative journalist working for The Independent, that the existence of a network of companies, used to channel donations to the party was revealed. Woolton wrote to Churchill in 1948:

"The Treasurers and I have been much concerned by the fact that we have been told by our lawyers that, in the eyes of the law, a political party is not a body that is capable of receiving money by will or deed. ...Our lawyers have, in fact, given us a very ingenious solution to a problem that, up to now, has eluded those concerned with political funds ... I am given to understand that a substantial legacy may be bequeathed to us as soon as we are in a legal position to receive it, and on this account I would not like to keep the solicitors waiting any longer than necessary."[6]

The 'ingenious' solution was to establish a number of companies which each bore the names of lesser English rivers, such as the Arun, Bourne and Colne, with aims which included 'to support and further the objects of the Conservative and Unionist Party.' These would be able to receive the kind of donations the party itself was not, since it was itself neither a company nor unincorporated association. The companies would also be able to take advantage of certain tax refunds available on these donations. The Independent story naturally brought a sober put-down from Central Office:

"Suggestions that there are hidden funds or backdoor methods for receiving large donations are heard from time to time. They are without foundation and are generally an attempt to smear the party."[7] But in trying to put the lid back on the financial genie, the party spokesperson failed to address one of the main thrusts of the Independent story, which, backed with quotes from relevant party figures, demonstrated that "the desire for secrecy among many industrialists was paramount during the 1950s, 1960s and 1970s." Later, Lord McAlpine told the House of Lords: "To claim that it was a secret operation is frankly rubbish. The details were released to the press by Central Office and reported by the Daily Telegraph when the companies were originally set up in 1949. The river companies have always filed their annual audited accounts at Companies House, as they were obliged to do."[8] Alongside the filed accounts of 500,000 other companies, anonymity in later decades was almost guaranteed. It remains a mystery why the Party had to establish half a dozen of these companies to get round the law, given that in the same year, 1949, they also set up a trust called the '1949 Conservative and Unionist Trust', which according to evidence given in court, was set up precisely to receive "moneys intended to be bequeathed to the Party should anyone make enquires at the time of drafting a will how best such a bequest should be effected."[9] The existence of the Trust was brought to the notice of the courts, as we shall see, when the Tories were intent on not paying Corporation Tax.

The desire to find new ways of fighting the Labour government had also led to the establishment of the body which became known as 'British United Industrialists' in 1947 by Lord Renwick, whose Times obituary in 1963 recorded that "He was, in fact, of the utmost importance to the party: though very few realised it, he collected more money for Conservatives than any other individual. . . . In one way and another, Lord Renwick has probably produced some £20 million for the Tory party since the war."[10] If that last claim were true, it would of course almost entirely demolish any credit Lord Woolton might deserve for successfully raising £1 million in 1947/1948, since the average annual figure determined by the Renwick obituary £20million total would be over £1million a year since 1945. However, the figure was probably just a kind way of bulling up the late Lord Renwick's reputation, since the total known income of the Conservative Party between 1950 and 1963 came to much less than £8million.[11] However, BUI is credited with raising £367,000 in two years after Lord Woolton's £1million appeal, which may give some indication of industrial support at that time.

However, the 'problem' about giving money to the Conservative Party identified by its solicitors only applied to the Conservative Party, since its main rivals were in fact unincorporated associations – each with a clear constitution and responsibilities defined between their various parts, and already accepting their duty to pay tax. But the 'national' Conservative Party, if that meant, for example, Conservative Central Office and all its departments was nothing more than the office of the leader of the party. Leaping ahead some-what, if we look at the party's lawyers' advice in the early 1980s, they were once again searching for a way to use their curious status to avoid paying tax. This became necessary when the Inspector of Taxes tried to extract £40,000 Corporation Tax, plus interest for each of the years 1972 to 1976 on the basis that it was indeed an unincor-porated association. The party successfully appealed against the decision, making the point that since the members of the party, who are in fact only members of their local associations, did not vote for their leader they did not have a sufficient relationship with him or her to warrant the description 'association'.[12] All that may now change, of course, with William Hague's determination to have leadership ballots. It is as yet a matter of speculation to see whether the party will find other tax avoidance schemes.

It is not known exactly how much cash was channelled through the river companies, although a total figure of £2,593,899 between 1954 and 1963 was identified in The Independent.[13] This represented over one third of the total donations received in the same period. Undisclosed funding on this scale was inevitably going to give the party a public relations headache, but the critics were not always to be found amongst Central Office's natural opponents. It is implicit that even by 1963 local associations were chafing at the quota system, perhaps feeling that the national party seemed well able to secure funding without them having to work harder. In a report on a review of party organisation that year, Selwyn Lloyd commented:

"I found some constituency treasurers adopting an attitude of hostility towards the quota. This attitude is out of tune with modern political necessities. The quota is not a tax levied from the centre: it is a means to provide the centre, party headquarters, with the resources to give a general service to all constituencies and supply financial help to those financially weak so that they can play their full part in the political activity necessary for the party as a whole."[14]

Apart from the quota, there were a number of ways the party could extract income locally, and perhaps in the majority of cases local associations could co-operate with these to help reach their targets. For example, a case came to light in a 1963 Commons debate on yet another attempt by Labour to force disclosure in company accounts of political donations. Ledger, Labour MP for Romford recalled how he had recently received a letter from the Conservative Party agent in the next constituency inviting him to contribute £50 to the Hornchurch and District Industrial Association – a Tory front organisation. The letter informed him that this would give him the right to attend four luncheons or four dinners at the House of Commons at each of which at least a junior minister would speak. The balance of the £50 was to go to Conservative Party funds.[15] It was to become a matter of widespread complaint amongst MPs in the late 1980s and early 1990s that the private House of Commons dining rooms were perpetually booked up with Tory fund raising dinners.

More underhand methods of extorting funds could be used too, as George Wigg, Labour MP for Dudley exposed in the House of

Price of Power

Commons in 1949:

"I speak for a Midland constituency... and I have many good friends there, some of whom are Members of the Conservative Party. They sent me copies of Conservative Party publications, some of which are confidential. For example, I am well aware of the methods employed by the friends of the hon. Member for Moseley in raising funds. It is as near political blackmail as anything can be. I have photostatic copies which I can show to any hon. Member.

A book is sent round to manufacturers, and all sub-contractors are invited to place their names in the book, alongside an adequate subscription. If they do not do so, a peremptory note is sent to them drawing their attention to the fact. I have got photostatic copies of a subscription list to the Conservative Party in the West Midlands which has been extorted – that is the right word – from business people, irrespective of their political views. They have got to pay, even though many of them, being intelligent men, are members of the Labour Party. They have got to pay; otherwise they know that their businesses would suffer."[16]

Wigg was interrupted by Sir Patrick Hannon, the said hon. member for Moseley and a leading scion of the industrial world, who suggested that all some industrial leaders were interested in was a 'desire to promote research in their respective industries'. Wigg responded with further details from his documents, which bore the heading of Conservative Party headquarters and the name of two industrialists, Sir Francis Joseph and Sir Hugh Chance, whom he accused of adopting "the methods of conspiracy... Great sums are extorted by blackmail from firms who have got to pay or go out of business."

Wigg's description of this method of fund-raising is remarkably similar to the method used today by so-called 'business to business'magazines to sell advertising, by getting companies to pressurise their 'valued' suppliers to support 'advertorial' features. There is an ever-present veiled threat that valuable contracts may go elsewhere if the support is not forthcoming. Thus it is not unreasonable to believe that such approaches were made on behalf of the Conservative Party, especially since Wigg said he had documentary evidence to back up his charge.

Additional pressure could be brought to bear in other, more legitimate ways, for example by the publication of lists of companies the

Conservative Party thought a Labour government may nationalise – although this would probably not affect the smaller, local suppliers of those companies. Nevertheless, the threat of nationalisation was always a good recruiter of funds from business to the Conservatives, especially once Labour had achieved enough electoral strength to be able to carry through its plans. However, the matter had to be dealt with using discretion, since as long as a Labour government was in power, it wouldn't do for businesses to be seen to be 'party political'. There were now virtually continual demands made and bills put before the Commons by Labour members to force companies to declare their political donations. Their enthusiasm for legislation could only be encouraged by the behaviour of some industrialists who didn't care to conceal their support for the Tories. One such, a Blackburn company Managing Director, Tom Hindle, sent a leaflet out in their pay-packets to all his 350 employees telling them "I am going to vote Conservative... I am convinced it is the right thing to do in this most critical election."[17] Clearly, the 'squirearchy' approach to electioneering was not yet quite dead by 1950.

Another example of blatant electioneering on behalf of the Conservatives by a company was that of the Tronoh Mines Company, who advertised in The Times against Labour in 1951. Their behaviour led to a prosecution on the grounds that it may have been an illegal practice under election law, but the Judge ruled that there was no case to answer, adding to the case law which was to allow ever–increasing amounts of money to be spent on behalf of political parties by other organisations who shared their views.

As the parties found new techniques, such as a more extensive use of advertising agencies and television, they also fell prey to the lengthening time-scales of electioneering, with a greater need to try to affect the opinion polls outside of official election periods. Given that most election law covers only the activity of local candidates, the national parties had a free rein to campaign more vigorously at other times without any limits on expenditure. It soon became apparent that the need for funds would expand exponentially.

The Conservatives were ahead of the Labour Party in exploiting the new 'mass appeal' doctrines of the powerful new advertising agencies, but fears were expressed on both sides of the political fence about the dangers presented. Senior Labour MP Gordon Walker said:

Price of Power

"I cannot believe that it is good for any business activity to get involved in this way in the political struggle. I am quite sure that the majority of our people do not want to see our political life "Americanised" by the introduction here of high pressure advertising techniques aimed at the hidden persuasion of the electors"[18]

Lord Hailsham, it was reported, had also seen the "dangers of political television slipping into Barnum and Bailey methods that will affront viewers who are seriously interested in politics and passing well informed, and do nothing to persuade the Admass who have no interest much beyond entertainment."[19] For the Liberals, Jo Grimond called for an inquiry into expenditure on advertising, but no doubt sensing that the Conservatives had nothing to gain from such an inquiry, R. A. Butler, for the government, saw no need for such an inquiry.[20] Given that Grimond's question was paired with one on company donations, and that Gordon Walker too was calling for an inquiry into the control of political expenditure, it was clear that the Tories could have little more than a tenuous sympathy with the calls for restraint on political advertising, by whatever means. In July, 1960, Gordon Walker MP moved an amendment in the Commons that "this House calls upon Her Majesty's Government to set up an inquiry into the control of political expenditure."[21] The debate that followed adhered to a well-established pattern that all similar debates took, that is with Labour attacking the secrecy surrounding Conservative Party funding, and with the Conservatives attacking trade union and co-operative society support for Labour.

As another general election approached, the Labour Party became increasingly determined to make the secrecy surrounding Conservative Party funding an issue. At the 1963 Labour Party conference, Tony Benn speaking on behalf of the National Executive Committee said that only 10% of the Tories regular expenditure had come from the constituency associations, and that British United Industrialists had collected 90% of the Conservatives general election campaign funds. He was speaking in favour of a motion which sought legislation that would make it illegal for a company to donate money for political purposes without the express approval at the annual general meeting of its shareholders; to ensure that such money be not tax deductible; and that all political parties be required to publish their accounts, with all sources of income disclosed.[22] At the same time, however, some companies were being more forthright: Lord Netherthorpe, Chairman of Fison's Ltd told his shareholders that the sum of £2,320 had been given to the Conservatives in "support of private enterprise". "The company was not interested with party politics as such."[23] Thus the lines were being drawn, with some company bosses showing their defiance of Labour's plans, whilst at the same time maintaining their defence that their actions were not 'party political'. But even whilst Labour were still in opposition, the party had discovered new powers to act – recognising the growing importance of local authority pension funds. Birmingham, Liverpool and London County Council alone controlled nearly £22 million worth of shares, and through their representatives on investment boards, they sought to add to the pressure for reform.

The matter came back to the House of Commons in June 1964, when Jim Callaghan introduced a clause to the Finance Bill which would force companies to declare political donations of £5 or more. He also said he possessed evidence which demonstrated that the tax payer was effectively subsidising company donations, as companies were treating them as business expenses. This was particularly true where 'front' organisations like BUI and Aims of Industry were concerned. This charge in particular upset the front organisations' directors. The spokesperson for BUI said "We are a very small body and we have no connexion with the Tory Party. We stand for one thing only – the protection of free enterprise and opposition to nationalisation."[24] If it were true, this denial would make many wonder why BUI didn't have a relationship with the Tory Party, if it was the democratic way of supporting free enterprise – but never mind. For the Economic League, its Director General, John Dettmar wrote in to The Times to say, "It can be stated quite categorically that the League neither gives nor receives financial support from any political party, neither is any part of its expenditure devoted to political aims."[25] Aims of Industry were more robust: "If Mr Callaghan had first taken the precaution of paying his shilling at the Companies Registry to inspect Aims of Industry's annual accounts deposited there – or had asked us to send a copy – he would have found what he proposed to say was a load of rubbish."[26] It was to be revealed later in the year that Aims of Industry had spent £21,000 prior to the election on a 'Free Enterprise' campaign, clearly in an attempt to influence the result. But Callaghan also claimed to have evidence of a nationalised company – the South West Electricity Board – giving money to the Tories, over eight years after nationalisation. His evidence was called into question, although he had made the charge in seeming good faith.

From the evidence of the few comments by company directors at the time, it is probably the case that a long period of Conservative rule had lulled them into a false sense of security – With Labour looking ever more likely to return to power, they could only blame themselves if their donations had been inadequate. The cost of fighting elections was rising inexorably, and with Labour firmly committed to forcing companies out into the open, things looked bleak for the Tories. Nevertheless, they had set up a formidable money gathering machine, with 'non-political' sounding associations or 'Industrialists Councils' established in most parts of the country, based in Conservative Regional Offices. Thus, for example, in Newcastle there was the "Northern Industrialists' Protection Association", in Leeds there was the "West Yorkshire Industrialists' Council" and in Birmingham it was the "Midlands Industrial Advisory Council". We shall return to examine these august bodies later.

Labour's election in 1964 at last brought the possibility of action on company donations, but it was not a legislative priority. For, although it was mentioned in the Queen's Speech in 1965, it was not until the passing of the 1967 Companies Act that the disclosure requirement was introduced, at a level of £50 or more. The 1963 Labour Party conference resolution demands for shareholders' approval and the publication of party accounts were dropped. The Conservative response was largely unsurprising, with Airey Neave MP for the Tories asking that fines or imprisonment should be imposed on any who discriminate against companies because of whom they donate their money to. He referred to an earlier call by Richard Marsh, the Labour Minister of Power, who said, "if firms want to get involved in politics, they must do so with knowledge that some of us are determined to hit back where it hurts".[27] Given that the law on accepting tenders for government or local authority work was still in the laxer pre-Poulson period, it may have been possible for companies to be barred on political grounds, but it is equally possible that Marsh was at one with the view, often expressed by Tories in defence of company donations, that if shareholders didn't like it, they could sell their shares. Another more surprising response from the Conservatives was that they decided that from 1967 they would publish their "accounts". There was a genuine fear on their part that the company disclosure rule would deter companies from giving money, and their own continued stance on secrecy would prove counter-productive. The Chairman of the Party was Edward du Cann, who told the 1967 National Conference that "financial secrecy can deter party members from subscribing,"[28] a view which was later adopted by progressive members with the arrival of the Conservative Charter Movement.

The Party was also stung into action to launch another Woolton style appeal, this time for £2 million. Lord Carrington, launching the appeal, outlined the problem: "The number of Conservatives who have even contributed in any year in the past totals just under 15 per cent of all our supporters. That is all and only about half of them gave in the last 12 months. But well over one third of the Conservatives – double the number who have ever contributed – say they would give money if they were ever asked to."[29] The former MP for Nottingham South, William Clark, and the firm of "professional consultants" Hooker, Craigmyle and Co. were put in charge of the appeal. It might thus be seen that the double edged effect of Labour's modest addition to the Companies Act was to give impetus to some accountability and grassroots activity in the Conservative Party. The appeal, it was reported, had raised £500,000 in the first three months of 1968, and was said by May to have already exceeded the whole income of the previous year. It was also reported that of the 1967 income of £650,000, over £400,000 had come from business – the remainder from quota payments.

According to The Times "Much of the £400,000 is paid by industrialists personally who sit down once a year and write cheques on their own account for £500 or £1,000."[30] No doubt quite unconnected with this group were a pop group called "The Idle Race" who pledged to give 50% of their royalties to the Conservative Party. Given that they had made only three records in 18 months, one suspects that their idleness never brought much in the way of cash for their intended beneficiaries – perhaps the story was an attempt by some Young Conservatives to broaden the party's appeal amongst Times readers.[31] By June, contributions to the appeal were nearing £1 million, with two thirds from business – but with only £130,000 so far declared in company accounts. The £620,000 shortfall in this regard could be explained by the fact that many companies' accounts would not have been published yet for the relevant financial year since the introduction of the Companies Act, but against that one-off likelihood it must remain the case that the vast majority of donations were not traced. Since the introduction of the disclosure requirement, the Labour Research Department has annually surveyed 5,000 company reports for company donations, leaving well over half a million companies unresearched. By January, 1969, Lord Carrington was able to announce the success of his appeal, indeed it had been more than successful, with £2,340,000 in the kitty, not counting £350,000 of regular income. If the two thirds ratio of business to other sources of income was maintained, then well over £1.5million had come from business: leaving the conservatives still the party of business, rather than reaching out to the 85% of Conservative supporters which du Cann's research had shown did not give anything to the party. Whilst well on the way to his target, Carrington berated the company donations disclosure clause:

"There was no doubt that this was aimed directly at us, and at our finances, with the hope that industrialists and businessmen would be dissuaded from stating publicly that they supported the Conservative Party by subscriptions.

I am glad to tell you that in an overwhelming number of cases that spiteful little trick has been conspicuously unsuccessful... If there be of your acquaintance any rich men, chairmen of companies, directors of companies who are still holding back for this reason, I hope you will tell them that never at any time have there been a better reason, in the interests of shareholders, employees and the nation to subscribe to the Conservative Party because if we have another Labour Government those businessmen will not have much business to do."[32]

Interestingly, a year later a report on the party's healthier than expected surplus explained that the rise was partly due to "appreciation in the market price of investments" – this under a Labour government, and with most commentators expecting it to be re-elected shortly.[33] One shareholder victim of the Carrington appeal was Mrs David Ennals, wife of the Minister of Health, who objected to the brewer Watney Mann's donation of £24,650 when she attended their annual general meeting. She was the only shareholder to vote against the donation, saying "I am stopping drinking Watney's beer, I drink a certain amount and the family do. I will try to drink other beers and supply the family with other brands."[34] Mrs Ennals would have found it difficult finding another tipple which was not supplied by a brewer who was not a member of the "beerage".

One of the hardships of being in opposition is of course the reduction in salary MPs who were once ministers have to suffer – although an opposition MP can have more time to nurse his or her "outside interests", with whatever rewards are available. Conservative MPs had always been expected to have other means. As we have seen, before the war, the rules of the selection game made life well-nigh impossible for those who couldn't afford to enter Parliament with a substantial income. But after the war, and no doubt due to the great extension of government that followed Labour's victory, (paid government posts had nearly doubled between 1930 and 1970 – up from 58 to 102) MPs placed a greater reliance on their parliamentary career to produce a salary one could live on.

The greatest "star" of this period, who found an MPs salary of £3,250 hard to struggle by on, was Reginald Maudling, who had first entered the Cabinet in 1957. As he says in his memoirs:

"There is, too, quite frankly, the question of money. People do not go into politics in order to make money, or if they do, they are very misguided. But on the other hand they cannot reasonably be expected to neglect their interests and those of their families. One of the ways you can offset [the absence of ministerial pensions] is by endeavouring to earn money in industry or commerce when out of office. It seems to me a perfectly reasonable system, and indeed a beneficial one to British industry, for which the advice of former Ministers should be of value. And there are many illustrious examples."[35]

With his legal background, his directorship of Kleinwort, Benson Ltd., the merchant bankers, and as Deputy Leader of the Conservative Party, Maudling would indeed be a good "catch" for many a respectable city firm. If at today's prices, for example, he had followed Douglas Hurd's metamorphosis into a director of the National Westminster Bank, he would be laughing all the way from the bank £140,000 a year richer. As it was, he relied on a former Tory MP and ministerial colleague, Lord Brentford, a senior partner in the law firm of Joynson Hicks and Co. for an introduction to the board of the International Investment Group, which was to manage something called the Real Estate Fund of America. Sadly, this grandly named investment fund was to turn out to be a modern-day South Sea Bubble – with hundreds of thousands of investors collectively losing a fortune. An idea of how IIG was run can be gleaned from Guillermo Gutierrez, its Latin American sales director. "Asked how many countries his sales area covered, he said 'Twenty nine'. Asked in how many it was legal to sell the fund shares, he said 'Only two.' Gutierrez said that one of his salesmen was accustomed to getting money out of Brazil by canoeing across the river into Paraguay."[36] Now it is unlikely that during his six month stint at IIG that Maudling would have been au fait with such detail: his job, apart from launching the fund, important though that was, was to serve as a politically respectable figurehead to give IIG a gravitas it would otherwise lack. Lord Brentford himself also served on the board, as did his son, the Hon. Crispin Joynson-Hicks. Even when Maudling resigned, after being warned of the real nature of IIG's provenance, he still felt obliged to give the originator of the fund, Jerome D. Hoffman, a letter saying REFA was "a good, sound investment." Judging by what he has to say in his memoirs, this may have been an early attempt at personal damage limitation – a standard defence of "I didn't know what was going on." Nevertheless, Maudling picked up an invaluable lesson from this and other experiences:

"One of the great advantages to me of my business appointments was that they made it possible for me to travel extensively. I think it is of very great value to this country and to the world generally, that both politicians and businessmen should be able to travel widely, and to meet one another. The problem, of course, is one of money. If I had not been a director of these various companies my ability to travel as a leading member of the Conservative Party would have been very much circumscribed and, as a result, the service I could render as a politician would have been very much limited."[37]

His was an example to be emulated by many Tory MPs, who sought the 'Club Class' lifestyle – but one would have thought that his might be an example which many latter-day jet-setting politicians could have learnt from, since his other, infamous, 'outside interest' was to cost him his job when he was to forced to resign as Home Secretary in 1972. This was precipitated by the now notorious Poulson corruption case. This has been well documented, so it does-n't need repeating in any detail here. What is of interest, however, are the names of the networkers who helped this particular ex-Chancellor of the Exchequer into the field of prefabricated concrete. Once again, Lord Brentford had a role to play, although that he acted for Poulson's wife Cynthia is not the most important feature of this connection. What was more useful to Poulson was that Maudling was a director of Kleinwort, Benson. As the bankrupt architect said at his trial: "He [Maudling] was a director of Kleinwort, Benson . . . One can get all the work one can possibly hope for if the finance can be arranged. It is an obstacle of all emerging countries that they haven't finance."[38] What this meant in practical terms, according to a wiser John Poulson, who wrote his autobiography after serving a seven year jail sentence was that:

"Reggie... never seemed to care about anything, provided the compensations, in privileged travel and luxurious accommodation made up for it. He arrived in Tehran on behalf of his bankers, Kleinwort Benson, who were financing a British-laid gas pipeline to the Soviet border. He was, as always, delighted to join us in being entertained by the Shah and his family. Reggie took advantage of the splendid banquets and dinners to which he and Beryl were invited by [myself]. He talked as if he represented huge financial interests with an ever-open cheque book, but I was beginning to realise that a lot of this was bluff. In Mexico where he accompanied Williams [an associate of Poulson's] and me or four or five times in vain search of local finance, we drew a frustrating blank. As Williams rightly said, "It was all very jolly. Reggie was always talking to bankers. But he never raised any finance.'"[39]

Of course, Poulson was bitter with Maudling, whom he saw as getting off scot-free. His final epithet for Maudling was that he was a "roguish parasite". But even allowing for that fact, Maudling's worth does seem to have been negligible – especially so given the money he was paid by Poulson.

The Conservative Party was to do much better – Kleinwort Benson have been stalwart funders of the Party, averaging £30,000 to £40,000 a year. They also provide another example of the "Triangular Relationship" referred to earlier, since one of Maudling's fellow directors was George Kennedy Young, a former deputy director of MI6. Another Kleinwort's man was ex-MI6 officer John Farmer.[40] Sir Rex Benson, another director, was a cousin and colleague of Sir

Price of Power

Stuart Menzies, one-time chief of MI6.[41] Merchant banks were always in need of "security work", no doubt not the least of which would be trying to fill-in the intelligence gaps left between the likes of Maudling's lunches and receptions. But there is nothing unique about this merchant bank/Conservative Party relationship. The triangular relationship would certainly extend to others, such as Hambro's (£30,000 to £50,000 donations) and Hill Samuel, known as the "spy bank."[42]

Kleinwort Benson were also later recommended as bankers to the Fayed brothers, during the time of their successful bid for House of Fraser. Kleinwort's were recommended by the Royal Bank of Scotland, the Party's bankers. The Party's account benefited from the Fayed's faith or gratitude to the tune of £250,000.

During the same period that Reggie the "roguish parasite" was imbibing Poulson's treats, another opposition heavyweight, Peter Walker MP, who was to become a Cabinet Minister in 1970, was providing a not entirely dissimilar service to Slater Walker Securities, the financial success story built on the "whizz-kid" share dealing of Jim Slater in the 1960s and 1970s. The company began to come unstuck after a merger proposal with Hill Samuel fell through. Its shares, once priced at 245p, fell in two years to just 10p. But that was after Walker had resigned to take up his ministerial duties again, following Ted Heath's victory in 1970. In defence of his innocence in all matters related to Slater Walker, Walker gives an account of the onerous duties he performed for his £2,500 p.a. directors fee between 1966 and 1970:

"I never on any occasion had an office at the company or even a desk. I was never involved in any press conference given by the company, nor directly in any of its publicity... I never wrote a letter on the company letter-heading. I played no part in any of the subsidiaries of Slater Walker... I was never involved in any of the negotiations for acquisitions made by the company. In the days the business was at Hertford Street I would perhaps call in on average once a week and have a half-hour talk with those who were there and I would attend a monthly board meeting. From the time the firm moved to the City I normally attended a two hour management meeting on Monday morning. I was made deputy chairman on the basis that the main shareholders and directors considered that it would be appropriate if I took the chair at the board meetings in the event of Jim Slater being absent. In fact he never was absent from a board meeting that I attended and therefore at no time did I perform any duty as deputy chairman. My relationship with this company was therefore never one of being involved in the detail of the company but one of being a person who admired the abilities and talents of Jim Slater and appreciated his friendship. I was able to give him advice and comments in a totally objective way. We frequently saw each other during this period on a social basis when business discussions could take place, and we frequently conversed on the telephone."[43]

This, then was the gruelling schedule that Slater was paid £2,500 a year for. It must have been purely coincidental that in the period after Walker had left the company to become a Cabinet Minister, various economic measures were taken by the government which conformed very closely to what Slater Walker desired. It would also be coincidental that between 1969 and 1973 Slater Walker gave £40,000 to the Conservative Party and £19,000 to various front organisations. Another person who was able to do rather well having met Jim Slater was Jeffrey Archer, who was given the task of raising money for the European Movement, in which Slater was involved. It was estimated that Archer raised £1.5 million for this organisation, helped along by a list from Slater of "forty up-and-coming young rich men who wouldn't mind making a name for themselves."[44] Archer took £150,000 in commission. One of the donations came in a single cheque of £300,000 from Michael Sobell of GEC. This was to be the first of two, amounting to £600,000 in total. Shortly afterwards Ted Heath awarded Sobell a knighthood, and the possibility of there being a connection was raised in the Commons. As a result, Sobell's second cheque never arrived – probably costing Archer another 10 per cent in commission.[45] Another business-knight-to-be was also a donor with Slater Walker connections, James Goldsmith, although he got his gong from Harold Wilson a few years later. Goldsmith gave £100,000 to help Heath with the European cause, and later became chairman of the ailing Slater Walker group.[46]

In 1971 Slater had given a talk at the Institute of Directors, and amongst the audience was Anthony Barber, Chancellor of the Exchequer. Slater made a threefold plea to "adequately reward managers" using "stock options, for further reductions in surtax, and for the restoration of tax relief on the interest paid on borrowed

Price of Power

money." The requests were "duly implemented" in Barber's second budget in 1972 and "soon seven Slater Walker directors, including Slater, were borrowing between them about £1 million from their company 'in the normal course of business.'"[47]

In the 1980s and 1990s share options became a useful 'management incentive' which was completely risk-free, since the beneficiary of this largesse need only take up the option if the shares had risen in value, not if they had gone down. The only danger was the risk of being called a 'fat cat', but by then the directors, particularly of privatised utilities, had become immune to the notion that they were either not completely infallible or the accusation that they had perhaps been handed a cut-price bargain which even a three year old could extract a profit from.

The 'Barber boom' of 1972, which resulted from a massive stimulus to the economy with tax cuts in his March Budget, fuelled the hunger of a number of politicians (almost, though not exclusively Tory: Jeremy Thorpe and John Stonehouse were sucked in too) to profit from the easy pickings in the financial markets. Secondary banks took advantage of relaxed credit controls, and lent large quantities of money which they themselves had borrowed. Much of the borrowed money went to finance a property boom, as well as personal spending. Between 1970 and 1974 lending to property companies rose from £343 million to £2,834 million.[48] Inevitably a reaction would come to stem the resulting inflationary pressure, and the government was forced to take deflationary measures, such as pushing up interest rates. As a consequence of this, some of the secondary banks, and other institutions associated with them, had to be offered a 'lifeboat' – to ensure that impending insolvencies did not threaten confidence in the City. Thus it was that Slater Walker Ltd, (SWL) the authorised banking element of the Slater Walker Group, was bailed out by the Bank of England in 1975, ironically when Labour was back in power. The support continued through until 1977 and was provided in three ways, according to the Labour Party's analysis:

First, the Bank offered £3.5 million for SWL despite the fact that its notional assets of £21 million were far outweighed by provisions of £46.6 million which would be required against bad debts and lost interest. Thus the Bank was prepared to pay roughly £28 million more than SWL would be worth without Bank support.

Second, while in previous rescues it had been the Bank's policy to give protection only to 'outside' depositors in order to maintain confidence, it was agreed in this case that £12.5 million of [Slater Walker] group deposits in SWL would continue to be credited to the Slater Walker Group.

Third, the group would be freed from its obligation to inject up to £25 million into the banking subsidiary taken over by the Bank of England.[49]

In effect, the "lifeboat" operation run by the Bank of England – with its directors drawn from the merchant banks and those whose behaviour was responsible for the crisis in the first place – provided a sort of share option scheme to ensure that their boardroom companions would be saved some of the grief. This was taking one step further the comment Tony Benn made in 1975 shortly after having been moved from being Secretary of State for Industry to the Energy portfolio "When the Tories are in office, they are automatically wired into the City, to the big companies. When we get in we are actually tied to the Tory pressure groups, so we go on pumping out Tory explanations for everything."[50] Amongst other banks which received support were Keyser Ullman, which was chaired until 1975 by Edward Du Cann MP, a former chairman of the Conservative Party and chairman of the 1922 Committee. "In 1973 he made a perfectly legal £90,000 profit when the bank of which he was Chairman paid a very high price for shares in a property company of which he was also Chairman."[51] The Department of Trade and Industry criticised Keyser Ullman for making loans of £21 million "on worthless guarantees" to a Christopher Selmes for an attempted take-over bid of a Trust, in a period the DTI described as "an era of asset stripping, easy loans and closely-knit sharedealings."[52] Keyser Ullman took £65 million from the "lifeboat" to stay afloat.

Keyser Ullman eventually became the new merchant bankers to Tiny Rowland's Lonrho group, which led to a new appointment for Du Cann as a director of Lonrho. The appointment was pressed on Lonrho by another senior Tory MP, Duncan Sandys, whose own tale is worth recounting. He was appointed chairman of Lonrho because "as Rowland understood… he was easily manipulated, greedy and already compromised. With Sandys as chairman, Rowland saw that he would have little difficulty in continuing to run the company unimpeded."[53] The only issue at stake was remuneration. Given that

Price of Power

Sandys had previously had a six year arrangement with Lonrho to act as a "roving ambassador" at £50,000 per year, he would first of all have to be compensated for the loss of his consultancy, to be re-employed as chairman. An added complication was that most of his consultancy money was paid into an account in the Cayman Islands, to ensure that he paid no tax on it. It was agreed that he would receive a one-off sum of £130,000, to be paid into the Cayman Islands. It was quite a struggle for Lonrho to find, in relative secrecy, the loose £130,000 necessary to complete the deal. Sandys was then to be paid £38,000 p.a. plus £2,000 in expenses, two thirds of this total via the Cayman Islands. Sandys was appointed in 1972, his duties to preside at board meetings and at the annual general meeting.[54] But such sums, even in the 1970s were unexceptional. In 1977, three resigning directors of the secondary bank First National Finance Corporation (FNFC) received £120,000, despite the fact that FNFC had required £360,000 of "lifeboat" support. The announcement of the payment was made after it was also announced that FNFC had made heavy losses for the third year running.[55]

Lord Woolton's remark in 1969 that "voters are consumers"[56] effectively sums up the relationship between the Conservative Party and the electorate: it is a business relationship, and the higher one gets up the greasy pole, the more expensive it gets. A revolving door between the Cabinet and the Boardroom caps the lot, lubricated by unaccountable deals. But sadly, not even a Treasurer of the Conservative Party seemed to have much accounting expertise, judging by Lord Chelmer's comment that:

"Conservative Central Office accounts do not show separately the amount received from companies because no precise figure could be given. It is not always known whether a donation is from a company, a partnership or from an individual. Broadly, however, a pre-appeal income of £650,000 would have included between £400,000 and £450,000 from all industrial and commercial sources, including any amounts received through outside bodies."[57]

The obviously taxing job of trying to add up the sums, used here as an excuse in an attempt to shrug off demands for accountability, nevertheless exposes one of the failings of the Companies Act 1967. This relates to the non-existence of any requirement on businesses which are unincorporated to disclose their donations. Partnerships, or businesses wholly owned by private individuals escape the net.

This must partly explain why surveys of corporate donations have always come up with a cumulative total far less then the income shown in the Conservative Party's accounts – limited though they are. However, The Times reported in 1974 that 160 City firms had received an appeal from the Party towards its fighting fund, and although "many of them are private" it was thought that a similar appeal in 1970 had raised £350,000, or about £2,000 each.[58]

The two 1974 general elections clearly made huge demands on all the Parties' fund-raising efforts, and perhaps for that reason the prospect of state funding for political parties gathered real momentum. Ironically, the Conservatives opposed state aid, but at the first opportunity took as much as they were entitled to. The first opportunity came in 1975 with the granting of "Short" money to opposition parties for parliamentary research support. Named after Edward Short, the Leader of the House who introduced the measure, it was attacked by the opposition, in the words of Norman Lamont MP, as a "very questionable use of public money"[59] and by the Conservative Political Centre as "wrong in principle" and "managerialist."[60] The money was allocated on the basis of £500 per Westminster seat won, plus £1 for every 200 votes cast, up to a maximum total of £150,000. The Conservatives' principled opposition was not to last beyond the day when the money became available, and as Lord Houghton of Sowerby remarked, in defence of his own state-aid proposals a year later, were it not for the £150,000 taxpayers' handout, the Conservatives would not have been able to balance their books in 1975/76.[61]

Lord Houghton was charged by the Labour Government in 1975 to review the whole issue of political party funding, in the context of whether or not state aid should be introduced. Once again, the Conservatives opposed the idea. It would be hard for them to make a convincing argument from principle since they had already accepted state aid, not only Short money, but as mentioned much earlier, through the secret vote in the nineteenth century of £10,000 p.a. for party use by government Whips. Clearly it was the Conservatives who would benefit least from any state aid, if measured as a proportion of their overall income as compared to the other parties. In a review period of actual central expenditure by the main parties covering the years 1967/68 to 1975/76 the Conservatives spent £12,321,000 as opposed to Labour's £6,748,000 (all at constant 1970 prices).[62]

Having accepted the need for some state aid, the Houghton Committee's proposal for an annual grant was based on 5p for each vote cast at the previous general election. Thus, in 1975, based on the October 1974 result, each party would have got:

Labour	£573,407
Conservative	£523,234
Liberal	£267,340
SNP	£41,982
Ulster Unionists	£20,389
Plaid Cymru	£8,317
SDLP	£7,710

Whilst such a sum would have contributed to something like 70 to 80 per cent of Labour's annual costs, the biggest beneficiary would have been the Liberals, who in an average year would have had three times as much to spend on central organisation than before. But the contribution to the Conservatives would only have been in the region of one third. Why should they support such a partisan measure? Another good reason why they would not in any case have supported Houghton would have been new disclosure requirements. Houghton was not simply advocating a handout. The taxpayer should, if supporting the democratic process in this way, have some knowledge of how the money was spent and what other income the parties received. He thus recommended amongst other things, that gifts or payments from other bodies or individuals up to and including £5,000 should be included in an annual return. Detailed expenditure accounts should also be provided.

This would have been a double blow to the Tories, giving a financial advantage to their opponents, whilst removing once and for all the cloak of secrecy they were still fairly comprehensively able to throw over their own accounts. Given that by this time the "shock value" of the Companies Act 1967 disclosure requirement had worn off, Conservative Party fund-raising had settled back into a pleasant routine. There was not enough justification to take the half a million on offer – if that is, Houghton's proposals had ever come about. Lord Thorneycroft, Chairman of the Party, greeting the announcement of Houghton's recommendations, told the 1922 Committee that the Conservative Party would not take the cash if it was offered, his statement being received with the obligatory rousing demonstration of backbenchers thumping their desktops. Although Thorneycroft had clearly dismissed state funding, a year later the party issued a "Contact Brief", an information sheet for members to campaign with, but also to respond to, which amongst other things asked "Do you think there is a case for financing political parties from State funds?"[63]

The leaflet also reiterated the poverty plea, suggesting ways local associations could raise more money, e.g. by raising the minimum subscription level to £1, introducing a family membership, charging members to see whether they've been left off the electoral roll and publicising the fact that "qualifying political parties" are exempt from Capital Transfer Tax (subject to a ceiling of £100,000). According to the leaflet, the average constituency association would raise about £9,000 per year – £4.5 million for all 552 associations in England and Wales. But given what we shall was the case in Hull, a situation which must also have applied elsewhere, there must have been some very well endowed constituencies to achieve this average. These may have had the benefit of a well-supported Conservative Club being located in their area. A study of these 1,500 or so clubs showed that they gave up to £9,100 and £20,000 to their local associations.[64]

On the ground, the Conservatives heavily outweighed the Labour Party in organisational strength. A comparison of party machines in 1972 found that Labour had 140 full-time agents, of whom 100 had to spend 60 per cent of their time chasing their own salaries. The other 40 were paid for by head office to work in the marginal seats – or at least 40 out of the 100 marginal seats identified. The Conservatives were blessed with 386 full-time agents, and it was reckoned that they were probably paid twice as much as Labour's.[65]

The field of regional organisation of political parties has not received as much attention as national organisation, but as the link between the national leadership of the party and its lay membership, the importance of the regional tier cannot be understated. With the growing importance of national media campaigns, there has been a concomitant decrease in local resources, reflecting the apparently diminished role of local organisation in winning elections. There has also been, since the 1960s, a retreat from the cities by the Conservatives, which has seen once mighty city organisations wound-up and forgotten. Some of these once all-powerful city organ- isations were, reflecting the local autonomy enjoyed by Conservative constituency associations, themselves fiercely independent of

Central Office. But they could not, resist the tide of change. In 1966 a committee, under Lord Brooke of Cumnor, was set up by Party Chairman Edward du Cann, to see if improvements could be made in Conservative city organisation. The committee found that the relationship between the city organisations and their local CCO outposts, the area offices, were characterised by clouds of suspicion. Of relevance here is the effect this had on fund-raising, since a local association may effectively block a local company's donations going to Central Office. Thus it was proposed to bring them under the control of the Central Board of Finance.[66] In return, Central Office would become responsible for the salaries of chief city officers. Such a move would not only of course be inspired by the desire to tidy up finances. Once the staff could be paid by Central Office, their allegiance would inevitably change. In some instances, however, the city parties had already become basket-cases, beyond any hope of reinvigoration. A study of the Hull associations (published in 1980) by Philip Tether, an active Conservative member, showed how weak the party had become. The combined nominal membership in the three Hull constituencies was put at 1,050, but only 180 were "visible", that is, active in any sense of the word.

A Conservative Club existed, part of its job being to help the party financially. But, according to Tether, "It has drifted away from the party's political wing and become to all intents and purposes an autonomous organisation. Financial donations have to be 'negotiated' and are not extravagant."[67] In fact, the club was keener to spend its money repairing the roof. The "Federation" of Hull constituencies, intended in part to co-ordinate some of the associations' activities, clearly was not successful. It had a five figure overdraft, but was supposed to collect money from local businesses. Money raised in this way was then intended to help fund constituency election campaigns. But the system was failing, and a lack of interest combined with a "proprietorial" attitude to fund-raising meant that few ordinary members felt any responsibility for it.

When it came to the quota system of funding Central Office, there was a decline of contributions from the three seats as a whole between 1976/77 and 1978/79 – precisely at a time, in the run up to a general election when one would have expected to find an increase. But as Tether remarked, even the local quota payments were made up from local company donations, and did not reflect any responsibility having been taken locally for fund-raising as a "political activity": "the assumption of financial responsibility by benefactors provides no incentive to develop a membership based party to seek new ways of raising funds."[68]

Tether's study may of course have been of a particularly bad example. But others too were failing to meet their quota: in Birmingham for example, the former bastion of local Conservative organisation and financial clout, only half of the associations paid their quota money in 1979.[69] These facts no doubt fuelled the opposition's and other claims that the party was in hock to big business for its support. Curiously however, leading figures in the party organisation always sought to deny that allegation. Perhaps this was partly motivated by the fear that the Labour government may still introduce new measures to curb such funding. In 1978 for example, Doug Hoyle MP had introduced a bill which aimed to put company donations on the same footing as trade union political funds – with the same bureaucracy, ballots and scrutiny.[70] But the party leadership also could not want it left unchallenged that anything like the Hull situation was endemic, that the "mass membership" of anything between 1.5 million and 2 million was chiefly made up from a non-active, social membership, largely drawn from Conservative Clubs. According to The Times, it was a common lament amongst party staff out in the field not only that "it gets harder and harder all the time to get people to devote themselves full-time" but in many places it was known that membership was socially rather than politically motivated.[71] The membership was therefore a great, soft underbelly which lent leadership claims to a mass membership some credence, and inter alia their claims to having many small donors, but probably could not stand up to any close scrutiny. The party's deputy chairman's suggestion in 1977 that "four fifths" of total income was "collected on the doorstep" is laughable.[72]

There is another interpretation one could put on the leadership's reluctance to be seen as too widely supported by business. That is, that in a big way, they weren't. This might be seen as odd from the point of view of all those company chairmen who ritually told their AGMs that Labour was a massive threat to their very existence. Yet according to the then Mr Alaistair McAlpine, a deputy treasurer at the time, only 12 out of the top 100 British companies donated to the Conservative Party.[73] This comment came at a period of intense speculation about the date of the general election, so it may be taken with a slight pinch of salt, given the usual pleas at such times of poverty. But one of the largest brewers, Bass, had only recently confirmed that they did not give money to the Conservatives. It was further revealed that the average company donation was only £200.[74] By this time, the number of companies in the UK numbered around 660,000; 5,000 of which the Labour Research Department was tracking on a regular basis for donations. Given the level of donations they were finding, there is corroborative evidence to support McAlpine's assertion. On this evidence, who could be forgiven for thinking that the 'menace' of a Labour government was still not quite great enough to thrust the vast majority of British business into the opposite camp? Or was it simply that, apropos Stanley Baldwin's suggestion that self-made millionaires become stingy with their hard-earned money, that they didn't see the Conservative Party as a good way of spending it – especially with the party's reputation for poor financial management?

Perhaps in these circumstances, a poacher's brief foray into the Conservatives' funding heartland may have borne fruit. In the mid-1970s, when the Labour government was toiling against constant and sinister right-wing pressures, Jeremy Thorpe made an effort to appeal to Tory financiers to support an anti-socialist alliance, based on the premise that proportional representation would form the basis of an anti-Labour majority. He held meetings with leading Tory-supporting businessmen, such as Sir Val Duncan of Rio Tinto Zinc, Jim Slater of the Slater Walker Trust, Maxwell Joseph of Grand Metropolitan et al, a gathering of donors who between them gave £45,750 to the Tories. Sir Ralph Bateman, president of the CBI as well as Chairman of Turner and Newall Ltd said his board had not yet discussed political donations (despite giving the Conservatives £15,000) "But they are very worried about the political situation. They will wonder what is the best way of giving money to preserve free enterprise."[75] Within two years, Thorpe was ignominiously finished in politics and the Lib-Lab pact was sustaining Callaghan's socialist government in power.

Chapter Five

THATCHER AND SONS

The 1979 general election is widely seen as the one in which British political marketing came of age. The 'new breed' of young entrepreneurs that had gathered around the Slater Walker altar were now to serve politics not as politicians, but as message fixers whose wisdom would be valued just as greatly as any minister sat at the Cabinet table. This reflected the growing importance of the media, not just the television and press, but outdoor advertising too. The Conservatives, steered by Margaret Thatcher's advisor Gordon Reece, appointed the advertising agency Saatchi and Saatchi in 1978 in anticipation of an autumn general election.

Their first major work, the "Labour Isn't Working" poster campaign, has become legendary for its supposed influence on the electorate and for creating the conditions which would influence Jim Callaghan's decision to delay calling the election. But it also pointed to a strategic gap between the Conservatives and Labour which had yet to close: the idea of a national campaign, as opposed to a campaign nationally which was no more than the sum of its local parts. An analysis of expenditure during the campaign[1] showed how the Tories gave nearly nine times less money to constituency campaigns than Labour, but spent more than twice as much on press, poster and cinema advertising. Given that there wasn't such a differential in total constituency spending by either party, or the amount spent to gain each vote (the Tories spent 49p per vote won, Labour 47p) then it can be seen that the question had become, in the awful American phrase, 'how much bang you could get for your buck', and the Tories were able to squeeze more out of their national budget.

Price of Power

The issue perplexed and irritated Labour, even though in constant terms the actual amount spent on advertising and publicity was not as great as in 1964. Denis Healey attacked the appointment of Saatchi and Saatchi as "selling Thatcher like soap powder… It is not surprising she has chosen Saatchi and Saatchi, specialists in detergents and deodorants to cleanse and sweeten the image of extremism and division which she has created by all she has said and done as leader."[2] These complaints echoed the earlier objections voiced by Gordon Walker when the Conservatives appointed Colman, Prentice and Varley in the 1960s as their advertising agents. Chelmer's view that the electorate was a market nevertheless appeared to reach its apotheosis with the appointment of Saatchi and Saatchi, as a consequence of the high profile the agency quickly acquired. The thrusting, new image the agency sought was not entirely risk free. Had their relationship backfired, i.e. if the Conservatives had lost the election, perhaps not a great deal more would have been heard from them, as opposed to any other agency. They may also never have been paid, since Alaistair McAlpine, Thatcher's long-serving party treasurer, arranged for their services to be employed on tick – a forerunner of the 'back-to-back' interest free loans that the party was able to sustain itself with in the 1990s. Saatchi's really had little choice – the Conservatives owed them half a million pounds for their election work, the party's credit rating had just risen enormously and it had wealthy backers, so when McAlpine told Maurice Saatchi, "We can pay you in a year's time" Saatchi would have no reason to doubt it.[3] When McAlpine said "I think of myself as a bit of an impressario… I introduce the right people to the right people"[4] it could be surmised that the Conservative Party bore more than just a passing resemblance to a theatrical production.

The idea of buying an election campaign on tick is a daring one, and became the hallmark of the Conservative approach. McAlpine's view was that it is better to be in power and broke, than in opposition with money in the bank. McAlpine, appointed to the post of Deputy Party Treasurer by Thatcher soon after her election to the leadership in 1975, turned out to be an inspired choice. He was not the conventional sort of person to occupy such a high ranking position; indeed, given his love of art and his relative youth he might by Conservative standards be classed almost as a 'bohemian'. His appointment was Thatcher's first step to clearing out the old guard from Central Office, for McAlpine was a thoroughgoing member of the 'one of us' school of Thatcher admirers, and like her was keen to get things done, without too much regard for other people's sensibilities. His attitude to political life was to be fully explored in his homage to Machiavelli, The Servant, where he wrote:

"The Servant is not a seeker after absolute truth, but one who will take the view that best suits the Prince. The Servant will then promote that view until it becomes an established fact. As the argument moves away from the truth to the perceived truth, so the Servant has the evidence of his newly made 'facts' to base his argument on. Even though it may be far from the truth, the fact, once established, will be generally agreed by all. Thus it will seem a true fact as opposed to a false fact, or a lie. Let not the Servant base his argument on the laziness of a lie when true facts can be so easily summoned by his own skill."[5]

Such an attitude would clearly stand McAlpine in good stead in the murky, secretive world of the Conservative Party Treasurers' Department. His philosophy might also accurately describe his leader's approach. The Thatcher decade was all about 'getting things done' – notwithstanding any 'facts' or reasoned dissent. She said of her Cabinet ministers that they could say what they liked, as long as they did what she told them to do.

This 'getting things done' philosophy infected her supporters on the backbenches, who flung themselves into the lobbies of commerce as never before to ensure that they could ease the path of business, against the pettifogging bureaucracy of democracy. Deregulation and privatisation meant that there were rich pickings available, and earnings would be high for those on the inside track. Thus the 1980s were dubbed the 'Enterprise Years', and Conservative MPs were able to feather their nests in an unprecedented fashion. 'Enterprise Years' is at least what Lord Young, businessman-turned-Thatcherite cabinet minister called them. "The Greedy Eighties" is what Ian Greer, political lobbyist par excellence called them. Reluctantly, the latter was to eventually expose what the former meant.

The first, most important act of Thatcher's government was to abolish foreign exchange controls. Money would be able to flow freely in and out of Britain without restraint. For the likes of Jim Slater, who professed a decade earlier not to use money to make

Price of Power

things, but only to make more money, this measure alone would have justified his faith in Thatcher. Although Slater had slid into obscurity by 1979, his philosophy prevailed. The new financial star who was to dominate the city in the 1980s was James Hanson. Anyone who recalls the buzzwords of the early eighties will remember the phrase 'leaner and fitter'; to a great extent, Hanson exemplified the practical application of that phrase. As the country's 'flabby' manufacturing capacity shed weight, the profits of Hanson's asset stripping rose accordingly. With both stock and property markets rising, anyone with the financial muscle could strip out companies' assets with relative ease, make a tidy profit – and by a circuitous route, send the proceeds to a tax haven where the British government would not be able to get its hands on them – even if it showed any willingness to do so. This was the real 'double whammy' the Tories delivered – a higher social budget to pay for the mess with reduced income to pay for it, unless that income could be produced from their own entry into the asset stripping market – privatisation. But in the early days of the Thatcher period, not all appeared rosy – the usual downturn in corporate donations after the 1979 general election seemed worse, and as the recession, much of it Thatcher-induced took hold, James Hanson felt obliged to give £40,000 to steady Mrs Thatcher's resolve: "he is concerned Mrs Thatcher is wavering in her economic resolve and the money is to demonstrate support for her policies."[6]

The eventual reward for the Conservative Party from Hanson was handsome. By 1987, the Hanson Trust had become the second biggest donor of funds to the Tories – £117,000. They have maintained their position as one of the Party's biggest (public) backers ever since, always making a six figure donation. Hanson wrote shortly before the 1987 election: "The world recognises, even if we ourselves find it hard to see, that the process of rejuvenating and reinvigorating is well underway."[7] Hanson's biographers described the 'special privileges' being such a large donor conferred:

"In the first instance Hanson found himself a political insider, courted by the Conservative Party's inner circle such as the former party chairmen Lord Parkinson and Kenneth Baker [Baker got a place on the board of Hanson plc]... On a second level, the act of donating up to £1 million to the party during the 1980s also meant that the patronage that governments can confer came the way of Hanson and his colleagues, including knighthoods and peerages and the power to command the presence even of the Prime Minister at corporate celebrations. Thirdly, and arguably the most important for a business, Hanson could use his financial firepower to inject his company into the political process: this happened at PowerGen…"[8]

In the case of PowerGen, Hanson was very nearly able to buy the soon-to-be-privatised electricity company outright. The government were persuaded to look at the option first by Sir Michael Richardson, at a meeting in May 1990 of business leaders and politicians at Clivedon, the former home of the Astors. Sir Michael was chairman of City brokers Smith New Court, who hosted the meeting. Present amongst the gathering was John Wakeham, the Energy Secretary. After confidential discussions took place, however, the potential deal was leaked into the open, and after a political row, the government retreated – especially after Hanson said they would not include any environmental costs in their bid. During the talks, Hanson revealed that new power stations employing only 40 people could replace those currently employing 850 – a good example of how the social economy would be expected to pick up the unemployment costs of Hanson's rejuvenating approach.[9] There is no doubt that Hanson's original proposal was a daring one, given that it flew in the face of the government's policy of extending the range of 'popular' share ownership amongst the British people. It would obviously be much easier for a friend of the party to be so dismissive of one its declared objectives. But Hanson was no friend of the British taxpayer: in the early years of Thatcher's government, it was found that Hanson, "despite declaring total European profits of £569 million, almost entirely from the UK in that period, cumulatively the company paid no mainstream UK tax at all."[10]

In the Heath era, business without a sense of responsibility was frowned on – publicly condemned even, as in the case of Lonrho, famously described as "the unacceptable face of capitalism." Even though Slater Walker at one time handled some of Heath's personal investments, there was never such encouragement given to rampant capitalism as that given by Thatcher. Naturally, such encouragement must have inspired new people to fund the Conservative Party, but it must have offended others, as the 1980s saw a marked downward trend in established business donations to the Conservative Party, as recorded by Labour Research. Perhaps a separate factor in the downward trend would be the recessions of the 1980s taking their toll on more traditional industries. The long term impact of the change from family owned or single proprietor-led businesses to large multinational corporations has also been credited with aiding the decline in business contributions to the party. In this respect the party's policies have clearly contributed to its own financial problems, given that it has led to an increasing reliance on large foreign donations, with the concommitant relationship that that implies, e.g. complete unaccountability and the use of offshore bank accounts.

An exemplar of the Thatcherite venality of the 1980s was her own son, to whom she was devoted not only in the normal filial sense, but as the very model of a Thatcherite businessman. Mark Thatcher unashamedly used not only his mother's name to promote his own business prospects, but also his access to Number 10 Downing Street as a base for doing business. He enjoyed an advantage which, by common consent, his business prowess on its own would not have given him – by a long shot. Mark Thatcher's big break came with an introduction from Victor Matthews, chief executive of the conglomerate Trafalgar House, which had given £40,000 to Thatcher's victorious 1979 campaign. In 1980 Mark Thatcher, with Matthews' help, was appointed as a consultant to Cementation International Ltd., which was bidding for contracts worth hundreds of millions in Oman. Mark Thatcher accompanied his mother on visits to Oman and other Gulf states, and there is no doubt that he was able to secure business through the special status he had.[11] When a potential conflict of interests was pointed out in the media, Margaret Thatcher genuinely couldn't understand what all the fuss was about – when she went abroad, she was 'batting for Britain'. The Cementation deal nevertheless propelled the accident-prone Mark Thatcher on to the front pages in a way which would clearly bring Thatcher's overseas visits into disrepute. Consequently, her trusted aide Tim Bell launched a public relations damage limitation exercise to prevent Mark getting more press attention. A group consisting of a former Central Office director of publicity, David Boddy, Michael Dobbs, an executive at Saatchi and Saatchi (and later a Central Office employee) and Sir Gordon Reece was called upon for advice. Boddy was to be paid a consultancy fee of £18,000, to paid for by Conservative businessmen, although he only saw £5,000 of it.[12] But their mission was doomed from the off – Mark Thatcher, although extraordinarily coy in his dealings with the media, was invariably crass when he did deign to speak to them, and only added to the speculation that he was making a fortune by abusing his unfettered relationship with his mother.

This speculation reached a peak later in the 1980s with the multi-billion Al Yamamah arms deals with Saudi Arabia. Once again, Mark was observed playing a shadowy role, often in tow with his mother. He was also a close friend of Wafic Said, a Syrian financier who acted as a middleman for the Saudis. Said gave Mark Thatcher a £14,000 Rolex watch as a token of his esteem, but more importantly, alleged-ly helped him reap at least £12,000,000, but possibly as much as £20,000,000 in commissions from Al Yamamah.[13] Inevitably, questions were raised as to whether the Conservative Party itself had benefit-ed from Saudi largesse.

The Saudi Royal Family could be doubly motivated to contribute; firstly because of the way in which Al Yamamah's system of commis-sions benefited them personally, which coupled with their admiration for Thatcher might induce them to donate; and secondly, because of Thatcher's unstinting support during the Gulf War. Ironically, Saudi Arabia's arsenal, acquired under Al Yamamah, was to be of limited use in the Gulf War, and pointed to the Saudi opposi-tion's case that the whole deal was yet another way in which the Saudi royal family was enriching itself.

The accusations that the Saudis were funding the Conservatives hit the headlines in an acrimonious and hotly denied series of reve-lations after the 1992 general election. The Guardian first reported that the Saudis had given as much as £7 million just before the 1992 general election. According to the paper, a meeting took place between a cabinet minister and Prince Bandar Bin Sultan, the son of Saudi defence minister, Sultan Bin Abdul Aziz.[14] In the 1980s, through Prince Bandar's close relationship with Wafic Said's close friend Mark Thatcher, Bandar was able to gain special access to the Prime Minister.[15] Whilst this close relationship, through Mark Thatcher would have been severed when Major became Prime Minister, there would have been contact between Major and the Saudis at the time that the alleged £7 million donation to Tory funds was being discussed. At the same time, in April 1992, Major was engaged in 'salvaging' Al Yamamah, which had run into financial problems due to low oil prices – the Saudis were paying for their arms with oil exports.[16] Conservative Central Office were at first hesitant in their

Price of Power

denial that the Saudis had made a donation, saying that, "To the best of our knowledge we have never accepted a donation like this". However, if the spokesperson was not at the very heart of Tory fund-raising, they wouldn't know about the donation anyway, as all matters were dealt with in strictest secrecy – even within Central Office. But the spokesperson added the rider that they didn't take money from foreign governments. The Saudi embassy also denied the story. The following day, John Major was 'incandescent', but whilst he was vehemently denouncing The Guardian's charges as 'utter fantasy' it was reported that he "twice refused a direct request to extend his denial of Saudi government or royal family donations to include private individuals or corporations within the Arab oil kingdom."[17]

The Guardian story was followed up in a full day's House of Commons debate on party political funding, called by Labour, when Clive Soley MP claimed to have a separate source of information pointing to the donation, and claimed that the minister involved was Michael Heseltine, who was at the time recovering from a mild heart attack at the Venice home of former Conservative Party treasurer, Lord McAlpine.

Over a year later, the claim resurfaced when Dr Mohammed al-Massari, a Saudi dissident said that "[King Fahd] was very keen to support both the Conservative Party in the British election and George Bush's Republican campaign for the presidency in 1992... the government was careful to ensure that its support for the Conservatives could not be detected."[18] Dr al-Massari claimed to have gleaned the information from a 'senior member' of King Fahd's staff.

The Saudis' preferred way of doing business, involving legions of middlemen and huge commissions, of course defies open examination. John Major's inability to deny whether other Saudi money was received casts a grave doubt over the source of any money that may have been given by people within the Gulf state – it would, as al-Massari indicates, be easy to conceal who was the original donor. But during the Commons debate, the Leader of the House of Commons, Tony Newton replying for the government, read a statement from Prince Bandar himself, saying that The Guardian's allegations were "untrue and wholly without foundation. No such meeting took place and neither Prince Bandar bin Sultan nor anyone connected with the Saudi Arabian government has made donations to the Conservative Party, whether directly or indirectly, or been asked for such donations. Also, HRH Prince Bandar was not in England during the month of March."[19]

Despite that, Business Age magazine, which had been taking a keen interest in Conservative Party funding, claimed in July 1993 that the Saudi royal family money was given in "much smaller donations... by individual Saudis." In the same article it also noted a potential role for Wafic Said and Mark Thatcher, by repeating a general view that "Everyone concerned has always denied that Said paid money into Tory Party funds via Mark Thatcher."[20] There would, of course be nothing to stop Said donating directly to the party – and it is clear, too that Mark Thatcher was more interested in what the Conservative Party could do for him – through his mother – than what he could do in return.

The Tories countered the growing concern over their funds by wheeling out Lord McAlpine, who was achieving something of a mythical status as a fund-raiser – a status all the more gilded given the party's appalling overdraft record in the Major years after McAlpine's departure from Central Office. Writing in the Daily Telegraph a couple of days after the Commons debate, he declared that in all his time at Central Office, King Fahd "never sent me a cent" and that if £7 million had been flown over in cash, "The poor dear things at Conservative Central Office would not have known what to do with several fork-lifts truck-loads of used fivers". The simple truth was that "most Tory money is raised by the selling of jam, more often than not sold for less than it will cost the donor to make the stuff."[21] But McAlpine's denial continued in the pattern of previous such denials. By lumping together local and national funding, it could be said that the sale of 'jam' was the major source of revenue, when in reality, the national pot was only in receipt of a relatively small amount of 'jam' money through the quota system.

McAlpine's attitude to accountability, however, was that it was nobody's business to know how the party got its money. He recalled in his memoirs, Once A Jolly Bagman, that "The Treasurers had rules that any donation from an individual was a matter kept confidential between the donor and the Treasurers. This was the rule long before I arrived at Central Office and I sincerely hope that rule will always be kept. A citizen in Britain is entitled to privacy as to which political party they support at the ballot box, so why should they declare which political party they support financially?"[22]

'Nobody read the accounts anyway', he once said, and if party members wanted to see how the money was spent, they need do no more than go to the stall at party conference and 'see our graphs of where the money went.'[23]

He also commented on 'rich foreigners' supporting the Conservative Party, suggesting that they 'mostly' had considerable economic interests in Britain and therefore contributed to the wealth of the country and employed large numbers of British people. As for wealthy Sheiks and Serb businessmen, "I never came across either of these bringing suitcases of money into Central Office. A suitcase is a useless way to deliver a large sum of cash; a cheque is far more convenient."[24]

This is a much more superficial denial than at first meets the eye, but is delivered with sufficient bonhomie and wit to take attention away from what is not being denied. As we find a little later, after the emotionally crushing defeat of his heroine at the hands of her own party, McAlpine's countenance becomes somewhat less cheerful: "Too many Members of Parliament were finding people who would give the Party money, too many businessmen believed that to be Treasurer of the Conservative Party was just the job for them. Senior officials in Central Office were in the pay of businessmen and promoting their interests, and I felt that the place was out of control... A warning was given to me about a particular businessman, and I passed the message on to two members of the Cabinet who were closely associated with him. Within hours, my words were repeated to this man."[25]

For one as defensive of the party's fund-raising as McAlpine had been (and despite his subsequent move to the Referendum Party) the above statement must confirm what a serious problem the party faced in defending its rectitude – particularly since he ascribed his discontent to a period which was still seven years away from the party losing power. Perhaps it may be suggested that he simply wished to cast aspersions on the kind of organisation John Major – someone he despised – ran. Revenge, or sour grapes might have something to do with it, since his memoirs were published at a time when they might only damage Major's already sagging reputation. But on the other hand, McAlpine had committed himself to the view, for all to see, that even whilst he was still treasurer, things had gone out of control and that MPs and senior Central Office staff were behaving badly. How long had this been going on?

One has to turn to the contemporaneously published memoir of Ian Greer, the lobbyist, to find out – or to begin the long search. Had Greer started his career a couple of generations earlier, he may have made it to the Conservative benches in the Lords. But the growing political corruption in the 1980s built up such a reservoir of public disdain, that what were once accepted as innocent activities – such as lobbying – became tarred with a lingering odour of disrepute. Coincidentally, Ian Greer shared some similarities with Maundy Gregory – both were gay and both were the sons of religious fathers; Gregory's a vicar, Greer's a Salvationist.

Both men's activities also contributed to changes in the way the establishment would regulate its affairs; in the former's case with the regulation of honours, the latter's with greater regulation over MPs' business interests. Ironically, although it was only Gregory who was to break the law, it was also only for him whom the Conservative Party sanctioned a generous pay-off. Greer was left, at a similar near-retirement age, with a folded business and a name that many of his erstwhile friends in the Conservative Party now sought to forget.

Greer started his career working for Central Office as an agent, a crucial apprenticeship for anyone about to embark on a career in the infant lobbying industry. Through his work he would get to know many politicians, and gain their trust. It is a reflection on the value of that apprenticeship that in later years, Ian Greer Associates (IGA) would send its employees out to work for candidates in elections – some of them even becoming candidates themselves.

For lobbying to work effectively, it must be seen to be a seamless part of the process, with the intimacy more of friendship than the less trusting nature of purely business relationships. Cultivating contacts, using the well worn route from the client's to the target's stomach, sharing in the ups and downs of a politician's career, getting to know their families – these are essential prerequisites of successful lobbying, quite apart from studying the client's case and presenting it to selected ministers.

The new clutch of young Thatcherite MPs elected in the 1980s were keen to follow in the footsteps of their forebearers, grasping at any 'outside interests' or perks that would enhance their status as members of what seemed likely to be a government without end. Whereas Tory MPs would once have to find the money to buy a seat in the Commons, they now found that the seat would become a source of income. Uncannily, many of them displayed the same characteristics as Thatcher's real son, Mark – bellicose, arrogant and ambitious. Greer became weary of the number of MPs demanding that he arrange Business Class travel for them. Such travel arrangements would no doubt be symbolic of their self-importance, but also perhaps more usefully, would present them with the opportunity of meeting businessmen for hours at a time – a relaxing contact building session on every transatlantic flight.

Greer's business appeared to grow exponentially during the Thatcher years. Greer describes a typical introduction of new business in his memoir, One Man's Word. Two Tory MPs, Michael Brown and Neil Hamilton had attended a conference in the United States organised by US Tobacco (UST), the manufacturers of Skoal Bandits, the nicotine enhanced chewing gum. While there, executives from the company explained to the two MPs that they needed a 'hard hitting lobbying outfit in London'. They suggested IGA, and indeed IGA were appointed. Greer then made a "new business referral payment" to each MP[26]. He does not reveal how much these payments were, but mentions that he also paid a similar fee to Hamilton for a referral from the National Nuclear Corporation, which was based in Hamilton's constituency. For this, the sum of £4,000 was paid.[27] It is easy to see how MPs would jump at the chance to help Greer. It was money for old rope. Not only would they personally be enriched, but their party would be too – everybody could be grateful all round. Greer estimates that:

"I have raised, directly or indirectly, around £750,000 for the Conservative Party over the years – something of which I am very proud. Many of my clients sought my advice as to how they should make donations to the party machine. I suggested that they should earmark their contribution for specific marginal seats. We also arranged for one client, ADT, to donate mobile telephones to a number of Conservative candidates."[28]

Greer's advice was not always understood. Whilst he was still on talking terms with Mohammed al-Fayed, the proud new owner of Harrods, just before the 1987 general election, Greer hinted that al-Fayed might help the Conservative Party with its funds.

Fayed revealed that he had already been tapped by Lord McAlpine for £250,000. "I tried to explain that the huge donation he had made, valuable as it was, would quickly disappear into Central Office coffers. From my experience, the candidate fighting the front-line marginal seat would be unlikely to benefit – and it was those I wanted to help."[29] As ever, Greer had a sharp eye on the main chance. Whilst it was obviously the case that the national party needed the money, giving large sums to head office would be of little use in cultivating his willing brood of Tory MPs. There would be no direct advantage he could play on for the lobbying business – as opposed to that gained by industrialists "coincidentally" finding themselves on honours lists, which statistically they were more likely to be than those who didn't help Central Office directly.

Greer happily acted as a courier between his business clients (such as DHL) on the one hand and deserving Tory MPs on the other. Some of the latter knew he could be relied on, and solicited money from him; others were blessed for no better reason than they were chums with one client or another. Greer's 1987 beneficiaries were:[30]

MP	Sum	Distinguishing feature
Norman Tebbit	£500	Chair of Conservative Party; admired by Dave Allen of DHL
Michael Portillo	£500	"enthusiastic whip"
Gerry Malone	£1,000	an assistant whip
Lynda Chalker	£2,000	Transport Minister and personal friend
Norman Lamont	£2,000	Greer's constituency MP, DHL office in constituency. Lamont was Financial Secretary at the time
David Mellor	£500	Home Office Minister
Sir Michael Hirst	£500	Chairman of Scottish Tories
John Moore	£1,367	Transport Secretary
Robert Atkins	£500	became a DTI minister in 1987
Andrew Bowden	£5,319	
Sir Anthony Durant	£500	Government Whip 1986 – 88
Gerry Bowden	£500	
Nirj Deva	£750	"working at IGA at the time"
Sir Malcolm Thornton	£500	
David Shaw	£500	"good friend of DHL chairman"
Gerry Vaughan	£500	former Trade minister
Ken Warren	£500	Chairman, Select Committee on Trade and Industry
John Lee	£500	Employment minister
Neil Thorne	£500	
David Trippier	£500	Environment minister in 1987

Another MP who was assisted by Greer's help – although he was one of those subsequently booted out in the 1992 general election – was Colin Moynihan, the former sports minister. In 1992, apart from personally driving some Tory voters to the polling station in Moynihan's constituency on polling day, Greer arranged "one or two or two" dinners at the Carlton Club, which were attended by sympathetic businessmen." At one of these dinners, executives from the Japanese Kobe Steel company expressed a desire to meet Margaret Thatcher, and Moynihan said he would do what he could. For that, he received a cheque from Kobe for £1,000, and he wrote his thanks to Greer, saying that Kobe were "keen to do what they can to help in the build-up to the coming election."[31] It is not known whether Kobe would fit the McAlpine criteria that foreign donations should come from companies having significant British interests, but then neither does McAlpine acknowledge Greer's not insignificant assistance in raising money for the party – most of it during his tenure as treasurer. In 1992 Lynda Chalker and Neil Thorne were supported once again, though not by the electorate, whilst Robert Atkins saved his seat. All got £250 from Greer. Elizabeth Peacock, the populist member for Batley and Spen, got the support of a worker from IGA after the Chief Whip Richard Ryder solicited support on her behalf from Greer: "It was a friendly request, and one to which I was happy to respond."

The most obvious feature of Greer's 1987 list is of course that so many of the recipients were already well advanced up the ministerial ladder – not what one would expect if they were a purely representative sample of candidates fighting what Greer then classed as 'marginal' seats. This clearly was not a random selection. As Greer makes plain in some cases, they were 'friends' (although they soon ditched him when he became persona non grata), but overwhelmingly they were well placed to be useful from the lobbyist's point of view.

Greer makes the point that he did not solely support the Conservatives, and lists a handful of Labour and Alliance recipients (one of these, Richard Holmes in Cheltenham he mistakenly lists with his Conservative beneficiaries) but this cannot be seen as much more than window dressing for the sake of maintaining the image of IGA as being 'non-party political.' He could more easily take the sting out of any criticism that may come along that his was 'an exclusive Tory outfit', but essentially such sophistry could be hardly more convincing than the old clichés trotted out by so many company chairmen that their donations were not 'party political', but were merely supporting 'free enterprise.'

The outstanding feature of the new Tory MP's venal code was that apart from earning some extra help with the mortgage, dining and first class travel should be about the grandest items their ambition allowed. This compares unfavourably with Reginald Maudling, who whilst his love of the good life has been described already, nevertheless wanted to use his connections to help fund a lasting memorial; in his case a new ballet theatre in East Grinstead named after his wife's ballet teacher, Adeline Genee. The Conservatives' latter-day lack of finesse was encapsulated in the popular imagination by the archetypal 1980s character, created by the comedian Harry Enfield, known simply as 'Loadsamoney.' For most people, Conservative MPs conjured up the image of a person who could hardly walk ten paces without seeking a consultancy, a commission or a place on the board.

By 1988, 58% of Tory MPs held company directorships, and 51% had consultancies, figures which were set to increase.[32] An average directorship might easily bring in an extra £5,000 or £10,000 on average, though many paid well in excess of that. Of particular value to companies would be MPs with ex-ministerial experience, especially in areas of privatisation. In addition to the headline grabbing privatisations of British Telecom or British Airways, there were piecemeal privatisations up and down the country, from hospital cleaning contracts to dustbin emptying. New firms sprung up to make their contribution to the Thatcherite revolution. One such was ADT, formerly known as the Hawley Group.

One of ADT's subsidiaries, Pritchard, showed what could be achieved by paying the second lowest wages in the cleaning trade whilst expecting the longest hours (for minimum overtime payments), and contracting workers to have been employed for five years before holidays could rise to just three weeks – two of which had to be taken between pre-determined dates. ADT moved its registered offices to Bermuda in 1984, helping it to slash its tax on profits from 27% in 1983 to 11% by 1987.[33] The Conservative MP on its board was Bowen Wells MP.

Later, ADT was to sell its contract cleaning businesses to BET, a conglomerate of which Norman Tebbit was a Director. As reported in Labour Research, Tebbit was just the person to hold down a few directorships as well as being an MP, since he had just lambasted nurses for 'moonlighting.'[34] Judging by Labour Research's survey reported in April, 1988, there were at that time 25 Conservative MPs "moonlighting" with interests in privatised or privatising companies alone.

Price of Power

Margaret Thatcher's third successive victory in 1987 also appeared to mark a high point in company donations to the Conservatives. Over £5,000,000 worth of donations were eventually traced by Labour Research, and by far the largest contributors were from 'City' interests. The breakdown was as follows:[35]

Banking, finance, insurance	£1,451,550
Other services	£113,650
Energy & water supplies	£14,333
Mining, metals, mineral products, pharmaceuticals	£449,250
Metal goods, engineering, vehicles	£657,533
Other manufacturing	£943,810
Construction	£461,925
Distribution, hotels, catering	£229,552
Transport, communication	£188,950

Of all the sectors which the above figures would be least likely to be a full reflection of would be the 'City' interests group, since that is where many businesses would not have to declare their donations, since they would be neither public or private companies covered by the Companies Acts. And the Labour Research figures will also be somewhat depressed since their sample covered only 3,000 out of a possible 600,000 firms.

The biggest donor in 1987 was the Hartley Investment Trust, which in the year ending March 1987 gave £167,000. The Hartley Investment Trust was a regular donor to party funds, but in the run up to the 1987 election had made a special effort to bring in more cash. Alan Lewis, the Chairman and Chief Executive sent out a direct mail letter to potential donors, asking for "substantial funds to meet a special requirement of the Conservative Party," namely, "providing the constituencies with modern technology and advanced management systems."[36] It was Alan Lewis's "considered opinion that if the Conservative Party do not win the next election, penal taxation, exchange controls and a breakdown of our traditional values will take place.' Perhaps he had in mind, when talking of 'traditional values", that useful traditional value of removing one's assets from the greedy eye of the Inland Revenue to some sun-kissed tax haven. Unluckily for Lewis's promotion of a 'patriotic' image, it was revealed that he had recently transferred £17.85 million of his shares in one of his companies, Illingworth Morris, to the Dutch Antilles. He denied that his 'personal' £30 million fortune had been moved abroad, but said that what he had shifted offshore had been for the benefit of his family's future.[37]

Another very traditional Tory, the doyen of the 1922 Committee, Sir Marcus Fox, member for Shipley, was a director of the Hartley Investment Trust. Sir Marcus was one of those MPs who had acquired a string of directorships and consultancies, and had taken a keen interest in seeing that NHS cleaning services were privatised. He was associated with Brengreen Holdings Ltd, a contract cleaning company which had given £5,164 to the Tory Party in 1984,[38] when he opened an adjournment debate in 1982 by opposing the closure of Shipley Hospital. He claimed that private contractors could help keep the hospital open by cutting the cleaning budget by 20%. He later joined the board of another cleaning company, Care Services Group, and continued his crusade on the hospital cleaning privatisers' behalf in a market worth £50,000,000 a year. Fox made himself very much a model for others to follow: "As a backbencher, and being a Conservative MP, I'm quite free to follow the interests I've got. The point is that Care Services is in my constituency, plus the fact that I've taken an interest in privatisation from the beginning… We agreed a certain figure to pay me for the time I put in and the expertise I've got that will help them."[39]

Bournemouth is not actually in the Shipley constituency, so it would be stretching a point to say that there was a significant 'constituency' interest in Fox's joining the board of Bournemouth-based McCarthy & Stone Ltd, retirement home developers (£2,000 to the Tories in 1987).[40] Here Fox was able to combine his public and private positions to promote the traditional rights of property developers to inflict excessive service charges on pensioners. McCarthy & Stone had come in for parliamentary criticism after MPs received complaints from old people in their sheltered accommodation. Labour MP Nigel Griffiths led a campaign to protect them, saying "We are facing the prospects of thousands of older people bankrupting themselves to feed the profits of unscrupulous developers."[41] He introduced a bill to curtail developers' profiteering by giving their residents new legal rights. Naturally, Fox was stirred into action and arranged a meeting between Griffiths and John McCarthy, and wrote a round-robin letter to other members defending the company. Given

Price of Power

his position as Chairman of the Commons' Selection Committee, Fox would have been able to influence the choice of members who sat on the committee stage of Griffiths' bill, had it got that far. This potential for a conflict of interests led twenty Labour MPs to sign a motion calling for his resignation. Bradford West MP Max Madden said "There could be suggestions that he was putting commercial interests before the interests of parliament. He could clearly influence matters by deciding which MPs go on which committees."[43] But surely Tory MPs were entitled to represent commercial interests? That, certainly could not be mistaken for anything but a 'tradition.'

Fox subsequently ran into a further storm of controversy when it emerged that he had failed to declare his directorship of three American companies, registered in Baton Rouge, Louisiana. The three companies, whose Chairman was Alan Lewis, were according to Fox, subsidiaries of Illingworth Morris, so he didn't have to declare them. Nevertheless, Sir Marcus, doyen of the Dales and backbone of the 1922 Committee faced the inevitable 'Top Tory faces sleaze inquiry' headlines, and even the ultra-Tory Yorkshire Post felt it had to devote some column inches to the story. Sir Marcus's fulminating response probably only stiffened the resolve of his Shipley electorate to dump him.

Another commercial interest which was generous in 1987, giving £249,325 – was the 'beerage' – brewers and distillers, the most loyal of Tory supporters. Their loyalty was stretched somewhat after the election, however, when a long awaited report from the Monopolies and Mergers Commission (MMC) recommended that the breweries should be limited to owning only 2,000 pubs each – meaning that they would have sell off 22,000 between them. When the Minister responsible, ex-businessman Lord Young, Secretary of State for Trade and Industry said that he was minded to accept the proposal, the brewers mounted one of the most effective lobbying operations ever seen. Eventually, Lord Young came under severe pressure:

"I ran into more trouble with the backbench committee and again with the 1922 Committee. Too late I realised what had happened. It was nothing to do with public opinion, which was uniformly for the proposals. It had nothing to do with the merits, which were rarely discussed. It had everything to do with the brewers' support for the constituency associations up and down the land. Eventually I had a meeting with the Chief Whips of both the Lords and the Commons. I was told quite firmly that they could not get my proposals through either House. I had to drop them."[44]

One rebellious Tory MP – on this and other matters – was Jim Cran, MP for Beverley. He received a call from a brewery chairman saying in "oblique terms that if I didn't back the brewers and the Brewers Society, then of course perhaps some money might be withdrawn from the Conservative Party at whatever level... I could see that in some circumstances perhaps some MPs might have to think about that twice."[45] The last comment rather understates just how pragmatic Cran's backbench colleagues were in the event. Perhaps it could be argued that every constituency had a 'constituency interest,' since they all had pubs. By 1994, the brewers' known cumulative reward for the party that had stood by them amounted to £2,278,047.[46]

The tobacco industry had a much more circumspect relationship with the Conservative Party. Being such a hot political potato, they did as much as they could to assert their commercial interests through lobbying groups, as opposed to head-on gifts to the party. In terms of direct donations, and perhaps signifying the perceived threat Labour then was to cigarette advertising, Rothmans appears to have been the first of many tobacco company to dip into its coffers to directly give the Tories £100,000 in 1992. But before then, others had helped out where they thought they could do so with as great effect, but more discreetly, such as BAT Industries' annual contributions of £4,000 to the Centre for Political Studies, or early gifts to Aims of Industry. Imperial Tobacco gave money to the Economic League.[47] The tobacco industry's problem was poor public relations. Even after she lost power, Margaret Thatcher caused a storm when she became a consultant to Philip Morris, the manufacturer of Marlboro.

The importance of building links with right-wing, libertarian think-tanks would obviously be a far more fruitful way of proceeding to influence matters. Thus, in the early 1980s, when Sir George Young, as health minister, sought to ban tobacco advertising, a sustained campaign was waged using the twin-pronged approach of parliamentary lobbying and making connections between individuals and groups which were in tune with Thatcher's libertarian instincts. They would fight against the 'Nanny State', although the industry's lobbying group FOREST (Freedom Organisation for the Right to Enjoy

Smoking Tobacco) went even further and portrayed Sir George Young as a German SS officer. FOREST was launched shortly after Thatcher's 1979 election victory, with £50,000 income a year, to:

"... restore and establish freedom of choice... There are a growing number of people in central government and local government, people in authority and people without authority, except self arrogated, Jacks in office and Jacks out of office, experts and self-styled experts, who apparently have decided to eradicate what has been an accepted element of our way of life for three centuries and more..."[48]

Hardly could a more resounding statement of Thatcherite philosophy be found. The first director of FOREST, right-wing Tory Stephen Eyres had edited Free Nation, the newspaper of the Freedom Association, Norris McWhirter's right-wing pressure group. Eyres had also served Thatcher free market loyalists Nicholas Ridley and Ian Gow. Through what is the usual channel, "the Conservative Chief Whip, Michael Jopling . . was left in no doubt that many Tory backbenchers were strongly opposed to what the government's Health Ministers were trying to do."[49] Other forms of lobbying were more direct, when for example Sir Anthony Kershaw, MP for Stroud helped to talk out a private members bill which sought to ban tobacco advertising. Kershaw, BAT's parliamentary consultant tabled 27 amendments to the London Zoo bill which preceded the hostile bill. Asked how he became involved in zoos, Kershaw replied "I've always been interested in animals."[50]

By far the most symbolic hot political potato of the 1980s was Thatcher's attitude to the apartheid regime in South Africa. She stood out against a worldwide tide of condemnation and increasing pressure through sanctions. In this, she was undoubtedly reflecting the views of a large constituency of Conservative Party funders. This is pointedly demonstrated by those British companies which donated £684,800 to the Tories in 1987 that had commercial interests in Namibia.[51] Namibia was illegally occupied by South Africa since a declaration made by the United Nations in 1971. Shortly afterwards, martial law was imposed, and between 1977 and 1983 5,000 Namibians were detained without trial. Torture and atrocities were the order of the day. Yet despite the illegality of the occupation and the brutality of the regime, the Conservative government's position was that: "on the question of the activities of British companies in

Namibia, we take the view that trade with and investment in Namibia is a matter for commercial decision only."[52] This laissez faire, amoral approach was not surprisingly identical to the attitude expressed by Conservative Party treasurers, who rarely refused a donation (if you believe McAlpine) or never 'refused a cheque' if you were to believe another Tory treasurer, Major Brian Wyldbore-Smith.

According to Pinto-Duschinsky, the Conservatives' total central income in 1987/88 amounted to £15,000,000, of which only £1,200,000 came from constituency quotas.[53] By 1988, Labour Research had managed to identify another £250,000 of corporate donations during election year, bringing the total up to £5,250,000. Hence, we are left with a gaping, unexplained hole of around £8,500,000 in income. In searching for an explanation, Pinto-Duschinsky identifies the possibility that the party's infant direct mail fund-raising effort contributed 5%, and possibly another 15% was contributed through legacies. Given the state of the party's growing deficit, it must be assumed that the remainder would have to be made up of loans, delayed payments and an overdraft.

So far as the direct mail was concerned, the 5% response was pleasing for the party. It was the first time they could make any significant use of a new kind of target voter – the owner of privatised shares. British Telecom had been privatised in 1984, but since then had lost not only a lot of its small shareholders who sold out, but BT's reputation had suffered because of its worsening service and burgeoning number of complaints. Nevertheless, a letter from Norman Tebbit was sent to BT shareholders in January, 1987, declaiming Labour's proposals for 'social ownership' and asking for a donation to the 'Fighting Fund.' Given that the letter made great play of 'protecting your pension', it was probably also sent to selected members of pension funds, access to which was probably made easier by having so many friends in the City. Tebbit recorded in his memoirs:

"The problem of political direct mailing is that many letters (at about 30 pence a shot) go to hostile voters, many friendly voters may not read what looks like junk advertising mail, and few who do will send their cheques. The heavy costs will normally take years to recover, but the privatisation programme gave us a great opportunity. The million-plus British Telecom shareholders, whose names and addresses are easily taken from the share register, were our first target...The programme shot straight into substantial cash surpluses, recruiting thousands of new members and becoming the most successful direct mail campaign in British politics."[54]

If the cost was £300,000 then the mail-shot delivered £800,000 to party funds – as well as delivering a political message to one million voters. Direct mail was to play a much larger role in subsequent general elections, especially since subsequent legal opinion altered the view that was held until 1987 that nothing targeted at individual voters could be sent after the dissolution of Parliament, for fear of breaching the Representation of the People Act which set limits on the amounts spent on local campaigns. By 1997 voters, particularly in marginal seats, could count on wading through a deluge of blue signed 'personal' letters.

The electorate did not have to wait too long after the 1987 election to reap the painful cost of a third Conservative victory, as the 'Lawson boom' fizzled out and the economy entered another recession. And as happens after every election, company donations to the party went into decline, but this time they didn't appear to recover. As a simple reflection of the downward trend of company profits, this may not have been exceptional. But the recession of the late 1980s/early 1990s spawned a new phenomenon which could only be described as the 'post-Loadsamoney' boardroom syndrome. For despite their fall in profits, directors discovered that largesse for themselves and their shareholders could still rise without restraint.

The departure of Thatcher and McAlpine, combined with the recession left the party with a financial hangover. Clearly somebody was going to get the blame. The party's accumulated deficit by the beginning of the 1990s was £11,814,000 and the Charter Movement, amongst others, were unhappy that reforms were not taking place to sort the finances out and to present a more accountable and positive image to the membership and the electorate alike. They were particularly harsh with ex-Party Chairman Kenneth Baker: "The Kenneth Baker era at Central Office can now be seen in all its horror. The Party has overspent in the last two years by an amount equal to approximately 50% of its income, setting new records for financial profligacy. Most of this overspending has been in adminstration."[55] But Baker was having none of it. Fully matching expectations of someone who had established a reputation as a slick 'houdini', he recounted in his memoirs:

"The current financial difficulties of Central Office have sometimes, and unfairly I must say, been laid at my door. The facts are
that when I became Party Chairman in July 1989 the decision to
modernise Smith Square had already been taken by my predecessor
Peter Brooke, and work was well advanced... The fact remains that
the period of appointment of Party Chairman bears no relation to
the period of the Party's annual accounts."[56]

But the criticism of overspending levelled by the Charter
Movement could be sustained without reference to the cost of
improvements at Central Office – which were themselves overspent
by two and half times. The Charter Movement rubbished Baker's
tenure having "departed the scene made desolate by his period in
charge. Not only did he fail to introduce reform but at no time has
he had to account to the constituencies for his stewardship."[57]

The accountability argument, which surfaced so strongly in the
Major years, had not been entirely dormant in the Thatcher years.
There was less pressure, perhaps, provided the party was doing well
under her leadership, but there were occasional murmurings of
disquiet amongst the constituencies. In 1984, for example,
Beckenham and East Surrey Constituency Associations tabled
motions for the party's Central Council meeting criticising the
absence of proper accounting for Central Office money. The present
position, according to Beckenham, is "inconsistent with the party's
public stand on matters of accountability and financial rectitude."[58]
If this was an attempt to shame the leadership into action, it was
clearly ill-conceived. The party's managers chose instead a motion
from Chester, calling for a greater fund-raising effort instead. Michael
Spicer, a party treasurer took the hint, and suggested that currently
the average constituency association quota payment was £1,250,
whereas it ought to be £50,000 in those seats with a sitting MP – or
approximately £6 per head of membership (assuming each association had between 6,000 and 10,000 members. But whilst the top
paying constituency, Surrey North West with £62,000, may have
suggested that such a scheme were possible, Spicer must have made
his assessment on a gross exaggeration of the membership levels in
many constituencies, which in some cases would be struggling to
get into three figures.

Even when the party published accounts, they were found wanting and it could be said, were deliberately misleading. "Accounts"

were published in 1985 – on two sides of a single sheet of paper. Eric Chalker, of the Charter Movement, said: "Any constituency treasurer producing such accounts would be thrown out of office by his fellow members" – it was "pathological secrecy." Councillor Don Hammond, the Deputy Leader of Ealing Council said, "I would expect better accounts from a sweet shop."[59] It was probably wise of Cllr. Hammond not to refer to a Grantham corner shop, but there may have been a slight possibility that the alleged rigging of that shop's scales could have been the inspiration for the comparison. It emerged the following year that what had previously been presented as a manageable £800,000 shortfall of income over expenditure was actually a deficit of £1.3million – entirely at Central Office. The difference could be explained by the removal of the cumulative constituency association accounts from the head office figures. Given that the local associations generally managed to stay within their means, and even show a surplus, the Central Office ploy of including these figures in their own was always bound to make the overall situation look better. This sleight of hand, however, was exposed by the local associations' representatives, and was not repeated.

Central Office did endeavour to demonstrate its entrepreneurial skills in other ways. The "Blue Rosette" Club was launched in 1986. Based on an idea of Graham Waterman, an executive on leave of absence from the Milk Marketing Board, the club entitled members to a food gift scheme, a wine society and a bookshop – including offers on Jeffrey Archer books.[60] For an additional £20, The Times reported, members "will be able to join the Membership Plus scheme, entitling them to a special discount shopping card, cheap health insurance and newsletters from Mr Tebbit… less affluent Tories could plump for a tea towel or Archer novel."[61] For the more affluent Tories, former Mars director Sir Christopher Lawson dreamt up another money-making endeavour: he commissioned cartoons of four living ex-Prime Ministers and one living Prime Minister, got them to sign each edition of 500 prints, and attempted to sell them for £1,000 per set. Contacted by the press, he expressed justifiable satisfaction at having sold 100.

Ironically, the Blue Rosette Club was undone by the very culture of secrecy which pervaded all matters financial at Central Office. The Party decided to adopt a new logo in 1989, but nobody told the Blue Rosette Club. Thus it was reported in 1990 that the Club: "sent out a catalogue of items bearing the old logo which members no longer wanted to buy. The company which had achieved sales of £100,000 a year crashed virtually overnight."[62] Some Tory MPs obviously thought that the culture of secrecy at Central Office was more a cover for incompetence and with it, self-denial – like a terminally ill cancer patient, who pretends to be healthy. One said, when Chris Patten took over as Party Chairman following John Major's election to the leadership, that "the reality is that the place seems to be coming apart at the seams."[63] A prescient remark, as it turned out.

Chapter Six

THE UNRAVELLING

Eventually, the chickens had to come home to roost. For years, the party had failed to exercise financial controls over expenditure and had failed to properly account for its income. Under the lacklustre and evasive leadership of John Major, the issue of Conservative Party financing was rarely out of the headlines, but from his re-election in 1992, sustained media scrutiny dogged the last term of his premiership on an unprecedented scale. Major's willingness to tackle the issues became ever more enfeebled as his majority dwindled; for a politician who was presented as an ordinary man of humble origins, a "Mr Clean" who failed his accountancy exams who nevertheless became First Lord of the Treasury, it must have been galling to have presided over an administration which allowed the word "sleaze" to dog his every move. The Conservatives' defeat in 1997 has been generally ascribed to the electorate's loss of faith in Conservative economic competence following the botched handling of the European Exchange Rate Mechanism crisis in 1992.

With or without the "sleaze" element, most commentators regard the electoral consequences as having been inevitable. But this being said, sleaze must have made matters much worse for the electorate, having coped with the prolonged effects of another recession, then to witness Conservative MPs and the Conservative Party indulging in an unscrupulous money-raking frenzy. All questions or criticisms – and many were raised by normally Tory-supporting newspapers – were met with the response that such lines of inquiry were part and parcel of a Labour-inspired smear campaign. It was as if all Mrs Thatcher's cracked fairy-tale mirrors had multiplied, preventing any

Conservative Member of Parliament from grasping the truth.

The party's growing burden of debt after the 1992 general election had reached £19 million, (which per head of staff member must have far exceeded the per capita debt of many third world countries; the kind of useless comparison Conservatives are fond of making when looking at Labour-run councils' debts) some £15 million of which was in the form of an overdraft facility given by the Royal Bank of Scotland – chaired by Lord Younger, the former Party Chairman.

The growth in Central Office debt and the downturn in the economy in the early 1990s led the Tories to look for new sources of funding abroad. The Middle and Far East were the principle areas scoured for donations, but some other sources were tapped which were notable for their idiosyncrasies.

Ironically for John Major, the foreign name which dominated the headlines, and came to symbolise all that appeared wrong with foreign donations during the early years of his premiership, was that of Asil Nadir. Ironic, since Nadir's gifts – and particularly sums amounting to £440,000 – had been given during the period of Thatcher's governments.

Nadir had been lauded as a great entrepreneur during the 1980s, perhaps more than any other coming to symbolise all that was good about the British go-ahead economy. Somebody who had invested £1,000 in Nadir's Polly Peck company in 1980 would by 1990 be sitting on an investment of £1,300,000 – a growth rate of 1,300 per cent and better than any other company in the world. Polly Peck eventually acquired FTSE 100 status, and looked set for further growth by the end of the decade.[1]

Some questions had been raised about the actual strength of the company, but since it had grown on the same principle that had propelled the British economy in the same period – borrowing – it did not stand out as being unusual. Only later, after its share price crashed by 75% when the Serious Fraud Squad let it be known that they were investigating Nadir's affairs did any uneasiness about him seriously come to the surface. Eventually it was alleged in Business Age magazine that Polly Peck was essentially built on arms trading with both sides in the Iran–Iraq War and that "those in the know knew the real source of those incredible profits that emerged year after year from Asil Nadir's company."[2] According to this account, the ending of the Iran-Iraq War in 1989 led to Nadir's crisis – which no amount of financial wizardry could avert. Allegations of Nadir's involvement in the arms trade are corroborated by Gerald James, whose book In the Public Interest described in detail his own company, Astra's heavy involvement in the Iran-Iraq conflict. James records:

"I have a letter on file from Panton Corbett of the merchant bank Singer and Friedlander advising me as chairman of Astra in 1983 to go and see Asil Nadir because he was heavily involved with the Turkish government on arms supplies; if we wanted any new contracts, perhaps he could help us get them. One man who has been linked with Nadir is Lord Erskine of Rerrick. Lord Erskine was also involved with the Conservative Industrial Fund."[3]

Nadir's meteoric rise was brought to a shuddering halt when he was charged with 18 offences of theft and false accounting amounting to £25 million. He was bailed for a record £3.5 million.

The problem for the Conservative Party was twofold. The £440,000 that it had admitted receiving from Nadir did not appear to have been declared as political donations by his companies. In the case of Unipac, this was on the tenuous grounds that a wholly owned subsidiary's donations need not be declared in the main company's accounts. The second, and perhaps more serious concern was whether the money was stolen.

Thames Television's This Week exposed the payments in March, 1992, and asked Sir John Cope, then a Conservative Party treasurer, to say whether the money would be returned. He said: "It is not my responsibility to ensure that they complied with company law." He later told The Independent, after being asked if the money would be repaid, "I'll wait and see the programme. It was all some years ago, before my time."[4] The Conservatives' embarrassment was made all the more acute in May, 1993, when Nadir jumped bail and fled to Northern Cyprus, where he would be safe from extradition. There followed revelation upon revelation of his links with the Tory Party, a number of ministers, and Nadir's alleged payments in an attempt to secure a knighthood. His alleged contributions to the Party rose from the admitted £440,000 to £1.5million.

Some of this extra money was reportedly used in an attempt to purchase an honour. An unnamed advisor to Nadir, who was to be paid a £100,000 commission if successful, said he approached Conservative Central Office, who suggested that he donate to the Conservative Industrial Fund, "'They were very cautious. They said

the money shouldn't go directly to them but to the Industrial Fund.'
Nadir is said to have pledged £300,000 to the fund over two years."[5]
According to the press, Nadir had been led to believe he would
receive a knighthood, but was bitterly disappointed that he had not.
He should perhaps have taken time to read Lord Davidson's memoirs
– to discover how what appears to be a promise in these delicate
matters often turns out to be much less than what it seems. There is
certainly something familiar about the Nadir knighthood affair, but
as ever, no proof of the allegations is available. Indeed, Nadir is
quoted later as saying "A knighthood? Why should I want a knighthood? I'm a socialist. I care about my people. You cannot buy status
and respect you know. You cannot put a wad of cash on the table
and say, respect me."[6]

For a 'socialist', Nadir gave generously to the Conservative Party,
and it has been suggested that he was their most generous backer
prior to the 1992 general election. It could only be seen as natural,
therefore, for links to have been made between his generosity, and
the concern for his welfare that was evinced by several leading Tory
politicians after Nadir had been charged. These included Michael
Heseltine, President of the Board of Trade, Michael Mates, a Northern
Ireland Minister, and Peter Brooke, then Heritage Secretary (who was
also Nadir's constituency MP). Representations on behalf of Nadir
were made by these and other Tory politicians to the Attorney
General Sir Nicholas Lyell.

The most controversial of the ministers implicated in the affair,
Michael Mates, eventually resigned over the issue, and in so doing
added a new twist to the story. He claimed that Nadir had been
brought down by MI6, who worked to destabilise Polly Peck prior to
its collapse in 1990.[7] The reason for MI6's involvement, it was
surmised, may have been that Nadir's interests in Northern Cyprus
posed a stumbling block to the resolution of the political division of
the island. Indeed, so far as Nadir's business in Cyprus goes, it could
be shown that, for example, his acquisition of commercial property
formerly belonging to Greek Cypriots was the source of diplomatic
activity, including an alleged intervention by Margaret Thatcher
when she was still Prime Minister.[8]

However, another explanation for MI6's interest in Nadir's business may have been to obtain information about arms supplies to
Iran and Iraq. As was revealed in the Scott Inquiry into arms sales to

Price of Power

Iraq, MI6 were heavily involved in spying activities with British companies such as Matrix Churchill who were involved in the trade with these countries. Such an involvement may just as easily have been beneficial to Polly Peck as the reverse. The suggestion was also made that Mates had been played along by Nadir to make allegations in order to ensure he could claim that if he returned to Britain he would be denied a fair trial.[9]

When the Mates row blew up, Major characteristically backed his beleaguered minister, passing off Mates's actions and particularly his gift of a watch to Nadir inscribed "Don't let the buggers get you down" as a small, forgivable error of judgement. Within days, Mates had resigned. But that was not the end of the Nadir affair for the Tories, since the spotlight was refocused on Nadir's donations to the party. A threat of High Court summonses forced the party to give a list of Nadir's donations to the trustees in his personal bankruptcy proceedings. These listed donations between October 1985 and March 1990 totalling £440,000 from Polly Peck International and Unipac Packaging Ltd.

The party accepted that the money had been received by the Conservative Industrial Fund and claimed that it had informed the bankruptcy trustees, Robson Rhodes. Robson Rhodes however said that 'repeated attempts to get the facts had been rebuffed.'[10] This claim was challenged by Paul Judge, the Conservative Party Director General, who sued The Guardian for libel, claiming that the suggestion left him "amazed, stupefied, worried and concerned."[11] Unfortunately for Mr Judge, the jury found that he had not been libelled. He was faced with legal bills of £300,000, which he would have to pay out of his own pocket, as his action had been launched in a personal capacity. Days later, The Guardian made the explicit claim that "Nadir gifts to Tories 'came from fraudulent deals'", based on a 'confidential' report by Touche Ross, the Polly Peck administrators. This report was revealed during the libel case and it showed that donations were made to the Tories at the same time as Nadir was siphoning money off from Polly Peck.[12] At last, it seemed that the party would have to honour its pledge to pay back funds if they were found to be stolen.

This pledge had been repeated by a spokesman for Norman Fowler, the party chairman, as recently as July of the previous year in no uncertain terms: "Bully for them if they have got new documents. We have always said we'll repay the money if it was stolen."[13] But there was a divergence of policy here, since Mr Judge had informed Touche Ross that "the donations had been 'legitimately received in good faith' and that the party saw no reason to return them."[14] A year later, in May, 1996, the new party chairman Dr Brian Mawhinney was still digging his heels in, claiming there was no evidence the money was stolen. He suggested that it was still open for the administrators to take action to recover the money. Lord McAlpine said 'it now appeared the money was dubious and should be returned to the receivers.'[15]

At the time of writing, the Tories have still not returned the money, and so the question naturally arises: what exactly is the standard of evidence they require before being forced to accept the money was stolen? Since Lord McAlpine has already said that receiving money in wheelbarrows full of used fivers was out of the question – for practical reasons – it may prove well nigh on impossible for any other form of money transfer to stand up to the Tories' strict rules on evidence.

In the age of electronic cash transfers, when millions can zip around the globe in less time than it takes to say 'sign here', it is clear that as long as a thief has a few honest pounds in credit, there can never be unequivocal evidence that anything taken from such an account would necessarily be stolen. Consequently, it is unlikely that the pensioners and others who lost their investment in Polly Peck will ever see a penny of the Tories' 'stolen' £440,000, still less the other £1,000,000 plus that Nadir allegedly gave to the party.

A further blow to John Major's credibility, and to the probity of the Conservative Party was delivered in 1993 when gifts from another disgraced businessman, Octav Botnar, came to light. Botnar had left the country and moved to Switzerland shortly before an arrest warrant had been issued for alleged tax fraud amounting to £97 million relating to his company Nissan UK. Botnar had been sponsoring the annual lunches of the Westminster Conservative Association, costing him £90,000. The last of the lunches he sponsored took place after the Inland Revenue had raided the premises of Nissan UK, but this did not deter Conservative Party officials, who took comfort from the fact that another Botnar company, Automotive Financial Group Holdings, was shown as sponsoring the meal.

Botnar had also, it was claimed, given £150,000 to the Tories between 1981 and 1983, depositing the money in one of their Jersey accounts at the suggestion of Tory Party officials who "preferred [this] to a less confidential donation made to one of the party's mainland funds, such as the Industrial Fund, because of rumours of alleged unethical business practices in Nissan UK."[16]

Two of Botnar's colleagues at Nissan UK, the managing and finance directors were eventually jailed for their part in the fraud. At first, Botnar had said he was too ill to return to Britain to face trial – he was after all 80 years old and suffering from stomach cancer. Perhaps being stung by what was said about him in his absence, he did a telephone interview on the Breakfast with Frost programme in which he said he would lose his self-respect if he did not come back to defend himself against the tax fraud charges. He also described some of the contacts he had made with leading Tory politicians:

"I had some contact with Mr Parkinson and then Mr Tebbit in relation to help the British side to bring about a decision for Nissan Japan in order to build a factory in UK. Because of a restriction, I wanted more cars in order to maintain my dealer network, to maintain the business, and so we have in a way co-operated. The company has made enormous effort in order to make it possible the cars that we'll produce then will be sold. That was a determined factor in order that Nissan is making donation."[17]

Following the decision of Nissan Japan to terminate their contract with Botnar in 1990, both the Lords Parkinson and Tebbit offered to help arbitrate, though both denied any knowledge of Botnar's previous or continuing support for the party. As it was, Botnar must have thought it wiser not to return to Britain, although he plainly maintained an interest in the country. In July, 1997, he gave £5 million to the Nuffield Orthopaedic Centre Appeal in Oxford.

The chairman of the Appeal's trustees, Lord Tebbit, said "This country owes a considerable debt to Mr Botnar. I do not believe that as Minister for Industry in 1981 I would have been able to reach agreement with the Nissan Company to establish the first Japanese car factory in Britain without his help. I know it is his wish to return here, not least to visit the grave of his daughter. I hope that will soon be possible for I would also like to show Mr Botnar what his support has already done to help the NHS in its work."[18]

In 1996, it was reported that the Inland Revenue was claiming £230 million from Nissan UK, although its assets were only valued at £80 million. Botnar himself had no assets in the UK, but had moved £250 million into a Liechtenstein bank. By November, 1997 Tebbit's wish to see Botnar return to the UK looked a step closer to fruition after the Inland Revenue agreed to the withdrawal of two arrest warrants, following Botnar's payment of £59 million in settlement of a corporation tax claim. He maintained his innocence of any fraud, saying "I have suffered five years of indignity during which time I have been unjustly branded as a criminal and a fugitive from injustice."[19]

The ranks of independently minded, multi-millionaire entrepreneurs who contributed to the Conservatives, but then came unstuck, was swollen by Nazmu Virani, jailed for his part in the downfall of the Bank of Credit and Commerce International (BCCI). Convicted in May, 1994 on charges of false accounting and providing false information, Virani confessed to giving "substantial donations to Tory Central Office over many years."[20] In addition, the Sunday Times had obtained documents which showed that he donated gifts worth £4,500 to the Putney constituency offices of David Mellor MP prior to the 1992 general election. Virani's personal fortune was estimated at £100 million.

Another published connection between the party and BCCI existed through the latter's sponsorship of fund raising dinners, usually held in a banqueting room of the House of Lords. These dinners, attended by up to 60 people, were addressed by Ministers, and guests would pay between £1,000 and £2,000 each. They were run under the auspices of the "Durbar Club" which had been founded to develop support for the party by Asian businessmen. In three years, the dinners raised £50,000 to purchase a new computer system for Central Office. On one occasion in 1988 the dinner's venue was at No. 12 Downing Street, and a senior BCCI executive, Kemal Shoaib was amongst the guests. Both Shoaib and Virani were close to one of the leading figures in the BCCI scandal, Ghaith Pharaon, who was thought to be acting as a front for BCCI through his ownership of a number of American banks.[21] Shoaib was accused in 1991 "of 'personal dishonesty' and fined £11.4 million by the US Federal Reserve for his part in the illegal purchase of an American bank."[22]

What makes the BCCI affair interesting in the present context is its fulfilment of the "Triangular Relationship" function Michael Pinto-Duschinsky has identified between the worlds of finance, intelligence and the Conservative Party. Whilst the known party donations of those embroiled in the BCCI scandal are relatively small, the potential for damage to the government's reputation was very great. After the bank was eventually closed down in 1991, the main question was who knew what and when, and it was evident that the Bank of England had dragged its feet long after intelligence reports had made it plain by 1989 what the true state of the bank was.

When tackled on the subject in the House of Commons by the then leader of the opposition, Neil Kinnock, John Major angrily retorted "If you are saying I am a liar, you had better say so bluntly." Given what we know now about the involvement of British, US and other intelligence agencies in the running of BCCI as a major intelligence-gathering asset, it is clear that there was probably very little that the British government didn't know about BCCI's various scams.[23] Indeed, it is only in the area of BCCI's political funding about which least is known.

Another case of the Triangular Relationship (unconnected to BCCI) was that of Mohamad Hashemi, an arms dealer who claimed to have given £85,000 to the Conservatives. His case – like so many – only seemed to come to light after the Serious Fraud Office had raided his premises, and he subsequently sought to demonstrate how well connected he was. A close relative of the Iranian President, Hashemi Rafsanjani, Hashemi claimed to have given money in order to gain access to Margaret Thatcher, which he did on a number of occasions. This was to ensure, he said, that the British Government would form a better view of Iran.

Following Hashemi's visit from the SFO, after allegations that he had obtained by fraud £1.3million from an American Company for the supply of equipment to Iran, he said "The SFO have ruined my life. I have served this country for years. Now it has taken everything from me."[24] Hashemi's claims to have worked for MI6 – specifically in arranging the sale of Chinese Silkworm missiles to Iran at MI6's behest – were naturally met with silence from the agency.

The revelations about Nadir, Botnar, and BCCI were all more or less shrugged off by the Conservative leadership, which sought to depict the behaviour of some of their erstwhile donors as simply that of a few bad apples – isolated examples of the risks taken when dealing with the go-getting wealth creators of the Thatcher period. The problem was that the revelations kept on coming, damaging the Tories right into the final, dog days of their government. By far the worst of these was the allegation that Serb money had been flowing into Central Office.

The seriousness of this allegation was that it directly confounded the 'rule' of Central Office that money would not be accepted if given by foreign governments – which presumably must have also meant on behalf of foreign governments too. The division of Yugoslavia into several vicious warring factions in the 1980s looked like becoming another insoluble problem, on a par with Northern Ireland, but on a larger scale. Attempts at peacemaking looked futile, and the role of the British government, and of Margaret Thatcher in particular, who expressed anti-Serb views, was to be pivotal.

The Sunday Times first broke the story with the headline "Serbs gave Tories £100,000" in May 1996, alleging that a Conservative parliamentary candidate John Kennedy, who had close connections to the Bosnian Serb leader Radovan Karadzic, had helped arrange one donation of £50,000 in 1994.[25] Kennedy dismissed the Sunday Times' article as "fantastic nonsense", and indeed a Serbian businessman resident in London, who was identified in an Independent story as being linked to the Kennedy Bosnian Serbian funding allegation, won libel damages against that paper.[26] The problem for the Tories was that Kennedy did have demonstrably a close relationship with Karadzic, and that he had developed other business interests which might lend credence to the story.

As a consequence, the party seemed unable to provide an outright denial that they had received money from this source – but they would hold an investigation, and if it was found that the Sunday Times was right, the money would be returned. The investigation was no doubt assisted by further revelations in the press. The following week, the Sunday Times gave prominence to claims that MI6 had "sent a detailed warning to John Major's private office that the Conservative party had received tens of thousands of pounds from Serbian sources linked to Radovan Karadzic, the Bosnian Serb leader, who is now accused of war crimes."[27]

The source of the MI6 tip-off was none other than an 'anonymous' Tory MP who had been elected in 1992, but who had continued to work for MI6 for nothing with the approval of the Prime Minister. According to this anonymous MP "The donation was well documented. The party has to be very careful about receiving money from foreign businessmen." An MI6 officer in 1992 had sent a report to

Price of Power

MI6's chief, Sir Colin McColl, who sent it up to John Major with the words "This should be treated as a hot potato."

Whilst the Sunday Times had agreed to maintain the MI6/Tory MP's anonymity, The Observer was under no such obligation, and they revealed that he was in fact the 'pro-Serb' MP Harold Elletson, who "ran an extensive network of private business interests in the region."[28] The paper said: "In Serbia, Mr Elletson gained access to a group of men who were secretly channelling money from the Serb regime to Conservative Party supporters on the eve of the 1992 general election campaign. More than £96,000 was dispatched in this way during Mr Major's main fund-raising efforts. There is no suggestion that Mr Elletson personally acted improperly by reporting to MI6 or was involved in this transaction. Many people would think he was carrying out his patriotic duty by helping the secret intelligence services."[29]

According to The Observer, the money was channelled through Kennedy – who was a business associate – and through Ian Greer Associates. But once again, the chief players denied the story had any foundation. Elletson described The Observer story as "schoolboy fiction", and Kennedy said the money came from 'Yugoslav industrialists.' After Labour had challenged the Conservatives to 'come clean' on the whole issue, John Major gave his characteristic response – urging Labour to "step out of the gutter" and charging his opponents to "Stop trying to tilt the newspapers in a particular direction."[30]

Sadly nothing more was heard of Dr Mawhinney's investigation into the Serbian funding allegations, nor whether any money was handed back; but in a post-election follow-up to the story, it was reported that another Serb businessman – who helps to run "a ruthless paramilitary unit accused of genocide in Bosnia" – admitted giving tens of thousands of pounds to the Conservative Party in the 1980s. This was one Giovanni Di Stefano, who for a time had run businesses in Britain, but who had fallen foul of the law for fraudulent trading. After serving three years of a prison sentence, he had gone to Yugoslavia. Di Stefano became the 'foreign affairs' spokesperson for Zelijko Raznjatovic, a Serbian commander named as a war crimes suspect, and in that capacity wrote to Robin Cook, the Foreign Secretary advising him that if any British soldiers sought to arrest Raznjatovic, they could expect to be shot.[31]

The Unravelling

In retrospect, it seems incredible given the gravity of the claims made in the press about the Conservative Party/Serb funding relationship, that the party chose not to issue a complete and detailed denial. The story had overtones of the kind faced by Thatcher during the Belgrano affair, namely that a government on the ropes was prepared to engage in very unseemly conduct for party advantage. In this case, there was the suggestion – clearly unmerited – that whilst British troops were in Yugoslavia trying to uphold a United Nations mandate, the British government was taking money from one side of the conflict which due to its aggression and criminal behaviour was subject to UN sanctions. Given the tedious regularity with which John Major had to deny his party's involvement with financial impropriety on so many occasions, his denials appeared to be wearing a bit thin. In these circumstances, and in a case so serious, one would have thought that the party would have nothing to lose by publishing the results of its investigation.

The argument against publishing the results (apart from the possibility that the charges were found to be true) was the 'spin doctors' nightmare – that the story would be kept alive – it would 'develop legs' if they responded to it in a substantive way. Given the media's appetite for fresh information and provided the party didn't supply any, the story would eventually die unconsumated, so to speak. Certainly, so far as the alleged sums from Serbia were concerned, the story did not rank as the biggest of the Tory funding scandal headlines. It could be forgotten, leaving little more than a bad taste. More prominent in the greater scheme of things were the links the party maintained with its Hong Kong friends. More prominent because of the amounts involved, and because of the delicate politics of British withdrawal from the colony and British relations with China.

The party became seriously interested in Hong Kong money in the early 1990s. Saddled with a debt, prior to the 1992 election of around £16 million, and facing an uphill climb to win, the party was desperate to gain substantial, single donations. Lord McAlpine had been drawn out of retirement to help, and an unofficial group of "super rich Establishment figures dedicated to saving the nation from socialism" had been working to improve on the work of Lord Beaverbrook, then the most senior of the party treasurers, who was perceived as being ineffective.[32] Beaverbrook was later to become bankrupt.

McAlpine had been out to Hong Kong many times to enlist support, and a stream of ministers found reasons to visit the colony, always finding time amidst their official duties at the taxpayers' expense to take leave to visit "fellow Conservatives." Some of the 'fellow Conservatives' who gave money to the party included:

Li Ka-Shing	£100,000 to £1m[33]
Sir Yue-Kong Pao	
Lord Kadoorie	
Gordon Wu	
Matheson & Co.	£10,000[34]
Tsui Tsin-tong	"six figure contributor"[35]
Ma Ching-kwan	£1,500,000[36]
Tung Chi-hwa	£50,000[37]
Rong Yiren	a 'private donor' who became Vice-Chairman of the Chinese government[38]

Mr Tung, who became the post colonial leader of Hong Kong, brought a barrage of criticism on his head when he said: "I have in the past made modest donations to the Conservative Party. This is a fact well known to everybody and, as a result, I am particularly sensitive that this should not happen in Hong Kong."[39] Where Mr Tung picked up this curious logic is not known, but it probably had something to do with his desire to limit the freedom of his pro-democracy opponents in the territory. Or, perhaps less likely, he had come to realise that foreign donations per se were corrosive of the democratic process.

Another of the donors, Ma Ching-kwan had at least 'substantial' business interests in Britain, but also had an "anxiety that his elderly father – wanted by Interpol and Hong Kong police on drug charges – should be allowed to return to the colony from Taiwan before he dies."[40] Whilst Ma junior was free of any criminal activity, the company he presided over, Oriental Press Group, had been established by his drugs-baron father and uncle whilst they were making a fortune from drugs trafficking.

According to Labour, the Conservatives took £3,675,000 in donations from Hong Kong prior to the 1992 general election.[41] But the indications were that this source would quickly dry up once the countdown to return to Chinese rule gathered pace. A visit to Hong Kong by a Lord Hambro, a party treasurer in 1995 apparently ended with Hambro meeting such a poor response that he offered his resignation.[42] The explanation for the poor response was broken into three parts: not wishing to back a loser – the Conservatives would not win again; hostility from the Chinese press; and anger over the policies pursued by Governor Chris Patten. In the end, Britain's last significant colonial possession reverted to its rightful owners at the same time as the Conservatives lost power: a poetic coincidence.

The final lap of the Conservatives' pre-1992 general election foreign fund-raising tour took their begging bowl to the door of John Latsis, the ageing Greek shipping magnate, who had previously supported the Greek Colonels' junta in the 1960s. His £2 million gift was at that time the largest single gift known to have been made to a British political party, but it wasn't the only time he had given, having previously donated £500,000.[43] Speculation as to why Latsis should be so generous to the Tory party led to no certain conclusions, but given that much of his fortune had been made in Saudi Arabia combined with Britain's support for the Saudis during the Gulf War, could in itself be a rich enough reason for Latsis to demonstrate his support. Looking at his business career, it is clear that he would actually befriend any regime that was friendly to his business interests – be it composed of right-wing colonels or democratic socialists.

Another possible explanation might be his gratitude to John Major for not removing the tax exempt status for wealthy foreigners who had set up a home in Britain. The 'foreign domicile' status meant that even though they lived in Britain, they would not have to pay tax on anything apart from their earnings actually made in Britain. This exemption is rare – only Luxembourg, Switzerland and the Channel Islands have similar tax rules.[44] At a dinner at Number 10 Downing Street, hosted by John Major to celebrate his first anniversary in office, nine of the 21 guests enjoyed foreign domicile status, and it was reported that the issue of tax exemption was raised: "The Prime Minister did say that he had considered this when he was Chancellor, and because of the representation which was received from the City, especially from the Greek community, it was not considered suitable to bring in the domicile amendment."[45]

As we have seen, John Major (or any leader of the party) trading as the 'Conservative Party' employed a number of measures to reduce their tax burden, so it is not surprising to find that a 'loop-hole' which could benefit their growing number of wealthy foreign donors was not going to be plugged. Another loophole was also employed to good tax saving effect – which also had the benefit of saving corporate donors the necessity of having to declare dona-tions in their company accounts. Known as the 'back-to-back' loan scheme, it entailed donors depositing money in Conservative Party interest bearing accounts, allowing the party to tap the interest. If the money was on deposit for less than a year, it wouldn't even show up in company accounts.

Given the party's peculiar status as a non incorporated body paying minimal taxes, this meant that the interest would not be taxed – although if it had remained with the lender, it probably would have. Thus, if tax had been due at 40% on £50,000, a saving of £20,000 could be made. The biggest known loan – later converted into an outright donation – reportedly came from Sir Graham Kirkham, the owner of the DFS furniture store chain.[46] Unfortunately for Sir Graham, news of the £4 million gift appeared at roughly the same time as he received his knighthood, but Central Office were quick to allay any fears of a connection by pointing to his generous support for chari-ties. It was later reported that his son Michael was actually responsible for the gift.

Another donor who used the loan scheme method was the bank Robert Fraser and Partners, which in turn had received substantial financial backing from Blackford Holdings, a Panamanian registered corporation. They in turn had received about £100 million from the Kuwaiti government.

The arrangement with Robert Fraser lasted for around three years in the 1980s, and the deposits amounted to about £200,000.[47] According to the Financial Times, these deposits would have netted the party 'tens of thousands' in interest – rather more than the bank's declared donations of £2,000 in 1986 and £5,000 in 1987. The Directors of the bank included former cabinet minister Lord Rippon, Nicholas Soames MP and Sir Dennis Walters MP. Other loans were made by Jim Wood, an expatriate British businessman who runs A&P, an American supermarket chain (loans: £2.5 million) and Michael Ashcroft, of the ADT Group (loan: £2.5 million).[48]

The full extent of the loan scheme is not known, but it is possible that it became an attractive alternative to companies who in the late

1980s and early 1990s were becoming hard pressed by the recession. Their ability to help the party in this way may in some way explain the downturn in straightforward donations reported at that time. According to a Labour Party survey in 1990, corporate donations which numbered 275 in 1988 had fallen to 199 the following year.[49] For some companies the explanation was obvious enough: British and Commonwealth, one of the largest donors, simply went bust, with debts of £1.3 billion. Another case was British Airways, whose stalwart Thatcherite Chairman, Lord King, had been a long serving and loyal supporter, finally lost patience with the government's policy of opening up more landing rights at Heathrow to BA's competitors. For Lord King, the free market had its limits.

The effect of the recession was measured by a study carried out by Pensions Investment Research Consultants, who surveyed the top 100 Stock Exchange companies. Sixty replied, and fifty-one of those said they would not be giving. Another problem was that some companies which had given money were taken over, and their new owners, even if they were themselves already donors, did not necessarily increase their contributions to match the previous combined total. Thus, when Hanson took over Consolidated Goldfields – once one of the biggest givers – Hanson's donation did not rise to take account of Consolidated's gifts.[50] Another survey carried out by the Financial Times in 1994 found that the biggest donors' contributions had fallen by 17.6% in real terms between the years 1986 and 1993, whereas the party's income over that period had actually risen by 16.2%. [51]

But another trend was re-emerging; that of company directors giving money privately from their own pocket. These donations clearly did not need declaring. Stanley Kalms, chairman of Dixon's, the electronics retail chain, gave a £100,000 personal donation. Others included Sir James Goldsmith (£250,000); Ray Tindle, a regional newspaper owner (£100,000) and Sir Philip Harris, a carpet millionaire and later party treasurer and peer (£100,000).

Of course, it is not being suggested here that any of these people were motivated by anything other than their honest support for Conservative policies. But having said that, for some of the less scrupulous, the publicity generated which had suggested a link between donations and honours may have been at the back of their minds. Why not give it a go? The continuing debate over whether there was a link between honours and certain wealthy businessmen depended to a certain extent on which newspaper surveyed which statistics, but by and large the bulk of the evidence seemed to support the notion that there was a link, and so did the comments of many who were closer to it all than the average commoner in the street.

For example, the eye-catching Sun 'Exclusive' headline story "£250,000 Tory 'Gift' In Suitcase Blocked by Tebbit" revealed that "several gifts of money have been rejected to avoid allegations of corruption", but then an 'ex-Tory official' went on to say:

"People give money, then they receive an honour – draw your own conclusions. If somebody said "Here is a large amount of money, now get me a knighthood," it would rule them out. But if he said, "Here's a million pounds to wipe out the party's overdraft" – in a few years they would probably get an honour.[52]

Few Tories would go on the record on the subject, but one who did was Macclesfield MP Nicholas Winterton:

"I think there is some reason to believe that a number of honours in this day and age are being given to... people for favours that have been done to a political party and perhaps financial contributions that have been made, rather than honours being given because of outstanding public service."[53]

The Sunday Times had little doubt: "How Tory donors pick up titles" was the headline, above the claim that "Heads of companies which donated £50,000 a year over the last decade were 10 times more likely to be honoured than the heads of firms which gave £5,000 on average."[54] Companies giving over £500,000 – 12 in all since 1979 found their boards decorated with 10 peerages and eight knighthoods. A later survey by the Labour Research Department found that 50% of the awards to businessmen in the Thatcher/Major years up until 1993 went to those whose companies donated to the Tories – but given that LRD had only looked at 5% of all company accounts, the actual correlation between awards and donations was much more pronounced.[55]

Of course, there were prominent businessmen whose companies had never been known to give to the Conservatives who had nevertheless received honours, and their existence could be shown to undermine the claim that the party awarded honours for cash. But the Conservatives were keen to recognise political service, and routinely gave honours to all and sundry. Long serving Tory MPs would get a knighthood on a muggins's turn basis; anybody promoted to the average-to-middling position of a Conservative regional director could expect automatically to receive a gong not dissimilar to a CBE. Why then wouldn't the party recognise the political service rendered by its donors? The answer is that it would always do its best to do so, provided that nobody explicitly asked for an award – in recognition of a long standing practice which would have as much to do with the need for deniability as the need to ensure each 'prospect' would give more generously, more often.

What of the Political Honours Scrutiny Committee, set up after the Lloyd George honours scandal, to police the system? Lord Carr, a former Conservative cabinet minister and committee member said "We did not feel at all embarrassed on this point in the time I was on the committee, although of course it was something we looked into pretty carefully."[56] But an erstwhile colleague – and Committee chairman – the Labour peer Lord Shackleton, took the opposite view: "There is an obvious gap here. It is highly likely that these secret donations are bypassing the scrutiny system and that honours are in effect being bought."[57] Shackleton was specifically referring to those donors who made private gifts from their own pockets, but his view necessarily begs the question as to how deeply the Committee delved into honours nominations. Under what disclosure obligations was the party of government bound to tell the Committee where its money came from? Given the irksome inability of several leading party figures to be able to say whether they remembered who donated what and when, and the obsessive secrecy of the Treasurer's department, it would be very surprising to find that a list of donations would be allowed to fall into the hands of a third party with all the danger that that entails, such as leaking.

However, according to John Major, the three-man committee would always be told whether proposed honours recipients had made political donations, and whether they were of good character. Major was commenting on the committee's role in the face of evidence which came to light just before the 1997 general election of how one man "with connections to top Tory party figures", Derek Laud, sought to 'swing' honours for his clients. Laud was the managing director of the Westminster lobbying firm Ludgate Laud, and two of his clients were John Beckwith, a property developer and Tory fund-raiser, and the industrialist Jeffrey Whalley.[58] Both Beckwith and Whalley were significant donors to the party. In the case of Whalley, his donations were referred to in a letter sent on his behalf by Sir Michael Grylls MP to party chairman Brian Mawhinney. The letter had been drafted by Laud. Beckwith would already be well known to party leaders for his work organising the "Premier" dining club, which charged guests considerable sums of money to attend dinners at which the Prime Minister and ministers would be present. The Observer, after taking legal advice, thought it had sufficient grounds to pass its dossier on Laud over to the police for investigation under the 1925 Honours Act, which prohibits the giving or receiving of money as "an inducement or reward for assisting or endeavouring to procure the grant of an honour."

But judging by the evidence published by The Observer, it would seem difficult to sustain such a charge. The problem, as always, would be to prove that the money was given for the purpose of purchasing an honour. Short of someone directly approaching a third party for this explicit purpose – as did Maundy Gregory – there is little to go on. Indeed, when it was alleged in the case of Whalley that the party chairman Brian Mawhinney asked for a list of his party contributions, this could easily be explained by the need of the Honours Scrutiny Committee to know the complete background of the man in question. The suggestion of any other motive was reprehensible, as was made clear by Central Office – it was merely

"a pathetic attempt to run a feeble election sleaze story... The newspaper in question has not got a shred of evidence that anyone has received an honour in exchange for donations. Our rules on party funding explicitly forbid accepting donations on any conditions whatsoever and the story should be treated with the contempt it deserves."[59]

For once, it is almost possible to sympathise with the overworked Central Office spokesperson – The Observer story, whilst interesting, did not prove its central premise. But what it did do was lift the veil of secrecy a little, exposing yet another role for at least one member of the phalanx of lobbyists who clung to the coat-tails of the Conservative establishment. In so doing, it removed yet another essential ingredient of the lobbyists' mystique, which is his or her ability to move freely and unnoticed within the circles of power.

The same, it seemed, could not be said for Richard Branson, who in a characteristic contribution to the honours debate, complained (if that is the right word) that his refusal to donate money had cost him a peerage, a knighthood or even an OBE. He said "the establishment think I'm fairly anti-establishment... I mean, I've had approaches from parties for donations in the past and always firmly said 'no.'"[60] Cynics may have concluded that Branson's intervention probably had more to do with the marketing of his brand than anything else, but one serious question does emerge – why hadn't he been offered an honour? In comparison to his 'merit' as a highly successful British entrepreneur, many other honours recipients had achieved far less in the business world. It could certainly be argued that Branson was on a par with Maurice Saatchi of advertising fame, who was awarded his ermine in 1996, or certainly with Peter Gummer, John Selwyn Gummer's brother, who ran the Shandwick public relations firm and was ennobled at the same time – a double reward for the 'industry' of persuasion which coincidentally had done so much for the Tories.

Curiously, it has been alleged that despite the fact that honours would always be distributed on 'merit', there was an unofficial blacklist of the heads of privatised utilities being honoured, on the grounds that it would be wrong to be seen adding to the rewards gained by these "fat cats."[61] Surely, these were the very people who were the living embodiment of the success of government policies? And why single out one group of fat cats, as opposed to another? There were indeed two types of fat cat: the first, more respectable variety were 'real' businessmen (and a few women) who had toiled continuously in the private sector; then there were those in the privatised utilities who came suddenly upon the riches they coveted. Their remuneration packages soared, when they discovered that they had joined that part of the workforce for whom market forces pushed prices up. They learnt quickly from their colleagues in the always-private sector what was called for.

The whole process, fortuitously enough, could be justified by referring to the recent report of the Greenbury Committee on corporate governance, which established the mechanism by which top executive's pay should be determined. This removed the responsibility for determining remuneration packages from company main boards to remuneration committees, comprising of non-executive directors. These dispassionate individuals rarely failed to recognise the overwhelming qualities of their colleagues, and consequently a great levelling-up took place.

The benchmark set by the private sector would sometimes be hard to pin down, but nevertheless it usually contained a mixture of pay, perks and share options. For example, Greg Hutchings, chairman of the Tomkins manufacturing group (annual donations to Tory party: £10,000 to £50,000) in 1996 earned £2.1 million in pay and share option gains. As has been noted earlier, share options are a risk-free method of payment. Another benchmark could have been that of Archie Norman, the chief executive of the ASDA supermarket chain who went on to become Tory MP for Tunbridge Wells and a party deputy chairman. In 1995 his remuneration package consisted of £548,000 pay, including a performance related bonus of £155,000, with the rest in cashed-in share options.[62]

Whilst one can justifiably praise Norman for his contribution to the turnaround of ASDA, which was on the rocks before his arrival, it is also possible to see the impetus his pay package would give to other executives – particularly to some who had set such easily achievable targets for 'performance' that they were virtually guaranteed excessive rewards.

It may never be known whether many of the privatised utilities' bosses became generous benefactors of the Conservative party, although one or two have been identified as such. Of all the people who did best out of Thatcher and Major's policies, these modest marvels of the boardroom probably had the most reason to keep quiet about their support for the party, since they already suffered extensive and sometimes humiliating public opprobrium. For a county branded as being inhabited by tight-fisted Tykes, Yorkshire seemed to have an abundance of stories to tell about the benefits of privatisation. Yorkshire Water plc became a by-word for incompetence, especially when its financial director was caught during the 1996 drought advising people to wash out of a plastic bowl – but failed to mention that he personally travelled out of the county to shower at his mother's. He – and his immediate boss, Sir Gordon Jones, the Chairman – had seen their salaries and share options rocket after privatisation. A fellow board member, Sir Giles Shaw was the Conservative MP for Pudsey.

The 'success' that companies like Yorkshire Water trumpeted was based on the original underestimation of their value, the monopoly they enjoyed, and large scale 'efficiency savings' bought at the cost of mass redundancies. Yorkshire Electricity consumers will have been thrilled to see the company, which was sold into the private sector in 1990 for £500 million, six years later being valued at £1 billion after handing out £1 billion back to its shareholders.[63] According to a survey by City analysts SBC Warburg, the water and electricity companies had so far given £5.8 million back to shareholders by 1996, and were set to give another £1.3 billion back by March, 1997.[64] In 1996, Sir Desmond Pitcher, chairman of United Utilities and former chairman of Littlewoods plc (£160,450 to the Tories 1990 - 92) and his colleagues were sharing a £462,400 bonus and pay rises of up to 30% Meanwhile, United Utilities had announced 2,500 job losses.

Further fabulous sums were to be made on the railways and other later privatisations. Hambros, the merchant bank, seemed to do particularly well out of both rail privatisation, where it earned fees associated with the sale, and the sale of MoD housing, where it was a partner in the consortium which made the winning bid. Hambros' chairman, Lord Hambro, as a party treasurer, no doubt considered the £368,000 donated to the party between 1979 and 1990 as money well spent.[65] Another sale was made of Her Majesty's Stationery Office (HMSO) which went for a 'knock-down' £54 million to a consortium called Electra Fleming. This comprised Robert Fleming, the bankers, and Electra Investment Trust plc, who between them had contributed around £567,000 to the Conservative Party. A spokesperson for the consortium reassured readers of the Eastern Daily Press that "Electra Fleming has made no donations to the Conservative Party with the exception of a one-off payment to the Millennium Club."[66]

Board members of the Electra Investment Trust included Tom King, the former cabinet minister, and Tory peer Lord Vinson of Roddam Dene. King was also chairman of the Millennium Club, which like the Premier Club, charged guests thousands of pounds to wine and dine with ministers. Oddly, the Electra Fleming bid was significantly lower than the bid from the runner-up – which came in at £65 million. According to the Cabinet Office, the losing bid was "less well defined."[67]

The concern about Tory MPs, like Tom King and Sir Giles Shaw having directorships, was one not entirely confined to the opposition benches – or so it seemed when in 1994 John Major warned, somewhat plaintively, that the Commons was 'above all a legislature' and not a 'hiring fair.'[68] But in a remarkable display of two fingers to the PM's authority, it was discovered only two months later that no less than 12 of his ex-ministers were among the 82% of Tory back-benchers who held between them 276 directorships and 356 consultancies with commercial organisations.[69] Of the 12 ex-minis-ters, eight held positions which were related to their former government posts. Major's pleas carried as much weight as Baldwin's pleas before him for auction-free parliamentary selections – in other words none at all.

It could be said that Conservative MPs' behaviour mirrored the changes in the British workforce that had occurred over the previ-ous 12 to 15 years – moving from full-time working to part-time working – except that the new Tory part-time jobs paid rather more handsomely than did those at the bottom end of catering or contract cleaning. The Tories' greatest opportunities for augmenting their salaries came with the fine-tuning of the quangocracy. By the 1990s there were fewer quangos, but the expenditure they were responsi-ble for grew until it exceeded the combined budgets of elected local authorities. These lucrative positions became a trump card for the party in a period in which Conservatives were being roundly defeat-ed at every level except Westminster. But power over local decision-making could still be obtained using patronage instead of the ballot box.

Companies who gave money to the party seemed to feature prominently amongst the membership of many quangos. A study by the Labour MP George Howarth, which was confirmed by a survey by the Observer, found that of 100 quangos covering 13 different government departments, there were 157 individuals with links to companies which donated to Tory funds.[70] John Major described this kind of research as "McCarthyism" since there had always been supporters of one party or another appointed to quangos. But once again, his bluster belied the truth – which was that Conservatives were being appointed disproportionately. It could be argued never-theless that many of the appointees were there because of their skills, disregarding for a moment the 33 failed Conservative parlia-mentary candidates who had found positions. But it was clear what kind of skills were thought most appropriate. The BBC programme

Here and Now discovered that directors of the FTSE 100 companies whose boards gave money to the party stood a one-in-three chance of getting a quango job. Half of the directors of Hambros had held quango posts, whereas among the top 282 executives of trade unions, just eight had held positions.[71] Some Tories did spectacularly well. A Conservative farmer and businessman, Michael Griffith notched up membership of five quangos, paying him a total of £57,313 a year. This made him an expert – to the exclusion of many others, no doubt – on conservation, the NHS, higher education and libraries, apart from the countryside. His explanation for his success was that "once you do a bit of public work, you get known."[72] There might lie another explanation for the Tories' dominance of quangos: "getting known" for public work might also mark out potential recruits for the honours lists.

Public disquiet over 'quango-stuffing' finally led to Sir Leonard Peach, the first Commissioner for Public Appointments to publish a new code of practice to ensure that appointments were made on merit. This covered the 8,300 ministerial appointments which presumably were felt to be the ones which were most susceptible to partisan patronage.[73]

By the middle of 1996, when Peach's report was published, the whole issue of 'secondary' political appointments was tightening like a noose around the Prime Minister's neck. The more he sought to allay fears of patronage and sleaze, the more interest there was. There could be no worthier contender for the epithet coined by Ralph Waldo Emerson: "The louder he talked of his honour, the faster we counted the spoons." Each instance of political 'moonlighting' brought fears for Major's wafer-thin majority. Some of these cases were interesting in that they showed up claims for Conservative MPs' business acumen for what they were – empty. Yet it was their 'experience' which merited so many boardroom appointments, and in a mirror-image led to so many Tory businessmen being appointed to quangos.

The earliest threat to Major's majority came with the possibility that up to 46 MPs would face bankruptcy and consequently disqualification as MPs because of losses they had sustained in the Lloyd's insurance market – or 'racket' as some called it. Many Tory MPs had found that being a Lloyd's 'name' was the route to worry-free earnings – double earnings in fact, since the liquid assets which they had earmarked for their Lloyd's commitment could be earning interest elsewhere so long as Lloyd's never called them in.

Among the losers in the early 1990s, following disasters such as the 1987 hurricane which devastated south-east England, were three Cabinet ministers, including Employment Secretary David Hunt (c.£50,000 losses); Attorney General Sir Nicholas Lyell (c.£60,000 losses); and National Heritage Secretary Peter Brooke ("I do not expect to be financially embarrassed").[74] The former Foreign Office minister Tristan Garel-Jones was thought to be out of pocket by £250,000. Other MPs were forced into straightened circumstances. One, Spencer Batiste, MP for Elmet, sold his mansion and moved into a flat. Eventually, a helping hand was extended to a list of MPs that was whittled down to 13 – these were the ones who faced bankruptcy. Lady Archer, the wife of one-time party deputy chairman, novelist and peer Jeffrey Archer, acting in her role as a member of Lloyd's council, reportedly devised a scheme which meant that the MPs signed over most of their assets, including their salaries, in return for an £18,000 living allowance. In exchange for this three year deal, they would not be made bankrupt. "This is an arrangement that is much more favourable than bankruptcy" Lady Archer said.[75]

However, Lady Archer also made it clear that no "special deal" had been made for MPs – they would have to take their place amongst the thousands of others seeking assistance from the 'hardship' arrangements she had negotiated. The public remained sceptical that in some way the party had not shifted heaven and earth to ensure that these 13 members kept their places on the green benches.

Three years later it emerged just how the party could lend a helping hand to one of its MPs who had got into difficulties. The member in question was Roy Thomason, who was elected in 1992 and had previously been a high-flying councillor, becoming Leader of the Association of District Councils. He had developed a property portfolio which included nursing homes and shopping centres, but his empire's value was badly hit by the property slump which followed the Lawson 'boom.' By 1996 it was reported that he had debts of £6 million, and one of his creditors, the French-owned bank UCB had started bankruptcy proceedings. With Major's majority down to two, this case could have led to him losing his majority altogether.

The Royal Bank of Scotland, which had established for itself a reputation as the bank that liked to say "Yes" to the Conservative Party's multi-million pound overdraft was called upon again, in the form of its chairman, former Secretary of State for Defence, Lord Younger. According to documents in the possession of the Sunday Times, Younger "instructed 'a senior gentleman at RBS' to investigate how the bank could rescue the beleaguered MP from his debts to UCB."[76] It also alleged that Younger used "British 'diplomatic channels' in France to press UCB's parent company to stop court action."

It may have come as no surprise therefore that three months later, Thomason was able to tell the press "I strongly deny the suggestion that I am threatened with bankruptcy proceedings," and that he had been 'able to reassure the whips that he is confident of resolving his financial problems by September.'[77] September was the time set by his constituency association to resolve the issue so that they could decide whether or not to proceed with a 'wounded candidate.' When the constituency executive met, they did indeed decide to open up the selection procedure, and Thomason was left pondering his options, which included the possibility of causing a by-election, which the Tories would almost certainly have lost. After two weeks, he came to the conclusion that he should stand down "even though my financial position has now been satisfactorily settled on a commercial basis."[78] With a solicitor's careful eye for wording, Thomason's own valediction appeared in the Register of Members' Interests on the 31st January, 1997:

"Gifts, benefits and hospitality (UK)

"Negotiations have been conducted over the past year by my lawyers with UCB Bank, Lloyds Bank, TSB, Midland Bank, Barclays Bank, Natwest Group and Royal Bank of Scotland concerning joint guarantees and similar matters given by me in relation to business activities before becoming a Member of Parliament. In so far as it may be said or perceived that I have benefited or am benefiting from any concessions which might not generally be available in respect of these negotiations or their outcome, I hereby declare them."[79]

Who could possibly suggest that such "concessions" are not generally available? Thomason was only registering the interest because, as he said, people may say that he had had special treatment, not that he thought so, presumably. But his registration of this interest, under the heading "Gifts, benefits and hospitality" would of course cover him whatever the case, since the category covered:

Price of Power

"Any gift to the Member or the Member's spouse of greater value than £125 or any material benefit of a value greater than 0.5 per cent of the current parliamentary salary from any company, organisation or person within the UK which in any way relates to membership of the house".[80]

Given that Thomason's problems were inherited from pre-parliamentary activities, his position could be described as clear-cut, except for the outcome described by the Sunday Times. For others, it appeared that great confusion attended decisions about what to register, and it could only be a matter of time before many MPs would fall foul of "The Seven Principles of Public Life" which Lord Nolan summarised in his First Report on Standards in Public Life. These were Selflessness, Integrity, Objectivity, Accountability, Openness, Honesty and Leadership. The Conservatives' shorthand for the Seven Principles appeared to spell "sleaze."

When exactly this word came to apply to the opposite of the Nolan Principles is not clear, but given that originally "sleazy" meant something 'thin or flimsy in texture, having little substance or body,' it was most apt. It also came to encompass MPs' sexual activities, especially after John Major's "Back to Basics" speech at the 1994 party conference. Major's problem was that he nurtured a romantic ideal that his party was a repository of moral values, which was a peculiar delusion for one whose parliamentary career had first flourished in the Whip's office where his colleagues' peccadilloes would be exhaustively researched, catalogued and saved for future reference.

Major's uphill struggle to contain the sleaze issue must largely be due to the fact that the behaviour of his MPs was probably not the usual province of the Whips – working for lobbyists, taking 'dodgy' directorships of consultancies, earning 'cash for questions' – these appeared to be routine and unexceptional activities outside the range of the Whips' concerns. Judging by the level of hurt astonishment evinced by some backbenchers when they were 'exposed' for having engaged in these activities, it is clear that they were somewhat bewildered as to why anyone should think they had not been standing foursquare behind all of Nolan's seven public virtues. Major's impatience grew every time the word 'sleaze' passed an interviewer's lips. On the Breakfast with Frost programme, he forcefully made his point by banging his fist on the desk, saying

The Unravelling

"I want it settled, I want it settled… Public life in this country is the cleanest, most free of corruption public life anywhere in the world. I know my Conservative Party. In it, as there are in the Labour Party and no doubt in the Liberal Democrats and other parties, are people who sometimes are not perfect. But the party as a whole is a straight and honest and honourable party. This constant, persistent determination to smear the longest-lived political party is a low piece of political trickery, and I bitterly resent it. It's very much my wish, my hope and my expectation that this will be cleared up well this side of a general election."[81]

In this, he was fully supported by one of his ex-ministers, Neil Hamilton, who said "Sleaze will be exposed as the hoax of the century."[82] A week after Major's breakfast TV appearance, a possible way forward was suggested by the Tory-supporting Spectator:

"The Conservative leadership must act now; no one else can or will do it for them. The whips must be empowered to prohibit all activities which exploit an MP's status to earn money. They must be apprised of all MP's activities and be the arbiters of what is legitimate, subject to appeal. MPs who cannot live on their salary and perks should retire. There may be a good case for paying MPs more, but not for letting them help themselves."[83]

But Major appeared to be caught like a rabbit, with a bad case of myxomatosis, in the beams of an oncoming juggernaut. With only months to go before the general election, it was too late to jump out of the way or clean up his MPs' act – and he was in any case too protective of "my Conservative Party" to recognise what was wrong with it.

Thus it was that just weeks before the general election, Sir Gordon Downey, The Parliamentary Commissioner for Standards, drew to a close an inquiry which he had been asked to conduct, not by John Major, but by the Speaker, Betty Boothroyd, into 'sleaze' allegations against several of his backbenchers and former ministers.

The publication of the Downey report was a feasibility prior to the election, but Major's calling of the election early – though not the derogation of Parliament itself – meant that it would not become public knowledge until after the election. This was in spite of Major's oft-repeated comment that the matter should be 'settled' before the election. Once the results of the inquiry were known, it turned out that Parliament would in any case have been unable to order any sanctions against those who had failed to declare their interests, since none of the MPs concerned were re-elected.

Most of the cases Downey investigated related to the MPs' relationship with Ian Greer Associates, and his controversial client, the Harrod's store owner Mohammed al-Fayed. Twelve MPs were originally implicated, of whom Norman Lamont, Nirj Deva, Olga Maitland and Gerald Malone were found to have no case to answer. For the others, the Commissioner's 'verdict' ranged from Michael Brown's 'persistent and deliberate' failure to register his interests (relating to the banning of the nicotine chewing gum, Skoal Bandits), to hearing Sir Andrew Bowden give a "positively misleading explanation of his representations" to an only slightly less dusty conclusion that Sir Michael Grylls had on one non-disclosure made a 'deliberate concealment.' [84]

The two most prominent MPs caught in Downey's sights were Tim Smith, a former Northern Ireland minister, who had resigned over the issue in 1994, and the former Trade and Industry minister, Neil Hamilton. Tim Smith said: "Although Al Fayed paid me fees [£18,000], there was never any suggestion of a specific amount per question and it cannot, therefore, be described, as far as I am concerned, as cash for questions."[85] Subsequently, Smith displayed what his colleagues described as "good grace and dignity" when he decided not to stand again as a candidate, after which moment all attention focused on the famously embattled Hamilton, who maintained his innocence of any wrongdoing.

Hamilton became the cause célèbre of the anti-sleaze lobby – not because his behaviour had been found to be so much worse than that of his colleagues who had failed to declare hospitality, fees and so on – but because he failed to comprehend what all the fuss was about. Protesting his innocence through several 'trials' – the election campaign, the Downey inquiry, the House of Commons Select Committee on Standards – Hamilton carried on digging his hole deeper and deeper. He became a symbol of the arrogance and political corruption of the Tory years. He exemplified the state of confusion many MPs seemed to experience about their role – between being elected to represent their constituents, or being a hireling of commercial interests. The defence offered by many of those who had this problem was that in the first place it wasn't clear in the self-regulating rules of the House what exactly they had to

declare, and secondly – and this seemed to be a particular Tory problem – they had to get an understanding of the business community
by being a part of it – a paid part of it, that is. Because neither of the
arguments could be found to be entirely specious, they felt they had
a case – but it wasn't much of one. Whilst it as true that members
such as the late Enoch Powell had objected in principle to members
registering their interests, the House had by a majority accepted the
need to have a register. The only intelligent approach thereafter –
and one which Lord Nolan made plain – was that if a member was in
any doubt, he or she should declare any gifts and payments, to be
on the safe side. The fact that some members couldn't make the
connection between what is a duty and what is plain common sense
contributed to the electorate's scepticism of its representatives'
wisdom. They had elected these MPs, surely to exercise some
wisdom, had they not?

The second defence – that MPs had to have experience of the
business community in order to understand its problems – on a
generous interpretation could carry some weight. Businesses as such
generally don't have a vote (although businessmen and women do)
so perhaps they were a category of interest that could, conceivably,
be neglected. But since in the real world businesses of every size
and shape have a myriad of specialist lobbies – the CBI, Institute of
Directors, Federation of Small Businesses, trade associations and so
on – the idea that somehow their views would be ignored couldn't
hold water. Indeed, so far as the Tories were concerned, they had
their own raft of regional 'Industrialists' Councils' which, although
chiefly set up as funding conduits for the party, could serve as confidential lightning rods for any problems.

But these 'defences' were just excuses – as the Spectator suggested – the real motivation for MPs joining the boards of so many
companies was simply a desire to boost their earnings. Perhaps this
was because they felt they could have earned more had they not
become MPs in the first place, and the sacrifice was too much to
bear. But this argument also did not go down very well with the
public, who thought MPs salaries had been increased more than
enough in recent years. The salary of an MP had risen in 1997 to
£43,860, from £9,450 in 1979. The majority of members who represent constituencies outside inner London also receive a living
allowance of £12,287. For many Conservative MPs therefore, a

133

combined salary more than three times average male earnings was deemed inadequate.

Ironically, the man at the centre of the sleaze scandal, Mohammed Al-Fayed, who had done so much to damage the reputation of Conservative MPs, and who had sought to use his wealth to influence the decision-making process during his battles with the government over the House of Fraser take-over, made a final extravagant flourish with his cheque book when he allied himself with the clean-up politics camp. He reportedly poured £1 million into an organisation called the "People's Trust" which sent millions of letters to voters urging them to obtain from their local parliamentary candidates statements of intent such as "I shall not be a slave to the Party Whips and will commit myself to act in the best interests of my conscience, my constituency and my country" or "I shall work full-time as my constituents' Member of Parliament, and not take back-handers from businessmen to act for them in the House of Commons or any other paid consultancies."[86] The "People's Trust" quietly folded after the general election. The electorate had chosen the ballot box to punish the miscreants.

It was perhaps in anticipation of their defeat that so many Tory MPs sought to make as much money from outside interests as they could before the fateful day. Could the same be said for the party itself? By August, 1996 Central Office had managed to pay off its £15.8 million overdraft. The accounts published in 1996 showed that donations of £18.8 million had been received.[87] Party bosses were necessarily 'bullish' about their good fortune, even though they still actually owed £8.5 million to local Associations and the various wealthy individuals who had lent the party money. Some of the success in the turnaround was due to the efforts of Lord Harris of Peckham, the carpet millionaire, who had reportedly secured one donation of £5 million – out of a total by early 1997 of £28 million.[88] In March, 1997 Tony Blair warned Labour members that the Tories could have up to £40 million in their general election kitty – giving rise to speculation that they were raising money for the eventuality of a hung parliament and an early second general election. Some commentators wondered how it would be possible to spend such a large amount of money in a such short period of time, without overdoing it. The danger for the Tories was that public overexposure to their propaganda could be counter-productive, since if they could not capture the mood of the public, they might only alienate it further. Despite much speculation at the time, with hindsight it appears that their attempt to portray Labour as a devil with demon eyes backfired. That campaign reportedly cost Central Office £10 million, but Tory strategists were most self-congratulatory on the two comparatively cheap newspaper advertisements which personalised their attack on a 'satanic' Tony Blair. The resulting acres of comment by the "sneering so-called intellectuals of Islington" was reckoned to have been worth millions in free publicity.[89]

As the party's funds grew, so the calls for accountability were renewed. Major had flatly rejected the idea on many occasions, most notably when feelers were put out by the Nolan Committee on Standards in Public Life, to see whether party funding could be included in its remit. Major was emphatic in his rejection of the idea – in the words of the Daily Telegraph he told Nolan that 'donations to political parties were none of the committee's business.' [90] It was, as always, 'nobody's business' – the Central Office rule being that "donations to the Conservative Party are a private matter between the individual or organisation concerned and ourselves."[91] The point that the party's stance was entirely analogous to that of its MPs – who did face income disclosure requirements – seems to have been completely missed by the party's leader and his subordinates. Perhaps – and this would be one of the weakest explanations available – perhaps it was simply because legally only individuals stood for parliament, and not parties per se, that the Tories believed that their 'private' affairs were just that. After all, every member of the legislature had by law to declare their election expenses and income within weeks of polling day. Wasn't this enough?

But other legal or regulatory tests could apply too – or so thought Austin Mitchell, Labour MP for Great Grimsby, who having acquired a copy of the 1994 party accounts, wrote to the Institute of Chartered Accountants to complain about the inadequacies of the audit, carried out by Coopers and Lybrand. Mitchell's complaints were described by 'Coopers insiders' as 'bearing all the hallmarks of political mudslinging of the first order,' Mitchell was merely 'jumping on the sleaze bandwagon.' Officially, Coopers declined to comment, even if only to defend their own reputation, as opposed to that of their clients.[92]

However, Mitchell's complaints were substantial, and look now as if they will only be answered by the force of legislation in the aftermath of the Tories' defeat. His most significant complaint was that the audit had not shown that, according to accountancy guidelines, the party was a 'going concern.' Mitchell wrote that

"By any standard the Conservative Party is insolvent to the extent of £9,829,000. Any application of the going concern standard/guideline should have resulted in Coopers issuing a going concern qualification. In fact they have given an unqualified audit opinion."[93]

Mitchell's concern was to establish what Coopers meant when they said they had 'complied with the Auditing Standards' and whether they had any relevant connections, which should have been revealed with the party or indeed any of its creditors. At the root of the problem, however, was the Conservative Party's vague legal status. This meant that quite apart from being able to avoid paying taxes on the same basis as their opponents, they could also 'pick and choose' how to reveal their income and expenditure. The Financial Times found in 1993 that the party's then new commitment to publishing a fuller statement and balance sheet was full of holes. For example, the balance sheet had shown as an asset the £5.9 million value of the Central Office property – actually held by one of the Conservative 'river' companies, the Bourne Association – but failed, in line with accountancy standards, to declare "a summary of the financial statements of each quasi-subsidiary."[94]

The Financial Times said "The Conservatives can claim that the party is not obliged to comply with accounting standards or company law. But its accounts state that they have been prepared 'in accordance with accounting standards and, so far as is pertinent, the Companies Act.'"

Why then was it so impertinent for the likes of Austin Mitchell, or for that matter the Charter Movement, to question the accounts? Whilst Mitchell's intervention may well have been unhelpfully partisan, the role of the Charter Movement was not. They may for example have had grounds to be concerned that if the party was ever declared bankrupt, then as members of it they could be held liable for its debts. Or worse still politically, their leader could, if the party was deemed to be the trading arm of the leader, be made personally bankrupt. And what of the local Associations' £5.5 million worth of unsecured interest free loans to Central Office? Could they be used to pay off debts? It is hardly likely that these disasters could ever be allowed to happen – but the Charter Movement, as members of the party, felt they had every reason to be told why. They got short shrift from successive party chairmen.

Such concerns, as it turned out, were unjustified. The final out-turn of the Conservatives' general election fund-raising efforts showed an astonishing boost in fortunes. In the year running up to the general election, they raised £38 million, giving them a surplus of £7.4 million at the end of March, 1997. They then proceeded to spend a further £10 million during the campaign itself, much of it on advertising with M & C Saatchi, leaving a final deficit of around £3 million – less than Labour's debt.[95]

In the short space of two years, therefore, the Conservatives had raised and spent in the region of £50 million – suggesting that no amount of money can save a party which has lost the trust of the electorate. Indeed, the publicity which accompanied the Tories' funding appears to have been counterproductive, making them appear more detached from the everyday concerns of ordinary voters. Many of the donors, perhaps recognising the bad publicity others had received, simply chose to remain anonymous.

The Independent claimed to have documents from Central Office which showed that at the beginning of the Tories' big fund-raising push to clear their £18 million overdraft in 1996, anonymous dona-tions of up to £2 million were received. The Party's explanation was that receipts were issued which said 'anonymous' on them, to protect the privacy of the donors. Nearly £7 million of donations were dealt with in this way.[96] Party staff, even senior figures, were not allowed to know the donors' identities, presumably on the prin-ciple that 'what you don't know won't harm you.'

Chapter Seven

A Fresh Future

As soon as the election was over, Major threw himself on his sword as expected. The ensuing leadership contest was remarkable not only for its bitterness, which further crystalised the Conservative Party's divisions over Europe – but also for the amount of money spent on the candidates' campaigns. With an actual electorate of only 164 MPs, the candidates managed to spend around £250,000 between them – roughly £150 per head. The eventual winner, William Hague, at £110,100, managed to spend more than twice as much as any one of his rivals. The bulk of Hague's finance came from Harris Ventures Ltd – Lord Harris of Peckham, the carpet millionaire's company. He gave £74,000, and was to be rewarded with the Treasurership of the party. Harris, whose company Harris Queensway went bust in 1988, had climbed back up the ladder of corporate donors. In 1992, he paid the salaries of two Central Office staff, although reports suggested he was rather coy about his support becoming public knowledge.[1]

The next most generous Hague supporter, coming in at £20,000, was David Steene, who was managing director of City Mortgage Corporation (CMC). In July of 1997 CMC came under fire for its excessive interest charges and redemption penalties. These meant for example that if a borrower missed one payment, the interest rates could double. CMC targetted the poor, the self employed and council house purchasers. One couple, who were evicted from their home, found that their £150 monthly payment for a £15,000 loan went up to £500 after one instalment was missed. Eventually, a CMC Victim's Association was established, and over 1,000 customers were considering taking legal action for redress. Steene said, "I am always concerned to hear of customers that have any problems with their loan."[2] The Office of Fair Trading, however, was moved to issue guidance prohibiting dual rates of interest and practices which were 'deceitful, oppressive and unfair.'[3] There was nothing unfair or oppressive about Steene's own pay, since in 1996 he was paid by CMC's US parent company, the Cityscape Financial Corporation, £578,000 for his efforts.[4] Hague presumably felt that none of the controversy surrounding his benefactor's business should rub off on him, since he said it was a 'personal' donation.

The second highest funded leadership campaign was that of John Redwood, who declared expenditure of £55,534.36. £44,000 of this came from the Conservative 2000 campaign, through its trading company, Wilfred Street Conferences and Publications Ltd. The remainder was paid for by the defeated Tory MP for Welwyn, Hatfield, David Evans, a former PPS to Redwood. Michael Howard spent £49,000 almost half of which, £23,500 came from Alan Hagdrup, a former director of Hanson plc. Ken Clarke, deemed by many to have the most gravitas of all the contenders spent a modest £42,000. Bringing up the rear was Peter Lilley, who spent £27,850. Both the Chairman and Treasurer of the Carlton Club's Political Committee, Sir Brian Goswell and Richard Simmons CBE respectively, supported Lilley's campaign.[5]

Hague's appeal – apart from his youth – was that he would bring radical changes to the way the party worked: "I think it is time to choose a leader from the new generation who has conviction and energy to make the changes that are required if we are to win the next general election and become the party of government again" he said.[6] In one respect he was appealing over the heads of the Parliamentary Party to the membership. Most polls had shown in the early stages of the contest that he was ahead of his rivals in constituency support, although this was not borne out in the party's official consultation when constituency chairmen plumped decisively for Ken Clarke.

Hague's election as leader in June was quickly followed by headlines which proclaimed he was to 'get tough' on sleaze. He made a speech on the 23rd July proclaiming 'The Six Principles of Renewal' which were Unity, Decentralisation, Democracy, Involvement, Integrity and Openness. The last – and least – of these dealt with the

Price of Power

party's funding. Hague said:

". . we must be open about our funding. In not being so in the past, we have often appeared secretive and defensive. And we have paid a political price for that. It is time to be much more open. We have nothing to hide and nothing to fear."

"And so I will instruct our Party treasurers that in future years we will list the major donors to the Conservative Party alongside our published accounts. But I want to go further than that. We have to recognise public concern across the Western world about the sources of funding for political parties. We must respond to that concern. We will publish new guidance later this year, and our intention is that in future years the Conservative Party will no longer accept foreign donations."[7]

The first commitment, wrapped-up in the common ploy of alluding to the 'appearance of secretiveness' – as opposed to the party's actual strict policy of secretiveness – suggests perhaps that the public got it wrong about the party 'with nothing to hide or fear.' The principle of secrecy, which had been protected religiously for the whole life of the party had after all been something which John Major had defended ad nauseum at the Dispatch Box until the very end. The right of an individual to financially support the party of his or her choice in complete privacy was enshrined as if it were a basic civil liberty on a par with the secret ballot.

It was not long after his election to the leadership, according to the press, that Hague had to go cap in hand to 'Tyke tycoons' in his native county, to get £2 million to tide the party over until the annual conference in September. It was reported that although the party had come out of the election campaign with a small surplus, it was unable to raise sufficient funds to cover its estimated £500,000 per month running costs.[8] In August, Hague appointed two new treasurers, Sir Graham Kirkham as senior treasurer, with Michael Ashcroft as his deputy. Between them, it was estimated the two men had a combined fortune of nearly £500 million.[9] For Ashcroft, his appointment realised a long held ambition – he had, it seemed, coveted a party treasurer's post at least since 1991, after Alastair McAlpine gave up the job, but he was unfortunately getting a bad press at the time due to accusations about his business practices, which he denied. Nevertheless, a Central Office spokesperson was moved to say in regards to a very generous back to back loan from Ashcroft: "I have to add that if Mr Ashcroft has in any way broken any laws of the country, then the money goes back to him straight away. This party is clean."[10] This rather wide-ranging commitment was later refined to the narrower standard response, following the Nadir debacle, that only stolen money would be returned. Ashcroft's problem was not that he was in anyway breaking any laws – he wasn't – but that the City found him 'too clever by half.'[11] The complexity of his business dealings, coupled with his activities in the former British colony of Belize gave the impression of a secretive political schemer. When he sold his company ADT on the day of the general election, he reportedly made £154 million.

One of Hague's alleged Yorkshire millionaire targets was Paul Sykes, who had earlier demonstrated his generosity to the party by sponsoring the election expenses of scores of Euro-sceptical candidates, and who had chosen Lord Parkinson to sit on the board of his computer company, Planet Online. Sykes' support of the Euro-sceptics led to criticisms of 'cash for policies' since he had set up a £500,000 "fighting fund for candidates prepared to pledge in their manifestos that they are against the single currency."[12] Sykes said that by early April, 1967 candidates had been in touch with him, and since 147 of them had already made up their minds about the single currency, his offer could hardly be described as a 'bribe.' In addition, he was reported to have given the party centrally a 'significant' donation to general funds. He said "My country's worth everything I have got. I never start out on something I cannot finish. And I am not going to run out of money."[13] By the day of the election, Sykes was said to have given between £1,000 and £3,000 to 237 Tory candidates. On the eve of the election the Guardian reported that in some cases the size of the donation under new parliamentary rules would mean that if the candidate was elected as the MP, he or she may not be allowed to speak on behalf of the cause for which the money was expressly donated. Thus it was that by polling day, the headline ran "Tories may repay Sykes" – but by then, the damage had been done. At the same time, in his own name, Sykes was running full-page advertisements in the press, urging Britain to "WAKE UP TO THE FACTS" and vote Conservative. He must have assumed that the previous press coverage had acquainted the electorate with who he was, since in one advertisement, simply entitled "A personal message from Paul Sykes," there was no explanation as to his background.[14]

Price of Power

The Sykes money had overtones of an earlier Euro-sceptical donation row, which had enveloped the doyen of the Conservative
backbench sceptics, Bill Cash. His 'European Foundation' received
money from the late Sir James Goldsmith back in 1996, coincidentally at the same time as Cash was introducing a Euro Referendum Bill
in the Commons. Cash denied that there was any connection, but it
was embarrassing for John Major to have linked in the public's mind
78 of his backbenchers who supported Cash's bill appearing to ally
themselves with the Goldsmith line, incidentally leading to speculation that they were as much concerned with protecting their seats
from Sir James' Referendum Party as voting for any matter of principle. But those 78 had also set the seal on the future Euro-sceptical
course of the party, leading to Hague's succession to the leadership.

The drift of the party was making it increasingly beholden to Euro-
sceptic business leaders, and for the first time, by autumn 1997, it
was becoming clear that some businesses, particularly those represented by the CBI, looked more to Labour for leadership than to the
Tories. Perhaps one could speculate that this trend was to have its
impact on donations, since even one of the staunchest of
Conservative corporate supporters, the Dixons chain, announced
that it would cease to give money to the party. Instead, Sir Stanley
Kalms, Dixons' chairman, was expected to give money personally.
This was reported to be another example of a "current corporate
fashion which states that companies should not fund political parties
and support should come from individuals instead."[15] One explanation was that corporations were increasingly not willing to give
money without shareholder approval – but another might be the
development of a more profoundly hostile relationship with a party
which appeared to be painting itself into a corner. So far as Sir
Stanley Kalms was concerned, however, he fully backed Hague's line,
co-signing a letter to the press giving his support to Hague's stance
on Europe. But it was significant that the other signatories to the
letter were largely drawn from a tight-knit, ultra loyal group of party
funders.

When Hague addressed delegates at the 1997 CBI conference as
'lemmings', for 'favouring a headlong rush towards monetary union',
he can only have confirmed the view that Britain's biggest businesses – those which were no longer run by the idiosyncratic
entrepreneur, but more the institutional type – had little in common

with the main plank of Conservative economic policy. But the split went deeper: David Heathcoat-Amory MP, the shadow Treasury chief secretary, described the CBI as a 'corporatist' whose "lifeblood is consultation . . [but] whose voice should not be mistaken with that of British industry as a whole."[16] So it was not Euro-scepticism alone that caused the rift, but a revived Thatcherite disdain for corporatism, and a trumpeting of individual entrepreneurial values. These would be better represented by bodies such as the Institute of Directors, who never had much time for consultation, and whose views might occasionally make even the Adam Smith Institute appear leftist.

The party's diminishing appeal to the business community was reflected by its dwindling membership. In the leadership endorsement ballot Hague called in September, 177,391 votes were cast, on a 45% turnout – suggesting a membership somewhat short of 400,000.[17] But it was widely reported that party officials thought the ballot a shambles – largely because there was no central membership list. This meant that allegations that members were voting more than once, that dead members' papers were being returned and so on could not be disproved. No-one knew how many people were eligible to vote, and since it was also known that some associations were padding their numbers by using higher but out of date figures, then even the estimate of membership put at 400,000 was likely to be on the high side.[18] Most independent observers agreed on a figure of 300,000. Compared to the days of Lord Woolton's membership drives of the late 1940s and early 1950s, when the party could claim over 2,000,000 members, then by 1997 the party had indeed hit a historic low. Another problem with the Conservative figures, however, relates to who qualifies as a party 'member.' It has generally been accepted that many Conservative Club membership rolls were included – even though many of these 'members' would only be interested in joining a local social club for the snooker tables or cheaper beer.

Despite its £250,000 cost, the endorsement ballot also failed to impress many members. It was not merely that Hague had given them no more choice than the 'back me or sack me' variety, but signals were being given that in future ballots, the voice of the membership would not be given much of a say either – 20% in an electoral college being the figure then touted. On top of that, many activists saw the leadership as seeking to centralise power. A

143

Price of Power

Yorkshire based millionaire, Peter Gregory, set up the Conservative Democratic Movement with £250,000 of his own money to challenge the party's lack of democracy. He claimed he was not against Hague in particular, but wanted a ballot with "candidates."[19] His group later united with the Charter Movement, the Party Referendum Steering Committee, and the Conservative One-Person One-Vote Group to advertise their concerns in the press.

In many respects, therefore, Hague's theme 'A Fresh Future', appeared as daring in its ambitiousness – one million members by the year 2000, for example – as it appeared cautious about engaging with membership demands. Grassroots Conservatives, after all, needed only to look at Tony Blair's leadership election to see that there could be a successfully conducted mass ballot, without undue weight given to MPs. They also blamed their own MPs for the election defeat, and couldn't see why this much diminished group should still exercise such sway over events.

On the other hand, the party's characteristic deference to its leadership, and its natural, heirarchical pecking order, will be difficult traits to eradicate, even if after such a heavy defeat at the polls it may appear that much of the slate has been wiped clean. The two aspects of autonomous local organisation

which are most precious to party activists – selecting their candidate, and controlling their own money – will not be given up lightly. The balance sheets of many better off local associations are healthier than that of Central Office, and the suspicion will naturally be felt that the new party structure will take away such local control members currently enjoy to order their own affairs. If this process starts with Central Office running its new, centralised national membership system taking a portion of membership subscriptions, the centre may also lead the questionning of the need for one local association – perhaps a safe seat – sitting on a six-figure balance, whilst other nearby marginal seats have very little. A new 'quota' system could be in the offing, redistributing the wealth to where the political targets are. As one ex-minister told the Guardian: "It will be an awful next election if we don't win back 100 seats. But the real effort should go into the 75 where elections are decided. That's where Central Office should direct its money and effort."[20]

The speculation about Hague's reforms ended when his detailed Fresh Future proposals were published in February, 1998. It would be churlish to say that for the Conservative Party, these reforms are anything but revolutionary. The creation of the party into a single entity, with the introduction of one-member, one vote ballots for many positions within the organisation, with one fell swoop takes on board, and perhaps goes someway further, than the demands of the Charter Movement's 10-point reform package.

So far as the financial aspects of Hague's reforms go, A Fresh Future does not add a great deal – indeed, there still remains a coyness about party financing. The creation of a centralised membership system provides the first additional source of funding, since it is proposed that £2.50 of a minimum national subscription rate of £15 should be retained by the central organisation. The quota system would remain, for the foreseeable future – thus the local associations may well feel that they will have to saddle an extra burden.[21]

One little reported aspect of Hague's proposed reforms will be the closing of the loophole that exempted the party from paying corporation tax. Once it has a centralised membership list, Central Office will no longer be just the office of the party leader, and the Inland Revenue will be able to assess its income for tax. Sadly, according to one source, the revenue gained will for some time to come probably be very little: despite Hague's wish to declare donations received over £5,000, it was said that since the general election, there hadn't been any.

The reform of the Conservative Party has been a long time coming, as Archie Norman, the former Asda chairman acknowledged: "What we are proposing is by far the biggest move towards democracy in the Conservative Party this century."[22] But as we have seen, there are those who believe that a fully fledged democracy within the party is still not on offer. The fear is that unless the party changes itself, then it will not convince the electorate that it once again deserves their support. But given the fact that well over nine million people still voted Conservative in 1997, the party insiders who claim that they can 'quickly' double their membership may have a point. After all, if despite the sleaze and the divisions there are still that many loyal Tories out there, then there is everything to play for, particularly since it will be felt that those nine million voters could be of a stronger metal than Labour's 11 million, many of whom switched to Labour for the first time in 1997 and may fall away again if the government fails to live up to their expectations. But this kind of thinking poses a conundrum for the Tories, many of whom have come to the conclusion that the blame for their defeat was peripheral to the usual causes of voter motivation – generally agreed to be the economic, 'feelgood' factors. If the electorate did feel good about the economy and their personal well-being, then perhaps they only booted the Tories out because they felt bad about sleaze and division. In other words, the defeat was a victory of form over content, the common Tory complaint that poor presentation was the problem all along. Such a view is only natural amongst those who clearly would have difficulty challenging the central tenets of their own political beliefs. The danger in this argument is that it could lead to a backlash against reforms which are perceived to be copying Labour's reforms of the 1980s, or are simply 'anti-Conservative.'

The leap from being an Edwardian political party to one ready for the 21st century is unlikely to be achieved in two years. The Labour Party refashioned itself from the kind of party it was in the 1940s (and remained well into the 1970s) in the space of about 12 years, between 1984 and 1996. An anti-reforming theme of much of that period in opposition was the traditional Labour belief that all it would take to beat the Tories the next time was 'one more heave.' Now, the Tories face a similarly redundant concept, 'We'll be back next time.' Historical precedent is easily quoted to support this view – notably the 1951 general election. For some Conservatives the issue is not if they will overtake Labour again, but how soon – how quickly that is, will the natural order return to British politics.

But the natural order is unlikely to return, least of all for the Tories. The internal reforming pressures both from the leadership and the grassroots will lead to the partial demise of the deferential body the party has always been. It may still be 'top-down' after the reforms are in place, but the grassroots demand for reform is bound to leave in its wake a greater expectation of policy input from the members, who in the past have been generally prepared to accept what their MPs told them and be little more than fundraising and campaigning fodder. Thus the internal changes will be made as quickly as possible whilst William Hague's 'iron' is still hot, so leaving as little opportunity as possible for the reactionaries to marshall their demands and the backing to push them through.

Change will also be forced externally on the party by legislation. This will include new rules on party funding, which will potentially force the party to reconsider its opposition to state funding. Having committed itself to ending foreign donations, and publicising all donations over £5,000, the party cannot be certain of relying on its recent, secret backers to maintain the income it grew accustomed to. Certainly at the national level, the party may have to reconcile itself to the fact that in normal, non-election years, its income will be no greater than Labour's. And with Labour attracting more commercial and industrial support, even some traditional Tory funders will divert more money as has already happened, into 'hedging their bets,' backing both parties simultaneaously.

But by far the biggest external threat to the Conservative Party however must lie in the prospect that reform will take place of Westminster elections. Perhaps Jeremy Thorpe, back in the 1970s, foresaw the shape of things to come, except for one detail – electoral reform could lead not to the creation of an anti-socialist alliance, but an anti-Conservative one. The existing agreement between Labour and the Liberal Democrats on this issue – at least to the extent of setting up an electoral reform commission under Roy Jenkins – if taken to its logical conclusion, could see the creation of a new centre left alliance which is, apart from anything else, 'business friendly.'

A move of this sort would alter the psephological battlefield beyond recognition, leaving those Tories of the 'We'll be back next time' school left without any historical precedent to turn to except perhaps, with supreme irony, the days of Ramsay MacDonald and the National Government. But in the new political millenium, there would be no short-term marriage of convenience coming to an end thus enabling a return to standard party politics.

If this scenario is likely, then Hague will have only one chance to launch a winning campaign at the next general election (quite apart from his own campaign to retain the party leadership). Hague has to be a man in a hurry, for if he cannot reform his party in time to ensure it is more successful at least by Labour's mid-term, then the Conservative Party could fragment. The impact on its funding would be disastrous. Indeed, if Paul Sykes is anything to go by, the fragmentation of support has swifty set in – Sykes has already torn his membership card up having decided that the party is not Euro-sceptical enough. With larger businesses increasingly deciding that the giving of donations is a matter for individual directors and not the shareholders' funds, combined with the loss of the protective cloak of anonymity, the party treasurers will face a completely new challenge.

To Labour supporting onlookers, who have witnessed repeated attempts by the Conservatives to 'nobble' their trade union funding, the sight of Conservative funding in turmoil will be richly entertaining. But even here there could be a crumb of comfort for the Tories, who could point to the loyalty of trade union members to the Labour Party as evidence that they too will have a core group of supporters willing, even in dire times, to keep the party going. Trade unionists not only supported their political funds in the ballots brought about by Conservative legislation, they also largely resisted all Conservative efforts to get them to individually contract out of paying the political levy. Well into the post war period, Conservative campaigns to convince workers to stop paying the levy failed to destroy the financial base of the Labour Party – indeed, one wonders how many workers seeing Conservative leafletters at factory gates took the opportunity to indulge in a little repartee at their opponents' expense.

A similar phenomenon occurred when Labour introduced the political donation disclosure requirement into the 1967 Companies Act. The Conservatives, at first fearful that it would force companies to give up making donations, found that it stiffened the resolve of many of their supporters, who had to decide to 'come out' – and when they did so, found themselves newly generous.

Thus, whilst the general political scene does not appear particularly likely to benefit the Conservatives, provided they appear politically credible, they have a chance of keeping themselves solvent – certainly by previous standards. But if they fail to appear politically credible, is it likely that any bank – even the Royal Bank of Scotland – would bail them out to the tune of £15 million again? (In February, 1998 their overdraft was 'strictly' limited to £3 million.) Unless the party can offer collateral – which now only exists at the local association level – it may find its overdraft facilities far less accommodating in the future. This surely adds one more pressure on the leadership to seek control over local association funds.

Another route to fundraising, the 'sale' of honours, which for the time being is closed off in any case, also looks set to diminish further. Perhaps those business world lords-in-waiting did not consider physically sitting in the House of Lords as a primary ambition – being so poorly paid in comparison to the boardroom – but if the second chamber is reformed, allowing for further democratisation, then even the attractive glow on that supreme gong, the peerage, might become tarnished. But that remains to be seen – the possibility of a peerage for a Conservative Party donor probably amounted to little more than what in business parlance could be described as 'added value' in any event.

Hague's efforts to present the Conservative Party as having turned a new leaf have taken some severe knocks, not least of which was the revelation that should the party's fundraising in 1998/99 fail, it would be bailed out by just two millionaires, Michael Ashcroft and Sir Graham Kirkham.[23] It was reckoned that it would take £16 million to put the Tories back on an 'even keel.' Given the Tories' new-found distaste for offshore tax havens, they remained remarkably silent on the fact that one of their benefactors, Michael Ashcroft, could not spend more than 90 days in the UK if he wanted to avoid paying British taxes.[24]

Nor has Hague helped his clean-up crusade by refusing to name previous donors, even to Sir Patrick Neill's Committee on Standards in Public Life, which is investigating party funding. Hague said "We cannot change retrospectively the basis upon which donations were received. It would be dishonourable to do so."[25] This unwillingness to co-operate – even to obtaining permission from recent donors on a confidential basis for disclosure to Sir Patrick's scrutiny – suggests that Hague has plenty he would wish to hide. Perhaps he feels he has done enough by banning future foreign donations (except from tax exiles) and fears the consequences should any more of the party's previous history escape the clutches of the party treasurers' safe. He perhaps feels that the pain threshold for transforming the party was passed on 1st May 1997, and that all that has to be done now is hope that time, and his reforms, will distance the new Tory Party from its past. But as the evidence suggests, this will be a much more difficult task to accomplish without more openness, as opposed to expressions of future intent.

The bottom line for party funding is tribal loyalty. All those old chestnuts put out by some industrialists about 'serving the greater interest,' 'defending free enterprise', and so on, whilst no doubt being sincerely held beliefs, nevertheless cannot conceal straightforward party loyalties. The question is, how small will the Conservatives'

Price of Power

funding tribe dwindle before extinction – or state funding – beckons?
The Tories have not demured at the possibility that just two multi-
millionaires may yet save it from bankruptcy. No doubt they will still
be assisted by anonymous support from the city (until the law
changes, at least). These are hardly the foundations on which the
Conservatives can reconstruct their political fortunes.

Chapter Eight

FRONTS AND CLUBS

nyone wanting to write a cheque out to 'The Conservative Party' was blessed with a choice which, in most cases, would have saved them using those actual words. The range and complexity of Tory party funding fronts set it apart from its rivals, and this never been adequately explained. We have seen how for some donors there was an oft repeated disdain for "party" politics – almost as if recognising the existence of party politics might mean recognising the primacy of the democratic process over market processes.

But a distinction should be drawn between organisations such as British United Industrialists, which were nominally separate from the party, and internal party fund-raising clubs. The dividing line would not always be obvious, particularly in the case of regional industrialists' 'councils', but the existence of a variety of destinations for donations could be and was used to obfuscate the accountability trail. Money given to the party could be deposited directly into a party account, or at the local level, a 'fighting fund.' But money sent through less direct channels would be paid into subsidiary accounts, such as those held with Adams Bank in Scotland (though this was denied by one of its directors), the Drummond's Bank 'Free Enterprise' account in London, or for overseas cash, a Barclays account, among others, in the Channel Islands.

The status of some of these accounts, like the financial status of the party itself, can be questioned. An account set up for the benefit of the party but not in its name, and run by nominees, clearly escapes all normal scrutiny. Add to that the paranoid secrecy relating to all party treasury matters, and it can be seen that there would never be much likelihood of outsiders (including party members) knowing the full story. This must surely have proved useful to those leading party figures who would insist that most of their money was sourced from the 'sale of our jam.' As we have seen with the Austin Mitchell complaint, there was no obligation on the party to reveal the extent of its subsidiaries' assets or liabilities in the party accounts.

But even at the local level, how true was it that even the local associations' funds were generated by jam sales, wine and cheese parties and the like? A report in the mid-1960s gave a clue to the more likely source of easy, 'big' money. Local associations set up their own businessmen's clubs, with names like the 'Spider Club,' the 'Knole Club' and the 'Chelwood Club.' For example, the Orpington Businessmen's Spider Club formed in 1965 included those businessmen who "want to give support to Orpington Conservative Association but who don't have time to go canvassing, or a personal inclination for it." Members were "solicitors, accountants and men of industry." The Sevenoaks-based Knole Club raised 'thousands' for the local association and membership consisted of "acknowledged business leaders, bank chairmen, great insurance chaps, all of whom live in the constituency."[1] They paid twelve guineas a year and "could attend two Commons dinners a year to have a completely off-the-record chat with a Cabinet minister."

These single association clubs, along with their larger counter-parts, the regional 'industrialists councils', would provide private and discreet platforms for visiting Conservative ministers to meet local business leaders – or at least those that paid for the privilege. There were, by the mid-1990s 10 regional councils, and they played a major, if somewhat low-key role in fund-raising for the party. Each council would comprise up to 12 Tory supporting business leaders, and according to Lord Laing, a former party joint treasurer, they might account for up to half of the total donations made to the party – a figure of £4 million has been reported, although this figure, as with all other estimates of Conservative income, has to be treated circumspectly.[2]

The most important of the councils was the City and Industrial Liaison Council, based in London. One of the party's most loyal bene-factors, the property developer Sir Nigel Mobbs chaired the council and also served on the party's board of treasurers at the same time as another city figure, Lord Hambro was a treasurer. The council was run by a full-time fund-raiser, Major-General Stuart Watson. The council would invite potential donors to meet Cabinet ministers, and one occasion an invite to meet Ian Lang, President of the Board of Trade, fell into the hands of the press. The meeting was arranged in liaison with Arthur Anderson & Co., the accountancy and management consultancy firm.[3] A spokesperson for the partnership said that the meeting was the initiative of just one of its partners, not the firm as a whole. Lang also courted controversy by embarking on a three month tour of the country attending Monday morning "Business Breakfasts" which he said would give "business people... the chance to give ministers direct feedback on our policies and priorities."[4]

The problematic part of this tour was that the 'Business Breakfasts' appeared to be concentrated in or near Tory-held marginal seats, but were organised by civil servants and cost the tax payer £250,000. But this further attempt to shore up business support probably came too late. The regional councils had found it increasingly difficult to meet their targets. An unnamed council chair said in 1994 "This year is bloody hellish. Everybody hates me [when I ask for money]."[5] Were the ministers more successful?

The existence of many Tory front fund-raising operations attracted attention for the first time at the end of the 1960s, after donation disclosure requirements in the Companies Act of 1967 began to filter through. This encouraged the regional media to ask questions of coy local party officials, whose defensiveness in those more innocent days did not run as far as outright denial, but rather a strained display of irritation that anyone should show an interest in their affairs. The Newcastle Journal probed the activities of the Northern Industrialists Protection Association (NIPA), founded in 1954 to "Defend free enterprise and to support the election of a government believing in the free enterprise system."[6] As ever, the military, in the shape of Commander Robert Reading made its presence felt. In 1970 he was the secretary of NIPA and told the Journal:

"We don't automatically support the Conservative Party. You never know what happens in politics and, I suppose, theoretically, that if the Liberals were in favour of complete free enterprise we would support them. As it happens, however, it's the Conservative Party that is doing it now... We feel that people are heartily fed up with party politics. The important thing is that many people feel the future of the country's success is bound up in the business sector."[7]

As the Journal's reporter put it, "it appears it is only coincidental that Commander Reading's office was located in the same building as the North-East headquarters of the Conservative Party." It was probably even more coincidental that NIPA shared the same telephone line as the Conservative Party. Amongst the activities NIPA undertook was "entertaining itinerant Shadow Ministers [Labour were still in power] and asking a question now and then in the House of Commons." According to the Chairman of NIPA, James Woodeson, the association did not do any campaigning itself. The sources of NIPA's income could be gauged by the list of its leading lights published by the Journal.

These shy but hard-headed businessmen didn't like their names 'splashed around' according to Commander Reading. A later report illustrated why, when it was discovered by Tyneside shipbuilder Swan Hunter's workforce that the company had given £60,000 to NIPA to fight nationalisation. The government were willing to pay £17million for Swan Hunter, whereas the company wanted £52 million, basing their estimate on the 'asset value of each share.' A leading shop steward found the company's valuation laughable, saying "Anybody who visits the yards can see the company's failure to invest in the yards . . . It is amazing that the firm manages to keep up any sort of production level with all the outdated machinery, tools and plant."[8] The attitude of the private sector to privatisations ten years later was notable for the reversal of roles given to the valuers and managers, especially in cases where senior managers were able to profit heavily from the undervaluation of state-owned assets.

By 1976 Commander Reading had been replaced as NIPA's secretary by a Col. Michael Knight, who was a little bit more forthcoming about NIPA's true role. He confessed that it had once given money to the Liberal Party; but "basically [our] money goes to the Conservative Party as an instrument in fighting for free enterprise. Contributions fluctuate, but more money comes in during elections. I don't know off the cuff how many contributors there are."[9] Col. Knight's more significant role in Newcastle was as representative of the Conservative Board of Finance. One of NIPA's biggest donors was Northern Electrical Industries (NEI), which had won a major contract for a power station contract in India, worth £300 million, after Mrs Thatcher had taken a 'personal initiative.' The contract was first revealed in a National Audit Office report, which led to complaints in parliament that were it not for a taxpayers' contribution of £119 million in aid, India would never have accepted the NEI bid. NEI gave NIPA £40,000 in 1981, but any connection with Mrs Thatcher's 'personal initiative' and the contract was denied.[10] NEI were also, as we have seen, involved in UN sanctions-defying links with Namibia during the period of South African occupation.

For many years, the most important of the Conservatives' front organisations was British United Industrialists (BUI). Formed in 1948 by Lord 'Bob' Renwick, with the approval of Lord Woolton, the BUI worked in relative obscurity until the donation disclosure requirement in company accounts gave it more prominence.

BUI had itself been a limited company, and thus would have had to declare in its own accounts where it donated money to – in its case, most of its income – after 1967. It changed itself in 1968 into an unincorporated association, thus evading the Companies Act disclosure requirement. Its Director General, Colonel Juan Hobbs told the Sunday Times in 1969: "We don't give any direct support to the Tory Party – we don't give a damn about party politics – but we do help by contributing to a special free enterprise fund. Much of our work is done through personal contact. We know a lot of people in the right places, and for instance, we can sometimes get questions asked in the House."[11] This answer, remarkably similar to that given on behalf of NIPA was of course nothing but a false trail for as we shall see, BUI's main purpose was to channel money to the party, although it did also appear to get involved directly in some industrial activity. Later in 1969, it was reported that BUI had carried out a 'small number' of 'anti-subversion operations': "If a company thinks that its plant is being disrupted by strikes designed to achieve political ends (by which is meant Communist or Trotskyist ends), then British United Industrialists reckons to be able to help – indirectly."[12] This help may take the form of publishing pamphlets or leaflets, though not in such a way as to identify their source. Two BUI paid-for pamphlets were written by Toby O'Brien, a former Conservative Director of Information Services.

The first year the Labour Party's Research Department investigated company donations to the Conservatives showed that in 1969, BUI received £282,952. Whilst most of this money would have passed to the Conservatives, theoretically to fund 'free enterprise' propaganda, some of it found its way to Conservative fringe organisations. In 1973, BUI became embroiled in an internal row at the Monday Club, which it was regularly funding, and threatened to withdraw support. The row erupted over a letter sent to Monday Club members by its chairman Jonathan Guinness, which attacked supporters of the late Enoch Powell. When asked whether as a result of this, BUI's Col. Hobbs had withheld £2,000, Guinness said "I am neither confirming nor denying that that involves BUI. We have all sorts of colonels who give us all sorts of money."[13]

The policy of reticence to confirm BUI's true role on the part of anyone connected to BUI began to unravel in the 1980s, when a series of damaging leaks finally confirmed what most people suspected. In 1987, internal BUI documents were copied to Labour Research. One of these documents was a 'Draft letter for companies who do not normally give political donations' written by the BUI Director General J.A.P. Forbes. This document is worth quoting in full, since it encapsulates, amongst other things, the 'line' that has been used down the decades by company chairman to defend their public 'non-partisan' facade.

"A Case for Financial Support for FREE ENTERPRISE Via British United Industrialists. This unincorporated association has supported the Conservative Party with a steady flow of funds since its inception in the forties when the late Lord Renwick went to the support and help of Lord Woolton, who at that time was struggling to raise funds for the Conservative Party. Very considerable capital sums were raised from industry in a matter of weeks and the results of that election are known to us all today.

"Each political party has its own fund-raising machine and possibly the most persuasive and most effective is that of the Conservative Party. The Liberal and Alliance Parties have their own machine, the Labour Party of course get most of the financial support from their union membership, which has now thanks to good Conservative union legislation, consulted its membership who have voted that they wish in the majority to continue to support the Labour Party. It is thought that the Labour constituency machinery on the other hand is weak and does not show the dedication of fund-raising support that is shown by the Conservatives in their own local party machines.

"BUI stands for FREE ENTERPRISE and in that capacity has examined the political spectrum and has clearly come to the view recently supported by discussions with Dr Owen, who clearly shows himself as an interventionist, that the only party who truly believes in the capital-owning democracy and will do everything in its power to encourage free enterprise in our nation is the Conservative Party.

"Many of our largest institutions in the country at Board level have taken the view that direct support for the Conservative Party would be dangerous in regards to their trade union relationships and could affect their negotiating position with an incoming government of a different colour or persuasion and with their chance of winning successful tenders with local authorities and even government departments.

"BUI would argue that FREE ENTERPRISE has to be fought for and that [gap] boom currently being enjoyed by many City institutions and the greatest [gap] of our companies' regards to exports across the country, came through an enlightened FREE ENTERPRISE government.

"Since the forties a number of people have followed Lord Renwick's magnificent example. He was involved in the Mr Cube case, while more recently the Freedom Association were behind the Grunwick Case, to name but two.

"BUI of course sympathise with certain financial and industrial sectors who believe that they should not support an individual political party, but it does suggest that there are other ways that those companies can support FREE ENTERPRISE. As BUI's Director General I would be only too willing to come and discuss with you any ideas that you and your Board might be able to help Free Enterprise [indecipherable]... and thus achieve Board approval for financial funding so that such organisations as the Centre for Policy Studies and the Youth Movement for Employment and Enterprise can further advance the principles of FREE ENTERPRISE."[14]

The letter, whilst specifically confirming BUI's Conservative remit, also shows how the organisation sought a wider role for itself at a time when the Alliance appeared to be a major new political force. Forbes commented in a further note to the letter that "Owen insists on a Tory Coalition but admits the Liberals (who are Socialists) could well join Kinnock and split the Alliance. Therefore the unity of the Alliance is an illusion." This confirms that Owen, in like manner to Jeremy Thorpe before him, was sniffing around the City for new

Price of Power

sources of funding for the party which was going to 'break the mould.' But the ascendancy of Thatcher, on the verge of another economic boom, was to prevent the Alliance breaking through.

There is also in Forbes' letter a reference to the Centre for Policy Studies (CPS), the Thatcherite think-tank established in 1974 with Sir Keith Joseph as chairman. In his 1987 annual report, Forbes claimed that without an 'initial cheque', CPS "would not be in existence today." But whatever the truth of this claim, it was inserted much in the same way as a finger in a leaking dyke, since it was becoming clear that despite BUI's previous success, the Conservative Party proper was adopting a more distant attitude to the semi-detached front organisation. Forbes wrote "...every attempt has been made by myself, the Chairman and other members of the [BUI] Council to get a full working relationship going with the fundraising side of Conservative Central Office. I think that an understanding has now been achieved but close co-operation and working together is, unfortunately, as far off as ever."[15]

It appears that the deputy party chairman, Peter Morrison, had "offered to assist if we end up with further disputes." The disputes were most likely about whether donors were channelling their money through BUI, or were destined directly for Conservative Central Office. Perhaps in the heady triumphalist Thatcherite days of the mid-eighties, companies were increasingly desirous to give directly to the party, either to ensure that credit (and honours) due would be awarded, or indeed to open direct links with ministers and the 'movers and shakers' of party policy to assist in the development of their companies' prospects. The very need for BUI and its own, separate secretive culture was being eroded by a new breed of control freaks, who were less inclined to show traditional Tory deference to retired Colonels.

Traditions were being eroded on the publications front too, since BUI was forced to publish its 'first and only publication' in 1987 to tell potential funders what it was for. In a letter in May, to Sir Michael Colman, of Reckitt and Colman plc., Forbes described a donation to BUI as "less emotive than a donation to the Conservative Party appearing as a note to your financial statements."[16] This presumably was a reference to the potential danger of a militant trade union reaction, but once again illustrated another reason for BUI's demise – the more mute function served by trade unions after eight years of anti-

trade union legislation and the background pressure of high unemployment had reduced the power of the unions to give management
an uncomfortable time.

BUI's declining usefulness for the party by September, 1987 led
Ian Weston-Smith, BUI's chairman to write that their "basic and
perfectly workable understanding is now in danger of disappearing
altogether." Weston-Smith adduced a twofold reason for this calami-
ty: Central Office's "financial pragmatism – get as much money as
you can from wherever" and a lack of "long-term thinking about how
to draw support from the vast majority of companies who make no
political donations."[17]

Weston-Smith and BUI had missed the boat, clearly not having
done much 'long-term' thinking themselves. This was the year, after
all, in which Central Office under the guidance of Chairman Tebbit,
launched their huge direct mail-shots to the shareholders of British
Telecom et al, and were courting a new breed of offshore entrepreneurs who were to cause so much grief later. Weston-Smith was
certainly right about Central Office's pragmatism, but he did not have
a strategy to match it.

Indeed, in an unhappily prescient comment, Weston-Smith
concluded his paper by commenting that BUI presented: "A face
acceptable to Scottish industrialists and the ability, through its
Council members, to offer a liaison role with industrial fundraising
groups throughout the UK." Whatever it was that stood BUI in such
a comparatively favourable light, three years later came to be embar-
rassingly snuffed out.

Conservatism in Scotland was, compared to England, an endan-
gered cause, with the number of its MPs dwindling from half of the
total in the mid-fifties to none by 1997. Even a review of local authorities which led to a much reduced tier of unitary authorities in the
1990s, thought by many opponents to be an example of 'gerryman-
dering' for the Tories' benefit, actually accentuated the decline of
Tory representation north of the border. Against this background,
Tory fund-raising was becoming increasingly problematic, despite a
loyal hard core of Scottish industrialists who, perhaps because of
their isolation, fought valiantly against the local anti-Tory tide.

For the 1992 general election, the party's Scottish Board of
Finance launched a £1 million fighting fund appeal which immediately led to controversy. The letter, from James Sneddon, honorary

secretary of the Board of Finance claimed that companies may find it 'preferable' to make contributions to the BUI, on the grounds that: "The attraction of the British United Industrialists arrangement is the exclusion of any disclosure of such payments as a political donation in the statutory accounts of your company."[18] The £1 million fighting fund was to be used for the benefit of the party's 21 'strategic' seats "where we are determined to either retain existing seats or regain seats, from other parties."

A day after the Sneddon letter was leaked, the party tried to calm the furore that had engulfed them – but they only made matters worse. A Scottish Conservative spokesperson said "We feel there is nothing dishonest about what was in the letter... We do not know anything about what happens to money given to British Unitied Industrialists."[19] This was in spite of the fact that BUI accounts had shown the Conservative Board of Finance receiving £20,900 before the 1987 election and possibly a total of £750,000 being passed over since BUI's inception.[20] Speaking for BUI, Alistair Forbes contradicted the claim made by Sneddon regarding the disclosure requirements: "That is not correct... My understanding is that donations in excess of £300 should be declared in the annual report and accounts and all donors are advised of that." He said BUI had not been consulted about the content of Sneddon's letter.

The association, desired or not, between the Conservatives and BUI on this occasion brought the value of the publicity-shy BUI into question. A survey by Labour Research in 1993 of company donations to the Conservative's election victory found that of 263 companies, donating a total of £3,907,602 to the Conservatives, only five gave a total of £74,500 to BUI.[21] BUI's inevitable demise appears to have taken place after the 1992 general election, and aroused very little comment. The 1994 edition of the Directory of British Political Organisations listed BUI as "no longer active."

The hands-on fund-raising approach adopted by Central Office in the 1990s represented a more dynamic response to solving the Party's huge debt burden. The new Premier and Millennium Clubs, where businessmen would pay thousands of pounds to attend dinners, some at 10 Downing Street, enlisted new fund-raisers who were altogether more entrepreneurial in their methods. One such club was called 'Team 1000', headed by a Party Treasurer the multi-millionaire 'cocoa king' Anthony Weldon. He resigned his position in

1994 after only seven months in office, after being accused in the United States of "bucketing, wash sales, illegal cross trades and fictitious sales" in the cocoa futures market.[22] Team 1000, in the form of Weldon, canvassed representatives of the defence and security industries for money for the Conservatives 'in return for valuable information.' A document prepared for this meeting by one of those present, David Bryan, a supplier of police motorcycle radios, said: "due to Team 1000's unique position within government it can arrange high level meetings and supply valuable information to companies."[23]

Determining what exactly this "unique position" was, was not hard to achieve. The Labour MP Barry Sheerman, concerned about the excessive use of House of Commons dining facilities by Conservative fund-raisers, told the Independent on Sunday: "I first became aware of this scam when I saw a mass mail-out of the Tory party Team 1000 fund-raising leaflets pitched at wealthy business people, which implied that entertainment at the Palace of Westminster was clearly one of the perks."[24] Mr Sheerman calculated that the Tory Party was raising £500,000 a year this way. The last official figures giving a breakdown of room bookings showed that Tory MPs had made 1,399 bookings in a year compared to 167 by Labour MPs. The Conservative response to Mr Sheerman's accusation was evasive, merely pointing out that the Team 1000 letter did not specifically refer to the use of House of Commons dining rooms.

The same evasion was in abundance when Conservative fund-raising events, either run directly or by one of the "Clubs" were held at No. 10 Downing Street. John Major was wont to say that the house was not used for fund-raising purposes, but as always this was only a partial glimpse of the truth. What happened was that whilst nobody would be so vulgar as to raise the issue of cash over their dinners, 'Guests would be contacted later by party treasurers.'[25] Naturally, in this most exclusive of streets, there was a touch of 'keeping up with the Jones's', since for £1,000 per head, members of the 'Quota Club' could dine at No. 11 Downing Street. Here, the Chancellor of the Exchequer, Kenneth Clarke in July 1995 entertained 18 guests who were bound not to repeat outside anything they had heard during their meal. The Quota Club was organised by Keith Brown, a manager of Morgan Stanley International.[26] Quota Club members, according to their invitation, were encouraged "to raise specific issues that are of interest to them and their businesses."

As its name suggests, the Premier Club was by far the most exclusive of these fund-raising dining clubs, charging guests £100,000 a year for the pleasure of being able to share access to the Prime Minister. Chaired by property tycoon John Beckwith, the Premier Club walked into a controversy waiting to happen when Beckwith's property consortium was shortlisted to bid in the privatisation of Ministry of Defence housing.

Chapter Nine

THE PARLIAMENTARY ROAD
TO PROBITY

Mr Winnick: To ask the Prime Minister if he will introduce legislation whereby political parties represented in the House would be required to publish detailed annual accounts of their finances.

The Prime Minister: I have no plans to do so.

Hansard, 18th March 1993

Mr Winnick: To ask the Prime Minister if he will introduce legislation whereby political parties represented in the House will have to declare all moneys received from overseas.

The Prime Minister: We have no plans to do so.

Hansard, 10th May 1993

Mr Winnick: To ask the Prime Minister if he will introduce legislation to require political parties that have received moneys from a source that has been shown to be criminal to return such funds to the appropriate body.

The Prime Minister: I have no plans to do so.

Hansard, 25th June 1993

Mr Spellar: When does the Prime Minister intend to stop hiding behind procedure and come clean about the secret sources of Tory Party funding?

The Prime Minister: I must let the Hon. Gentleman into a secret. There are a great many secret sources and they are all cheese and wine parties up and down the country.

Price of Power

Hansard, 19th October 1993

Parliament has often considered the issue of party funding, approaching the subject from various angles at least since Lloyd George's fund became notorious. But the debates have been generally uninformative, stale and repetitious, whilst reforms have been few and far between. In the past, the incentive for whichever government has been in power to do something has never been paramount – it is only when a party is powerless that it feels it should do something about it. Thus even Margaret Thatcher claimed that she had backed off taking a tougher stance on reforming the political levy for fear of appearing too aggressively partisan:

"On the face of it, it would have been fairer to base the system on a principle of 'contracting in' and some argued for change. But 'contracting in' would have wreaked havoc with the Labour Party's finances because of its heavy dependence on the unions... If we brought forward radical proposals on the eve of a general election, we would be accused both of attempting to crush the Labour Party financially and of unfairness on the matter of corporate donations."[1]

Such uncharacteristic political generosity on the part of Thatcher needs to be considered with a hefty pinch of salt. Thatcher's other trade union reforms, such as the ballots on political funds themselves, were designed to weaken financial support for the Labour Party. Indeed, as has been noted, there was a period between 1928 and 1946 when by law trade union members had to 'contract in' in any case.

The unprecedented publicity, most of it bad, given to party funding – chiefly the Conservatives' – prior to the 1997 general election has presented the new government with the most significant opportunity yet to reform the whole system (if 'system' is the right word to use in the British context.) Prior to the 1997 general election, Labour promised to reveal the identity of its own donors who gave over £5,000, and promised to make illegal foreign donations to all political parties. Other issues raised were reforming tax rules which penalised some parties more than the Tories – who had won their case against the Inland Revenue in 1981 – and whether or not shareholders should be allowed to vote on whether their companies should be allowed to make political donations. Back in 1994, Gordon Brown, the Shadow Chancellor also considered the possibility that shareholders should simply have the right to 'contract out' – a near automatic way of reducing company donations, since the sheer effort involved in the task of processing such contracted out shareholders would have outweighed in many cases the value of the donation in the first place.[2] This proposal was still being touted by Robin Cook shortly before the general election.

Late in 1997, six months after coming to office, Labour gave Lord Neill QC's Committee on Standards in Public Life the task of reviewing all aspects of party funding. Tony Blair, writing in the Times, gave readers an indication of where legislation may be forthcoming:

"I will be recommending the toughest possible set of rules. If there is one lesson to be learnt… it is that the current rules do not work. I believe there to be a powerful case for national limits on electoral expenditures. We will also be ready to limit individual and company donations to a modest amount. At the same time we stand ready to publish names and amounts. We will be ready also to consider any proposals Sir Patrick has for state funding of political parties. We have to be clear that we can avoid opportunities for front organisations to receive money. We have to be sure that that there are arrangements in place for a proper policing of the system. And we have to be clear that we can ensure foreign funding is banned for good."[3]

It may be judged from these comments that overall party political spending could be reduced. Indeed, that appears to have been the effect of the last major overhaul of political expenditure, the 1883 Corrupt and Illegal Practices Prevention Act. The 1880 general election cost the parties £94 million in 1997 prices, more than twice what was actually spent in 1997.[4]

But if the effect of reform is to reduce the global amount of money available, then either the parties will have to learn to spend their money more effectively, or they will have to contest elections on a more financially uncertain basis. This follows from the fact there will be more elections to fight – for the Scottish Parliament, the Welsh Assembly, annual local council elections, referenda on the London-wide authority, European Single Currency and proportional representation for Westminster elections, directly elected Mayors, possible English regional elections and so on. The implications of more democracy have yet to be absorbed by the political parties.

Arising from these considerations, the Tories' traditional opposition to state funding may be dropped. They have in any case, as has previously been noted, always accepted the taxpayers' money when it was offered, so their opposition if voiced during Lord Neill's review will stem less from principle than they would want the electorate to believe. Lord Neill's consultation document notes that most countries have some form of state assistance for political parties, even if only in the form of tax relief on donations (which is of no benefit to the millions of non-taxpayers whom traditionally might be considered Labour supporters.)

The other question more particular to the Conservatives, the issue of company donations, has strangely lost some of its partisan hue. Six months before the 1997 general election, the Labour Party was able to announce it had received £6 million in major contributions, including corporate donations.[5] Many commentators believe that the Conservative Party has lost its appeal to the full spectrum of the business community, for reasons mentioned earlier. In any case, fewer and fewer company donations are being made, perhaps as a result of media exposure, but also through greater pressure from institutional investors such as the pension funds. Thus, even without a review, there are changes taking place in corporate political donations which are unprecedented in the time scale of this study.

Lord Neill's Inquiry's consultation period ended on the 27th February 1998, and the Labour Party's proposals, met with a strangulated whimper of anguish from Central Office, were that:

- a limit of £15 million should be placed on each party's election
  expenditure
- donations form non-UK residents and companies to be banned
- corporate donations to be made only with shareholder approval
- audited accounts to be published annually
- £5,000-plus donations to be revealed each quarter
- a new Electoral Commission established to enforce legislation[6]

The Conservatives' own response to Neill led to accusations that Hague had committed a 'U-turn'. Contrary to his publicly avowed desire to promote openness, the Tory response stated: "We believe that tighter rules on disclosure will both discourage giving to parties and encourage the pursuit of ways to avoid the rules. We believe there is a perfectly honourable case to be made for anonymity."[7] Nor did the Tories want to see shareholders being forced to ballot before companies gave political donations, even though trade union members had such a right. In no small way, therefore, the 'Fresh Future' Hague promised did not appear to penetrate too deeply so far as the reform of party funding was concerned.

Lord Neill had a week earlier signalled his desire to Radio 4's In Committee programme to have a lower donation disclosure level of £1,000. Clearly, if that could be taken as a measure of his determination to take a strict line on party funding – a line which would inevitably cause the most discomfort to the Tories – then the subsequent legislation could be no less radical then the 1883 reforms. Those reforms were made when elections were fought not as national campaigns, but were conducted almost entirely at the local level. Technology has now created a 'national' electorate, the campaign for which requires regulation.

A radical, reforming report from the Neill Committee will be a real test for the reforming agenda Hague has set his party. The electorate know where most of Labour's millions come from – and have known that fact since the party was created. But in Central Office, where even senior campaign staff were denied that knowledge about their own funding, there has to be a culture shift of seismic proportions. When John Major – quoted above – jokingly lied to the House of Commons about the Tories' secret funding, he was not out of tune with his party. Yet the fronts and 'clubs', the overseas bank accounts, the back-to-back loans – an era of fund-raising expertise is about to be consigned to the shredder.

REFERENCES

Introduction

1. Gracchus, *Your MP,* Victor Gollancz, London 1944 p.26
2. Paul Mercer, *Directory of British Political Organisations,* Longman, Harlow, 1994 p.78
3. Emma Nicholson, *Secret Society,* Indigo London 1996 p.96
4. *Whittakers Almanack 1996,* J. Whittaker & Sons, London 1996 p.610

Chapter One: Money for Honours

1. Ken Young, *Local Politics and the rise of party: The London Municipal Society and the Conservative intervention in local elections 1894 - 1963* Leicester University Press 1975 p.15
2. *ibid* p.15
3. John Walker, *The Queen Has Been Pleased: The British Honours System at work* Secker & Warburg, London 1986 p46
4. *ibid* p.47
5. *ibid* p.48
6. Gerald Macmillan, *Honours for Sale: The strange story of Maundy Gregory* Richards Press, London 1954 p.21
7. *ibid* p.21
8. Robert Blake, *The Unknown Prime Minister: The life and times of Andrew Bonar Law 1858 - 1923* Eyre & Spottiswoode London 1955 p.100
9. Lord Beaverbrook, *The Decline and Fall of Lord George: and great was the fall thereof,* Collins, London 1963 p. 243
10. *ibid* p.299
11. *ibid* p.300
12. *The Times* 18th January 1923
13. *The Times* 19th January 1923
14. *The Times* 19th March 1923
15. Tom Cullen, *Maundy Gregory: Purveyor of Honours*, The Quality Book Club, London 1975 p.103
16. House of Lords debates, col. 139 29th June 1922
17. House of Lords debates, col. 142 29th June 1922
18. *The Times* 4th September 1923
19,..John Greenwood, *The Conservative Party and the Working Classes - the Organisational Response*, University of Warwick Department of Politics Working Paper No. 2, 1974 p.31
20. *The Times* 2nd October 1924
21. Keith Middlemas, *Politics in Industrial Society: The experience of the British system since 1911,* Andre Deutsch, London 1979 p.132
22. Cullen *op cit* p.103
23. Middlemas *op cit* p.132

24. H.J. Hanham, *Elections ad Party Management: Politics in the time of Disraeli and Gladstone* Harvester Press, Sussex 1978 p.370 "The Secret Service money was of considerable value to the party in office, because it enabled it to provide for ordinary recurrent expenses without appealing to its supporters and also to accumulate a small surplus. The whole sum of £10,000 was paid over without question, and without any provision for audit, or for the return of unexpended monies, and was spent at the entire discretion of the Chief Whip." The sum of £10,000 in 1880 would be equivalent to £602,000 at current prices.

25. *The Times* 26th January 1926

26. Robert Rhodes James, *Memoirs of a Conservative: J.C.C. Davidson's Memoirs and Papers 1910-37* Weidenfeld & Nicolson, London 1969 p 290

27. Rhodes James, *op cit* p.290

28. *The Times* 1st February 1927

29. Michael Pinto-Duschinsky, *British Political Finance, 1830 - 1980* American Enterprise Institute, Washington D.C. 1981 p.111

30. quoted in House of Commons debates 15th December 1949

31. Lewis Chester, Stephen Fay, Hugo Young *The Zinoviev Letter: A political intrigue* Heinemann, London 1967 p.80 The dispute about whether the letter was forged or not appeared to have been settled by 1998 - with the publication of KGB archives, which showed that "the letter was forged in Riga, the Latvian capital, by a Lt. Ivan Dmitrevich Pokrovsky who was in touch with British intelligence and used snatches of Zinoviev's speeches 'with something extra added.'" - *Daily Telegraph,* 15th January 1998

32. Cullen *op cit* p.152

33. Rhodes James *op cit* p.289

34. *ibid* p.289

35. *The Times* 1st March 1926

36. *The Times* 28th January 1928

37. Gracchus *op cit* p.30

38. *The Times* 29th January 1928

39. *The Times* 28th December 1928

40. *The Times* 10th April 1929

41. *The Times* 1st April 1930

42. *The Times* 16th May 1930

43. *The Times* 9th February 1931

44. Gracchus *op cit* p.25

45. *ibid* p.24

46. Richard Cockett, *Twilight of Truth: Chamberlain, Appeasement & the Manipulation of the Press*, Weidenfeld & Nicolson, London 1989 p.58

47. *The Times* 16th March 1932

48. *The Times* 29th April 1932

49. David Butler & Gareth Butler, *British Political Facts 1900 - 1985* Macmillan, London 1986 p.179

50. *The Times* 4th April 1933

51. *The Times* 30th March 1933

52. *The Times* 28th March 1935

53. *The Times* 5th October 1935

54. *The Times* 9th October 1937

55. *The Times* 3rd October 1944

56. *The Times* 27th September 1948

57. The Earl of Woolton, *Memoirs,* Cassell, London, 1959 p. 345

58. The Earl of Kilmuir, *Political Adventure,* Weidenfeld & Nicolson, London 1964 p.159

Price of Power

Chapter Two: The Triangular Relationship

1. Pinto-Duschinsky, p.107
2. Donald McCormick, *Murder by Perfection*, John Long, London, 1970 p.134
3. Wulf Schwartzwaller, *The Unknown Hitler,* Berkeley Books, 1990
4. McCormick, p134
5. James and Suzanne Pool, *Who Financed Hitler: The Secret Funding of Hitler's Rise to Power 1919 - 1933* Macdonald & Jane's, London 1978 p.488
6. *The Whitehall Gazette and St. James Review,* London, January/February 1932
7. *The Whitehall Gazette and St. James Review,* July 1930
8. McCormick, p.134
9. Martin Gilbert, *Prophet of Truth: Winston S. Churchill 1922 - 1939,* Minerva, London 1990 p.457
10. Pool, p.308
11. Cullen, p.149
12. McCormick, p.133
13. Donald McCormick, *The Peddler of Death*, Macdonald London 1965 p.187
14. Robert Neumann, *Zaharoff: The Armaments King,* Readers' Union, London 1938 p.157
15. *ibid* p.250
16. Simon Haxey, *Tory MP,* Victor Gollancz, London, 1939 p.64
17. Cockett, p.10
18. Pinto-Duschinsky, p.123
19. *Truth,* The Truth Publishing Co., London, 10th May 1940
20. *Truth* 24th November 1937
21. Pinto-Duschinsky p.124
22, Richard Spiegelberg, *The City: Power without accountability,* Blond & Briggs, London 1973 p.73
23. Aytoun Ellis, *Hier of Adventure, The story of Brown, Shipley & Co. Merchant Bankers,* Brown, Shipley & Co, London 1961 p146. In this official Brown, Shipley history, Ellis described their relationship with Brown Brothers, Harriman: [in 1918 their formal partnership was severed because of war taxes amongst other things] but despite the "dissolution of partnership the two firms continued without any change in name or constitution, and each continued to act - though not exclusively - as agents of the other. Almost half a century has passed since that decision had to be taken, yet the ties that bound the two branches though technically severed, have never really been broken." Brown Brothers, Harriman were dealing extensively with German interests, including those of Fritz Thyssen, a key financial backer of Hitler. A senior partner at Brown Brothers, Harriman was Prescott Bush - the father of U.S. President, George Bush. In 1936, Prescott Bush hired a lawyer, Allen Dulles, the future director of the CIA, to 'hide' assets made from Nazi transactions by the companies he was associated with, which included Brown Brothers, Harriman and Shroeders Bank, of which Dulles was himself a director. Eventually, Bush was charged under the U.S. Trading With the Enemy Act. The shares in an affiliate of Brown Brothers, Harriman, United Banking Corporation were suspended. According to one source, Bush was a former World War One U.S. military intelligence officer who had liaised with the British Secret Service and had been trained by Stewart Menzies (who became head of the British Secret Service during World War II). "Menzies knew that there were too many British investors in Brown Brothers, Harriman to make an issue out of their aid to Nazi Germany. It was better to bury the scandal." - John Loftus and Mark Aarons, *The Secret War Against the Jews,* St Martin's Griffin, New York 1994 p.360/1. Loftus and Aarons also refer to "a U.S. Congressional investigation in which it was revealed that Herman Abs, the president of the Deutsche Bank, used an 'old school tie' in Britain to arrange for Nazi money to con-

tinue to flow through American cut-outs during the war." *op cit* p. 67. This view of Dulles contrasts somewhat with the sympathetic hearing he gets in Leonard Mosley's *Dulles: A Biography of Eleanor, Allen and John Foster Dulles and their family network,* Hodder & Stoughton, London 1978. Here, it was Dulles' brother John Foster who was seen as the pro-Nazi sympathiser, rather than Allen, who apparently argued with his brother over the issue. Nevertheless, the anti-Semitic nature of their law firm, Sullivan & Cromwell is not at issue.

24. Andrew Boyle, *Montagu Norman,* Cassell, London 1967 p.166
25. *ibid* p.137
26. Fritz Thyssen, *I Paid Hitler,* Hodder and Stoughton, London, 1941
27. Pool, p. 312
28. Thyssen, p. 146
29. A survey of sources on this can be found in Chapter 2 of George Bush: The Unauthorised Biography, by Webster G Tarpley & Anton Chaitkin, published on the Internet at www.radix.net. The authors of this publication describe their findings as amounting to "The Hitler Project" and it certainly makes interesting reading, although the word 'Project' perhaps overstates the case on the evidence available.
30. Adam Lebor, *Hitler's Secret Bankers: How Switzerland profited from Nazi genocide,* Pocket Books, London, 1997 p.108
31. Boyle, p.312
32. *ibid* p.312
33. Christopher Andrew, *Secret service: The Making of the British Intelligence Community,* Sceptre, London, 1986 p.636
34. Alvin Finkel and Clement Leibovitz, *The Chamberlain-Hitler Collusion*, Merlin Press, Suffolk 1997 A highly relevant analysis of appeasement, placing Chamberlain's policies in an economic context can be found in *Profits of Peace* by Scott Newton (Clarendon Press, Oxford, 1996). Here, the search for peace was linked to the search for economic stability, with Montagu Norman playing a key role, in support of an overall anti-Bolshevist strategy: "The penetration of Germany by British capital had been encouraged by Montagu Norman, governor of the Bank of England. For Norman this process was central to the construction of an Anglo-German financial partnership which would thwart French and American aspirations to continental hegemony. But Norman's vision went further: the governor's objective was a working European economy whose prosperity would be guaranteed by co-operation between its two leading members. At the same time the rebuilding of Germany as a flourishing capitalist state would provide a guarantee that Bolshevism would fail to spread beyond the borders of the Soviet Union." (p.58/59) British merchant banks were at the fore with credit to German industry right up to 1939. The city's influence, through such bodies as the Anglo-German Fellowship and some newspapers, came from the very heart of the Conservative body-politic.

Chapter Three: Maundy's Friends

1. Walker, p.92
2. *ibid* p.92
3. *Whitehall Gazette and St. James Review*
5. Rhodes James, p.280
6. *ibid* p.282
7. Stuart Ball, *Baldwin and the Conservative Party: The Crisis of 1929-1931,* Yale University Press, London 1988 p.83
8. Rhodes James, p.285
9. G.R.Searle, *Corruption in British Politics: 1895 - 1930,* Clarendon Press, London, 1987 p.73
10. Rhodes James, p.288

Price of Power

11. *The Times,* 22nd February 1933
12. *The Times,* 3rd March 1933
13. Cullen, p150
14. Searle, p.123

Chapter Four: A New Dawn

1. *The Times,* 27th February 1945
2. *The Times,* 4th October 1947
3. *The Times,* 3rd May 1948 According to Gerald James, the solicitors who 'couldn't be kept waiting' were Trowers and Hamlins, of New Square, Lincoln's Inn. William Gosselin Trower set the River companies up, and his son Anthony became a director of the Bourne Association. (James, op cit p.158) The amounts of money channelled through the river companies cannot be traced after 1982, when new companies act dispensations came into force which meant that small companies no longer had to submit anything more than a balance sheet to Companies House. But immediately prior to that, the political donations paid by two of the associations showed a wide range of values:

Financial yr. ending	Arun	Bourne
1978	£19,500	
1979	£1,500	
1980	£17,050	£207,000
1981	£21,000	£76,000
1982	£1,655	£50,000

The Bourne Association was responsible for the lease on 32 Smith Square, so its balance sheet dwarfed that of the other river companies. Interestingly, according to the articles of association of all the river companies, it was stated that if any property remained after winding up it should be "given or transferred to such charitable institutions having as their object the promotion of the Christian religion."
4. *The Times,* 27th September 1948
5. *The Times,* 27th February 1950
6. *The Independent,* 27th December 1988
7. *The Independent,* 29th December 1988
8. House of Lords debates 7th November 1989
9. *All England Law Reports* 1980 p.52
10. Quoted in *The Independent,* 16th January 1989
11. *The Independent,* 16th January 1989
12. *All England Law Reports,* p.42
13. *The Independent,* 16th January 1989
14. *The Times,* 7th June 1963
15. *The Times,* 26th June 1963
16. House of Commons debates 18th July 1949 Thirty years later a similar form of 'blackmail was still being used. In 1980 Margaret Thatcher had to denounce a letter sent out by the Conservative Board of Finance, Newcastle Upon Tyne, to businesses which said: "I am writing to you for the reason that I have noticed your firm has received or is receiving government grants for buildings and plant. You may, I hope, feel in view of this that you would like to make a small recognition to the Tory Party. In brief, what I am meaning is a donation to the central fund, which is made through this office and passed to London." The firm's managing director responded furiously to this "impudence" and pointed out that since the Tories came to power the whole process of government grant giving had ground to a much slower pace, and that the grants were in any case originally conceived by the Labour government. Mrs

References

Thatcher said the letter had been withdrawn, and recipient firms phoned - but there was no knowledge of any phone call at this firm. *The Times,* 29th October 1980.

17. *The Times,* 18th February 1950
18. *The Times,* 24th November 1958
19. *The Times,* 11th September 1959
20. *The Times,* 8th July 1960
21. House of Commons debates, 21st July 1960
22. *The Times,* 4th October 1963
23. *The Times,* 6th December 1963
24. *The Times,* 20th June 1964
25. *The Times,* 25th June 1964
26. *The Times,* 27th June 1964 Whilst the Economic League and Aims of Industry supported the Conservative Party, unlike BUI they do not appear to have been used as funding conduits as such. After the war, Aims of Industry, more so than the Economic League, took on a propaganda role which has continued to the present day. Prior to the 1992 general election the re-named Aims, which shared offices with BUI, was taking money from firms advising them that such donations could be "categorised as a payment subject to VAT and not as a political contribution." This was despite Aims launching a 'pro-Conservative general election drive with national advertising stressing the "dangers of returning to socialism."' *Observer,* 14th April 1991. JAP Forbes, the BUI Director General was also a Deputy Director of Aims.
27. *The Times,* 19th April 1967
28. *The Times,* 7th June 1967
29. *Conference Report,* National Union of Conservative Associations, 1967
30. *The Times,* 6th May 1968
31. *The Times,* 10th June 1968
32. *Conference Report,* National Union of Conservative Associations, 1968
33. *The Times,* 4th October 1969
34. *The Times,* 1st February 1969
35. Reginald Maudling, *Memoirs,* Sidgwick & Jackson, London 1978 p.143
36. Charles Raw, Godfrey Hodgson, Bruce Page, *Do you sincerely want to be rich?* Andre Deutsch, London 1971 p.306
37. Maudling p.146
38. Michael Gillard and Martin Tomkinson, *Nothing to Declare: The Political Corruptions of John Poulson,* John Calder, London 1980 p.180
39. John Poulson, *The Price,* Michael Joseph, London, 197? p.138
40. Stephen Dorril and Robin Ramsay, *Smear! Wilson and the Secret State,* Fourth Estate, London 1991 p.298
41. Stephen Dorril, *The Silent Conspiracy: Inside the Intelligence Services in the 1990s,* Heinemann, London 1993 p.306
42. *ibid* p.306
43. Charles Raw *Slater Walker,* Coronet Books, London 1978 p.378
44. Patrick Fitzgerald and Mark Leopold, *Stranger on the Line: The Secret History of Phone Tapping,* The Bodley head, London, 1987 p.164
45. *ibid* p.164
46. Dorril and Ramsay, p.242
47. Raw, p.349
48. *Regulating the City,* Labour Party 1982 p.4
49. *ibid* p.6
50. Tony Benn, *Against the Tide: Diaries 1973 - 1976,* Hutchinson, London, 1989 p.401
51. *Regulating the City,* p.7
52. Alan Doig, *Corruption and Misconduct in Contemporary British Politics,* Penguin, London 1984
53. Tom Bower, *Tiny Rowland: A Rebel Tycoon,* Heinemann, London 1993 p.204

54. *ibid* p.209
55. *Regulating the City* p.16
56. *The Times,* 14th July 1969
57. *The Times,* 5th January 1970
58. *The Times,* 12th February 1974 Very rarely would the names of any private donors in this category seep out, although *Private Eye* reported a few in 1983. They were:

Akroyd & Smithers	£7,500	(1979/80)
	£10,000	(1981/82)
Bisgood Bishop	£2,000	(1979)
Hoare Govett	£2,000	(1978)
	£2,500	(1979)
Smith Brothers	£1,000	(1980)

As *Private Eye* said "These payments are likely to be only a hint of the scale of contributions in 1983 from the 250 Stock Exchange firms." (12th August 1983)
59. *The Times,* 3rd January 1975
60. *The Times,* 14th March 1975
61. *The Times,* 16th September 1976
62. Committee on Financial Aid to Political Parties *Report,* Cmnd. 6601 HMSO London 1976 p.92
63. *Contact Brief: Financing Political Parties,* Conservative Political Centre, 1977
64. Philip Tether p.67
65. *The Times* 20th December 1972
66. D. J. Wilson, *Power and Party Bureaucracy in Britain: Regional Organisation in the Conservative and Labour Parties,* Saxon House, London p.117
67. Tether, p.6
68. *ibid* p.28
69. *Daily Telegraph* 24th September 1979
70. *The Times,* 21st June 1978
71. *The Times,* 10th October 1977
72. *The Times,* 8th October 1977
73. *The Times,* 7th October 1978
74. *The Times,* 26th August 1978
75. *The Sunday Times,* 18th May 1975

Chapter Five: Thatcher & Sons

1. *The Times,* 10th March 1989
2. Ivan Fallon, *The Brothers: The Rise and Rise of Saatchi and Saatchi,* Hutchinson, London 1988 p.162
3. *The Sunday Times,* 16th October 1983
4. Alistair McAlpine, *The Servant,* Faber and Faber, London, 1992 p.11
5. *The Times,* 21st January 1982
6. Alex Brummer and Roger Cowe, *Hanson: The rise and rise of Britain's most buccaneering businessman,* Fourth Estate, London 1995 p.193
7. *ibid* p.194
8. *ibid* p.185
9. *ibid* p.287
10. Paul Halloran and Mark Hollingsworth, *Thatcher's Gold: The life and times of Mark Thatcher,* Simon and Schuster London 1995 p.100
11. *ibid* p.108
12. *ibid* p. 184
13. *The Guardian* 22nd June 1993
14. Halloran and Hollingsworth p.178

15. *ibid* p.178

16. *The Guardian* 23rd June 1993

17. *Sunday Telegraph,* 16th October 1994

18. House of Commons debates col. 1264 22nd June 1993

19. *Business Age* July 1993

20. *Daily Telegraph,* 25th June 1993

21. Alistair McAlpine, *Once a Jolly Bagman,* Weidenfeld and Nicolson, London 1997 p.251

22. *The Sunday Times,* 16th October 1983

23. McAlpine, *Once a Jolly Bagman,* p.252

24. *ibid* p.264

25. Ian Greer, *One Man's Word: The untold story of the Cash-For-Questions affair,* Andre Deutsch, London 1997 p.62

26. *ibid* p.108

27. *ibid* p.108

28. *ibid* p.39

29. *ibid* p.30

30. *ibid* p.109

31. *Labour Research*, May 1988

32. *ibid*

33. *ibid*

34. *ibid* December 1988

35. copy of letter dated 29th January 1987

36. *The Sunday Times,* 22nd February 1987

37. *Labour Research*, August 1984 Not surprisingly, Alan Lewis's responsibilities as a director came under the scrutiny of the opposition: during a House of Commons debate on party funding, Margaret Beckett noted: "In the run-up to the 1987 general election [Hartley Investment Trust] gave £167,000 to the Conservative party, which was the largest corporate donation to the Conservative party ever recorded - so far, at any rate. That company is breaking the law. It should have filed accounts for the year ending March 1991 by the end of April 1992, and for the year ending March 1992 by the end of April 1993. It has failed to do so. That company is chaired by Alan Lewis, and the hon. Member for Shipley (Sir M. Fox) - the chairman of the 1922 Committee and a member of the Conservative board of finance - is a non-executive director. So let us hear less from the Conservative party about the people who legally give money to the Labour party and declare their donations." Hansard House of Commons debates, 22nd June 1993 col. 178

38. Mark Hollingsworth, *MPs for Hire: The Secret World of Political Lobbying*, Bloomsbury, London 1991p.70

39. *ibid* p.71

40. *Labour Research,* December 1988

41. *Leeds Other Paper,* 2nd June 1989

42. *ibid*

43. Lord Young, *The Enterprise Years,* Headline, London 1991 p.344

44. Hollingsworth, p.68

45. Labour Research Department figures

46. Peter Taylor, *Smoke Ring: The politics of tobacco,* The Bodley Head, London 1984 p.129

47. *ibid* p.134

48. *ibid* p.137

49. *ibid* p.143

50. *Labour Research,* November 1987 and December 1988

51. *Labour Research,* November 1987

52. *Parliamentary Affairs,* Vol.42 No. 2 April 1989 p.198

53. Norman Tebbit, *Upwardly Mobile,* Futura, London 1989 p.313
54. 1991 Report of the Charter Movement
55. Kenneth Baker, *The Turbulent Years: My Life in Politics,* Faber and Faber, London 1993 p.292
56. 1991 Report of the Charter Movement
57. *The Sunday Times,* 18th March 1984
58. *The Times,* 28th September 1985
59. *The Times,* 25th August 1986
60. *The Times,* 16th September 1986
61. *The Sunday Times,* 23rd December 1990
62. *The Sunday Times* 23rd December 1990

Chapter Six: The Unravelling

1. Tim Hindle, *Asil Nadir: Fugitive from injustice?* Pan Books, London 1993 p.4
2. *Business Age,* June 1993
3. Gerald James, *In The Public Interest,* Little , Brown and Company, 1995 p.114
4. *The Independent,* 4th March 1992
5. *The Independent,* 15th May 1993
6. *The Independent,* 19th June 1993
7. *Daily Telegraph,* 20th June 1993
8. *Business Age,* June 1993
9. *The Observer,* 4th July 1993
10. *The Guardian,* 22nd September 1993
11. *Daily Telegraph,* 25th January 195
12. *The Guardian,* 30th January 1995
13. *The Sunday Times,* 3rd July 1994
14. *The Guardian,* 30th January 195
15. *The Guardian,* 22nd May 1995
16. *The Independent,* 26th June 1993
17. Quoted in *The Scotsman* 5th July 1993
18. *Yorkshire Evening Post,* 4th July 1997
19. *Daily Telegraph,* 5th November 1997
20. *The Sunday Times,* 13th November 1994
21. For further BCCI background see, e.g. Nick Kochan and Bob Whittington, *Bankrupt: The BCCI Fraud,* Victor Gollancz, London 1992 or James Ring Adams and Douglas Frantz, *A Full Service Bank,* Pocket Books, New York, 1992 The Durbar Club was founded in 1982, with an annual membership fee of £1,000, with aims to "provide means of regular contact between the financial and economic leaders of the Asian community and the top echelons of the business, political and social structures in Britain, together with the top-tier leadership of the Conservative Party" as well as to "raise funds for the Conservative Party and generally to assist the party." One Asian businessman said that there were at least 200 Asian millionaires in Britain. The Durbar Club's chairman and secretary was Mr Narendar Saroop. *Financial Times,* 24th January 1983
22. *The Sunday Times,* 30th October 1994
23. Loftus and Aarons, p.394
24. *The Sunday Times,* 9th February 1997
25. *The Sunday Times,* 19th May 1996
26. *Daily Telegraph,* 27th March 1997
27. *The Sunday Times,* 26th May 1996
28. *Yorkshire Post,* 29th April 1997 Sykes' fear was that "There is no half way house. A single currency means ultimately a single country. To achieve a single currency without having a single country would be a world first - there is no such thing."

29. *The Observer,* 22nd December 1996

30. *The Guardian,* 23rd December 1996

31. *The Sunday Times,* 27th July 1997

32. *The Independent,* 7th October 1991

33. *The Sunday Times,* 6th October 1991

34. *The Independent,* 7th October 1991

35. *The Guardian,* 26th June 1993

36. *The Sunday Times,* 16th March 1997 Until January, 1998, it was believed that Ma Ching-kwan's donation was £500,000, but thanks to allegations in the Ma-owned *Oriental Daily,* that figure had to be revised upwards following the claim that the Tory party had reneged on a deal with Ma, allegedly designed to ensure the dropping of drugs trafficking charges against his father. Ma met John Major at No. 10 Downing Street in 1994, just two months after Central Office issued a receipt for £1 million. As usual, Central Office spokespeople said that if their money had come with conditions attached, it wouldn't have been accepted, and that if it was proven to be stolen, it would be returned. The Ma family's unhappiness appears to have first come to a head when they saw the prospect of Major's defeat in April, 1997. Ma Ching-kwan wrote to Party Chairman Brian Mawhinney on April 1st saying "there appears to have been no satisfactory outcome to the explicit expectations of my family prior to and during the period during which the various donations... were made." (*Daily Telegraph,* 21st January 1998) Dr Mawhinney, Mr Ma was told, was too busy with the general election to reply – curious, given that a simple rebuff would have taken only two minutes of his time.

37. *Daily Telegraph,* 20th April 1997

38. *The Observer,* 20th June 1993

39. *Hong Kong News,* 23rd April 1997

40. *The Sunday Times,* 16th March 1997

41. *Daily Telegraph,* 1st March 1996

42. *Daily Telegraph,* 13th March 1995

43. *The Guardian,* 19th September 1991

44. *The Guardian,* 13th March 1993

45. *The Guardian,* 4th March 1992

46. *The Sunday Times,* 26th May 1996

47. *The Financial Times,* 24th October 1994

48. *The Sunday Times,* 27th September 1992

49. *The Guardian,* 6th October 1990

50. *The Independent,* 16th March 1992

51. *The Financial Times,* 19th December 1994

52. *The Sun,* 16th June 1993

53. *The Guardian,* 6th June 1992

54. *The Sunday Times,* 27th September 1992

55. *The Guardian,* 16th June 1993

56. *The Independent,* 7th January 1991

57. *The Observer,* 27th June 1993

58. *The Observer,* 6th April 1997

59. *East Anglian Daily Times,* 17th April 1997

60. *Daily Telegraph,* 13th January 1997

61. *Daily Telegraph,* 31st December 1996

62. *The Guardian,* 20th August 1996

63. *Daily Telegraph,* 2nd August 1996

64. *The Guardian,* 30th July 1996

65. *The Guardian,* 4th September 1996

66. *Eastern Daily Press,* 3rd December 1996

67. *The Observer,* 15th September 1996

68. *Daily Telegraph,* 15th November 1994
69. *The Guardian,* 6th January 1995
70. *The Observer,* 4th July 1993
71. *Daily Telegraph,* 30th November 1994
72. *Daily Telegraph,* 21st December 1994
73. *Economist,* 27th April 1996
74. *Today,* 3rd June 1993
75. *Today,* 1st June 1993
76. *The Sunday Times,* 25th February 1996
77. *Daily Telegraph,* 2nd May 1996
78. *Daily Telegraph,* 19th September 1996
79. *Register of MPs' Interests as at 31st January 1997,* HMSO London 1997
80. *Code of Conduct for MPs,* Category 5
81. quoted in *Daily Telegraph,* 7th October 1996
82. *Daily Telegraph,* 21st March 1997
83. *The Spectator,* 15th October 1996
84. *Daily Telegraph,* 4th July 1997
85. *Daily Telegraph,* 21st March 1997
86. leaflet produced by the People's Trust 1997
87. *Daily Telegraph,* 29th August 1996
88. *The Sunday Times,* 23rd February 1997
89. *The Guardian,* 13th August 1996
90. *Daily Telegraph,* 15th May 1996
91. copy of Conservative Central Office letter 3rd November 1996
92. *Accountancy Age,* 3rd November 1994
93. copy of Austin Mitchell letter 27th October 1994
94. *The Financial Times,* 28th October 1993
95. *Daily Telegraph,* 14th February 1998
96. *The Independent,* 23rd January 1998

Chapter Seven: A Fresh Future

1. *Labour Research,* April 1992
2. *Daily Telegraph,* 15th July 1997
3. *The Times,* 19th July 1997
4. *The Times,* 29th July 1997
5. *Register of MPs' Interests as at 31st October 1997,* HMSO London 1997
6. *Daily Telegraph,* 31st May 1997
7. speech given by William Hague downloaded from Conservative Party WWW site
8. *Daily Telegraph,* 29th June 1997
9. *Daily Telegraph,* 2nd August 1997
10. *The Independent,* 7th April 1991
11. *The Financial Times,* 29th May 1993
12. *Daily Telegraph,* 15th March 1997
13. *Daily Telegraph,* 12th April 1997
14. *The Yorkshire Post,*
15. *Daily Telegraph,* 24th August 1997
16. *Daily Telegraph,* 9th November 1997
17. *The Guardian,* 8th October 1997
18. *The Times,* 6th June 1997 The difficulty in assessing what constitutes membership of the Conservative Party, and in drawing comparisons with other parties' membership levels, is well summed up in *True Blues* (Paul Whiteley, Patrick Seyd and Jeremy Richardson, Clarendon Press, Oxford, 1994): "The lack of a clear definition of a Conservative party member means that the party is quite vague as to what consti-

tutes a member: individuals are expected to neither declare their attachment to a particular set of attitudes, ideals or policies, nor to pay a minimum level of subscription. A member of the Conservative Party can be someone who feels very strong attachment to Conservative ideals or, on the other hand, someone whose political identification is weak. Another aspect of this vagueness is that an individual can pay whatever subscription to the local party association that he or she pleases; and, in fact, our survey shows that there were some people clearly identified as members, both in terms of the local records and in terms of their own perceptions, who paid nothing at all to the local association by way of a subscription." (pp 24/25) This last category could include MPs who, as was discovered when Neil Hamilton's membership was queried, are members of the party by virtue of being a Conservative MP.

19. *Yorkshire Evening Post,* 6th October 1997
20. *The Guardian,* 21st July 1997
21. *A Fresh Future* downloaded from the Internet February, 1998
22. *The Guardian,* 25th November 1997
23. *The Observer,* 7th December 1997
24. *The Guardian,* 16th February 1998
25. *Daily Telegraph,* 22nd November 1997

Chapter Eight: Fronts and Clubs

1. quoted in Peter Paterson, *The Selectorate: The case for primary elections in Britain,* MacGibbon and Kee, London 1967 p.137 Every town of any size probably has - or had - some version of these clubs. In Aberdeen for example, there was the Deeside Business Club, described in the local *Press and Journal* as "a fundraising subsidiary of the Conservative Association." (31st October 1996)
2. *The Financial Times,* 19th December 1994
3. *The Independent,* 6th June 1996
4. *Sunday Business,* 17th November 1996
5. *The Financial Times,* 19th December 1994
6. *Newcastle Journal,* 29th April 1970
7. *ibid*
8. *Newcastle Journal,* 5th June 1975
9. *Newcastle Journal,* 16th June 1976
10. *The Guardian,* 2nd July 1990
11. *The Sunday Times,* 25th May 1969
12. *Daily Telegraph,* 4th July 1969
13. *The Guardian,* 24th July 1973
14. copy of letter from Forbes
15. copy of BUI Annual Report 1987
16. copy of letter 5th May 1987
17. copy of BUI's chairman's report dated 8th September 1987
18. *The Scotsman,* 2nd July 1991
19. *The Scotsman,* 3rd July 1991
20. *ibid*
21. *Labour Research,* July 1993
22. *The Guardian,* 2nd March 1994
23. *Daily Mirror,* 28th February 1994
24. *Independent on Sunday,* 16th October 1994
25. *Financial Times,* 22nd January 1994

Chapter Nine: The Parliamentary Road to Reform

1. Margaret Thatcher, *The Downing Street Years,* Harper Collins London 1994 p. 275

Price of Power

2. *Daily Telegraph*, 22nd August 1994
3. *The Times*, 17th November 1997
4. Lord Neill Committee on Standards in Public Life, Consultation document on party funding, downloaded from the Internet 15th January 1998
5. *The Guardian*, 22nd November 1996
6. *The Guardian*, 27th February 1998
7. *Sunday Times*, 1st March 1998

Other works

Robert Blake, *The Conservative Party from Peel to Thatcher*, Methuen, London 1985
David Butler and Dennis Kavanagh, *The British General Election of 1987*, Macmillan Press, London 1988
Jamie Camplin, *The Rise of the Plutocrats: Wealth and Power in Edwardian England*, Constable, London 1978
Colin Chapman, *Selling The Family Silver: Has Privatisation Worked?* Hutchinson, London 1990
Alan Clark, *Diaries*, Weidenfeld and Nicolson, London 1993
Michael Crick, *Jeffrey Archer: Stranger Than Fiction*, Hamish Hamilton, London 1995
A. J. Davies, *We, The Nation: The Conservative Party and the Pursuit of Power*, Little, Brown and Co. London 1995
Keith Ewing, *The Funding of Political Parties in Britain*, Cambridge University Press, Cambridge 1987
Elizabeth Forsyth, *Who Killed Polly Peck? The Corporate Assassination of Asil Nadir*, Smith Gryphon, London 1996
Wyn Grant with Jane Sargent, *Business and Politics in Britain*, Macmillan, London 1987
John Giuseppi, *The Bank of England*, Evans Brothers, London 1966
Richard Griffiths, *Fellow Travellers of the Right: British Enthusiasts for Nazi Germany 1933-39*, Oxford University Press, Oxford 1983
House of Commons Home Affairs Select Committee, *Funding of Political Parties* 2nd Report HMSO London 1994
Mike Hughes, *Spies at Work*, 1 in 12 Publications, Bradford 1994
H. Montgomery Hyde, *Norman Birkett: The life of Lord Birkett of Ulverston*, The Reprint Society, London 1965
Richard N. Kelly, *Conservative Party conferences: the hidden system*, Manchester University Press, Manchester
David Leigh and Ed Vulliamy, *Sleaze: The Corruption of Parliament*, Fourth Estate, London 1997
Alistair McAlpine, *Letters to a Young Politician From His Uncle*, Faber and Faber, London1995
R. T. McKenzie, *British Political Parties: The Distribution of Power within the Consevative and Labour Parties*, Gregg Revivals, London 1992
Michael Moran, *The Politics of Banking*, Macmillan Press, London 1984
Philip Norton (ed.) *The Conservative Party*, Prentice Hall, London
"The Pied Piper", *Rats!* Victor Gollancz, London 1941
John Ranelagh, *Thatcher's People*, Harper Collins, London 1991
Laurence Rees, *Selling Politics*, BBC Books, London 1992
Terry Smith, *Accounting for Growth: Stripping the Camouflage from Company Accounts*, Century Business, London 1992
Margaret Thatcher, *The Path to Power*, Harper Collins, London 1995
Hugo Young, *One of Us*, Pan, London 1991

An extract from
LAWYERS ON THE SPOT
by Donna Leigh-Kile

...Top judges in Britain have become third-age rebels. They outmanoeuvred and outflanked the former Tory government in the past two years with skills a matador would envy - notwithstanding their average age of 60. Whether they maintain this role under the Labour government is the subject of riveting speculation amongst the legal profession.

The time-worn, vicious swipe that judges dwell in ivory towers loses its sting when one considers that they opposed the Conservatives, who were forced to compromise on the down-to-earth issues of minimum sentences, asylum seekers and police bugging. Due to extremely unusual and outspoken criticism on policy from the massed ranks of the judiciary, the minimum sentences bill was modified, allowing judges to impose a lesser sentence 'in the interests of justice'; senior judges ruled that it was illegal for the government to withdraw benefits from asylum seekers whose applications to stay in the UK had not yet been determined; and they won a change in the police 'bugging' bill stipulating that authorisation must be obtained from a judge, not just a chief constable, when the police want to tap 'phones.

There has also been an explosion of judicial review cases, overturning all sorts of decisions made by central and local government and financial regulatory bodies in the last few years, making it one of the most fashionable areas of law in which to practise. "Indeed, the way the judiciary has taken on the government makes the Bar appear reactionary in comparison," says radical barrister Quincy Whitaker. Another barrister says that the judges' independent stance in the 1990's follows decades of toeing the government line, particularly in the late1960's and 1970's, which coincided with a number of grave miscarriages of justice, some of which are only now coming to light.

Despite praise for the judiciary's current collective show of strength from those within the legal profession, many lawyers, clients and the public view some individual judges as proof of the principle that people rise to the limits of their capacities, and then a bit more. No lawyer questioned for this book could explain why otherwise some good, even excellent, lawyers undergo a complete personality change or become incompetent when they take to the Bench. It is called 'judge-itis.'

"I do wonder what happens to these very sensible barristers who go mad when they get on the High Bench," says a long-time barrister's clerk. "Whether it's the power, I don't know, but they suddenly change for the worse. The opinions you know they held at the Bar are sometimes completely at odds with the decisions they are making as judges.

"I said to one barrister whom I've known for twenty years and who was about to become a judge: 'Don't get like some of the others.' He told me to keep calling him 'Andrew'. There are some who insist that you call them Mr. Justice So-and-So, even when you have been on first-name terms with them for years and years."

Bouts of overweening self-regard on the bench, or ignorance of sex practices and pop stars, resulting in judges being ridiculed by the press, disguise far deeper concerns. Partisan judges, who violate the basic tenet that justice should be done and be seen to be done, are the bane of lawyers' lives and have, in their view, seriously damaged the public's faith in the legal system.

Dick Ferguson, QC, was involved in the penultimate appeal of the 'Birmingham Six', at which Lord Chief Justice Lane uttered the famous words: "The longer this hearing has gone on the more convinced this court has become that the verdict of the jury (in the original trial) was correct."

Ferguson says: "What happened in those 'miscarriage-of-justice' cases, and there were a number of them, not all Irish, was that the establishment, as represented by the top echelons of the legal profession, refused to countenance the possibility of error by the lower courts. Instead of approaching the appeals with an open mind, they approached them determined to uphold the convictions.

"Even when the evidence had reached a stage where it should have been obvious to them that it was time to admit failure, they still tried to cling to the convictions. And it was only when the convictions were finally wrested from them that they gave up. Of course, that much publicised delay has done irreparable damage to the image of our legal system."

Bias is no less invidious at county court level. Barrister Jacqueline Perry recalls representing a man seeking custody of his children, as their mother had a history of abandoning them and then reclaiming them for short periods. "The county court judge, however, made it clear during the early part of the case that he believed a child's place was with his mother and, no surprise, ruled in her favour. My client felt with good reason that he hadn't had a proper hearing. This is an example of a judge who had made up his mind and wasn't prepared to listen to anything else."

An extract from
Power and Corruption
by Stephen Moore

...It is the sort of situation which would warrant the immediate despatch of James Bond 007 – an idyllic island in the Caribbean is taken over by a sinister criminal organisation.

In one of Ian Fleming's novels it would have been the evil organisation SPECTRE which seizes control. Bond would have despatched the villains with the help of a Walther PPK, a gorgeous girl on his arm and a vodka martini at the bar.

Yet the reality in the 1990s is just as dramatic.

The beautiful Caribbean island of Aruba, only five miles wide and 20 miles long, was 'bought' by elements of the Sicilian Mafia along with its 65,000 inhabitants. Everything of importance on the island was taken over by the mobsters, controlling elements of the police, politicians, customs and, most importantly, the banks. The 'ownership' of their own State offered wonderful opportunities for corruption on a previously unthinkable scale. Its very existence was founded on corruption and criminality.

Aruba lies just off the Venezuelan coast. During the age of discovery and conquest it was ignored by the Spanish, who described it as 'barren and useless', despite its beautiful long white beaches, and instead it fell into the hands of the Dutch and became part of the six Dutch Antilles.

Sleepy and ignored it was the perfect off-shore Shangri-La for the Mafia. For years they kept their ownership quiet, transforming Aruba into a staging post for cocaine smuggling. At the same time they bribed officials and used the island's banks to launder their money – channelling vast sums obtained from drugs, extortion, murder and prostitution across the world.

The authorities only discovered the Mafia's presence after a dramatic and violent police raid on offices in Caracas, the capital of Venezuela. Investigators seized computer disks concerning deals involving the Cuntreras family, one of the most dangerous Sicilian

184

Mafia clans. The Cuntreras had been living in Venezuela for years and visiting Aruba for lengthy holidays. But the disks and other documents showed they had been doing more in the Caribbean than soaking up the sun.

The information seized by the police proved that more than 60% of businesses and economic life on Aruba was owned and controlled by the Mafia.

When the American authorities belatedly realised what was going on there was little they could do. One of their most expensive satellites was moved off course to 'sit' on top of the island and spot smugglers boats and cocaine drops in the ocean, but it was a difficult task even when the clouds allowed vision. One of the largest hauls of cocaine ever discovered in Britain came via Aruba.

Investigators came to the conclusion that the Mafia wanted Aruba not only to create the perfect base for corruption and crime, but also as a bolt-hole they could flee to when they needed to escape the law and avoid extradition to America, Europe or, more specifically, Italy.

Their fears soon seemed justified. In September 1992 Venezuela agreed to extradite back to Italy three of the most dangerous Cuntreras brothers: Guiseppe, Pasquale and Paulo, a trio known as the Black Emperors and reputedly worth more than $1 billion each, earned from drugs. Back home they were arrested and thrown into Italy's top-security Pianosa prison.

Investigators claim the Black Emperors took part in the appalling murder of Judge Giovanni Falcone, who was blown up shortly after he arranged for their extradition to Italy. They then assassinated Paulo Borsellino, Falcone's successor.

According to the US Drug Enforcement Agency the Cuntreras were the main force behind the acquisition of Aruba, a buying spree which started in the early 1980s, when the Black Emperors were frequent visitors to the island with their 'beautiful' wives. They stayed at first in Spartan accommodation, were kind to their kids and avoided ostentatious displays of wealth, according to locals. Meanwhile they were arranging the purchase of restaurants, banks, hotels, cafés, and every type of local business.

Organised crime was hardly a newcomer to the region. From the arrival of pirates and buccaneers centuries ago to the more recent arrivals of fugitive financiers and money launderers, every criminal wants a home in the Caribbean. The island was quick to welcome

the latest arrivals with their new investment and the Aruba government took little action, perhaps through fear of reprisals.
Exceptionally, one member of the gang was arrested in 1988 and the
Aruban authorities requested military assistance from Holland as
protection. The Dutch took the request seriously and sent a frigate
and a force of soldiers.

The Aruba experience shows that while the Mafia's global power
has been under attack, the income from organised crime, the ability
to hide it, to launder it and the ability to use it for corruption still
poses great threats to international order...

Index

Index

Index

Index

Index

Index

Index

Index

Index

Index